BORN TO SHOP
HONG KONG

THE SUPER-SHOPPER'S GUIDE TO NAME
BRAND, DESIGNER AND BARGAIN SHOPP

OTHER BOOKS IN THE SERIES

SUZY GERSHMAN

BORN TO SHOP HONG KONG

THE SUPER-SHOPPER'S GUIDE TO NAME-BRAND, DESIGNER AND BARGAIN SHOPPING

FIFTH EDITION

HarperPerennial
A Division of HarperCollinsPublishers

HarperCollins books may be purchased for educational, business, or sales promotional use. For information, please write: Special Markets Department,
HarperCollins Publishers, Inc., 10 East 53rd Street,
New York, NY 10022.

FIRST EDITION

Designed by C. Linda Dingler

ISSN: 1067-3830

94 95 96 97 ◆/RRD 10 9 8 7 6 5 4

To Willie, Jane and Roger
where East meets West;
Greenwich and Hong Kong merge

BORN TO SHOP HONG KONG
Editorial Director: Suzy Gershman
British correspondent: Ian Cook
Paris correspondent: Pascale-Agnes Renaud
Executive Editor: Carol Cohen
Assistant to Executive Editor: Pat Bear
Line Editor: Jill Parsons
Associate Editor: Erica Spaberg
Manager, Publishing Reference Technology: John Day
Computer Production Editor: Douglas Elam

The currency used in Hong Kong is the Hong Kong dollar, which is also signified by a dollar sign. All prices quoted in this book are in U.S. dollars unless otherwise noted. Although every effort was made to ensure the accuracy of prices appearing in this book, it should be kept in mind that with inflation and a fluctuating rate of exchange, prices will vary. Dollar estimations of prices were made based on the following rate of exchange: $1 (U.S.) = $7 (H.K.).

CONTENTS

Central; Western; Hollywood Road; Lan Kwai Fong;
Wan Chai; Causeway Bay; Happy Valley;

4 HONG KONG DICTIONARY

5 MARKETS AND MALLS

6 THE HEART OF HONG KONG

PREFACE

What's going to happen to Hong Kong on July 1, 1997 when the Chinese take over from the British? Beats me. In fact, second guessing what will happen while this book remains on the bookshelves is a major task. Hong Kong is changing at such a remarkable pace that I am simply dizzy. Every day that I read the newspaper I learn of more controversy in Hong Kong.

What will the future bring? No one really knows.

Yet everyone agrees that there's too much at stake for it to all go up in smoke. Or down the tubes. Or out the window. I feel safe in assuming we can all shop while Rome burns. Or something like that.

Surely the interest in 1997 has spawned a major tourist thrust of immediacy: everyone wants to get to Hong Kong before 1997. So get packing. The time is now.

Hong Kong has already undergone three major financial events: the city survived the horrors of the bloodbath at Tiananemen Square and its aftermath of canceled trips and fewer visitors; the city has survived the brain drain when anyone who was going to flee from the Chinese fled, taking with them a lot of local talent. Furthermore the city has survived the international recession which burned the U.S., the U.K. and parts of continental Europe. In fact, Hong Kong wasn't hurt at all: the city has been booming.

Fears of the future can slow that boom at any time, of course. There's questions about continued contracts and the proposed new airport scheduled to go to Lantau Island. Yet locals remain optimistic and opportunistic: the biggest question that local wags ask is how fast the sky-line of Kowloon will change once the airport is removed from Kowloon peninsula.

Already the laws affecting the flight path have been changed and high rise buildings—with shopping malls beneath—are springing up and down the harbourfront. Perfectly fine buildings are being torn down so bigger and better ones can replace them; even the venerable Peninsula Hotel is getting a new tower.

Change is in the air.

This book is meant to reflect those changes and bring you as up to date as possible. Under the circumstances, up-to-date can change at an up-to-the-minute pace. I'm dancing as fast as I can.

Speaking of change, the format of this book has changed slightly. There's also a big juicy chapter on Macau; a first. Macau has been in previous editions, but never to this extent. Maybe that's because one of the big changes in Hong Kong is that Macau has changed too.

You'll also notice the influence of travelling with a photographer—photo ops are marked; there's a new section on buying used cameras and on film and processing. While Ian doesn't much like to shop and other *Born to Shop* editions from HarperCollins have a section called *Cook's Tour* for women who get stuck with a man who hates to shop, please note that Hong Kong swept Ian off his feet...and his credit cards. He earned his stripes in street market warfare. He now owns five watches. There is no Cook's Tour in this book. But plenty of Ian's personality. (British.)

Shops in Hong Kong open and close at an amazing rate, so there is a chance that any given address may have changed since we went to press. If you are going out of your way for only one listing, please phone ahead. As with all *Born to Shop* books, the same basic rules apply:

- No store can purchase a listing in this book or any book I write; I accept no advertising or paid announcements of any kind.
- Work is done anonymously. The stores never know I have "officially" visited them, no matter how many times I return.
- While I do have some local contacts and friends who pass on suggestions for these pages, each selection in this book is my personal choice.
- For British readers, note that I now use a British subject (Mr. Cook) to help with the reporting of these books so that an accurate British perspective can be brought to the pages. I am fully aware that we don't speak the same language at all.
- I update the book regularly, but if you catch a change before I do, please drop a card to *Born to Shop*, HarperCollins Publishers, 10 E. 53rd Street, New York, NY 10022.

Please note that it has always been policy to mention brand names of goods seen in stores, outlets and street sources, but I cannot promise you that these same designer goods will be available when you go there. Good luck.

ACKNOWLEDGMENTS

This is the first Hong Kong edition with HarperCollins; it simply couldn't have been done without a lot of help from old and new friends: I owe heap big thanks to an international cast of thousands.

No matter how many times I go to Hong Kong I always wistfully remember the very first *Born to Shop* trip when Judith Thomas and my sister, Dr. Debbie (that's Debra Kalter, M.D.) and I holed up in a single room in an almost luxurious hotel in Causeway Bay and did the town right. Not only were we all so young then, but we could carry much bigger packages. Thanks for the memories, ladies.

These days I travel with Ian Cook who has become an integral part of this edition, both as photographer and as British correspondent. Also as chief package carrier. You'll note as you read this new edition that Ian, his wife (yes, her name really is Bumble) and five children have become running characters in the text—after all when you go to Hong Kong to shop for seven people, you pick up a lot of information. I thank him for loving Hong Kong as much as I do, for putting his chewing gum behind the gap in my front teeth on the cover photo and for his invaluable street smarts.

His friends Willie and Jane Chan, and his godson Roger Chan, have become an important part of my Hong Kong family; even though Jane hates to shop, she has spent a lot of time faxing me information and guiding me toward local secrets. Roger checks pages for me. And I send him basketball cards. You'll see them as running characters in this text also.

My old friends Peter and Louisa Chan, have continued to add to the depth of this book; that's Peter on the cover, fitting me for one more suit. And yes, we are standing on the edge of the hot tub at The Regent Hotel, overlooking Causeway Bay. And yes again, Ian *is* standing in the hot tub to get the shot. They drained it for him. Thank you Karl Grebstad.

The suit I'm wearing on the cover, by the way, was made by Danny Chen at Irene Fashions Ltd., a division of W.W. Chan Tailors Ltd. Danny has been making my clothes for a number of years; no one makes me look better. Especially when the suit has both sleeves sewn into it.

The Regent now shares honors with The Peninsula as *Born to Shop* headquarters. The two hotels are so different and yet so much part of Hong Kong that you'll just have to try them both (even in one trip)—I thank Felix M. Bieger, Rolf Heiniger, Lynn Grebstad, Sian Griffith and Sheila Arora for their help and their hospitality.

When it's time to work from Central, I hang out at The Hilton. My thanks go to Mr. James Smith and his entire team for the warm welcome there.

My antiques headquarters on Hollywood Road continues to be Honeychurch. The Vessas were one of Judith's best discoveries in Hong Kong and I thank them for their help, their lessons and their hospitality. Hugs to my best antiques friends Glenn and Lucille.

The dictionary section of this book was originally put together by Judith Thomas, a portion of her original reporting remains. Thanks, Jude. My new editor throughout this text is Erica Spaberg; I thank her for helping me to weave together the old and new portions of this book. This book is the same but dramatically different (just like Hong Kong itself).

Thanks also to the gang at the Hong Kong

Tourist Association in New York and in Hong Kong. Mary Testa-Bakht and Edith Wei in New York have become my constant phone mates; Stephen Wong and Karisa Yuen-Ha Lui in Hong Kong have been devoted to the cause. They have faxed and fact-checked and double-checked for me to make sure we've got things straight and I thank them from the bottom of my shopping bags.

For the Macau section, I am indebted to local help from Dottie Furman in Los Angeles. Aldevina Russ in Macau made our trip sparkle with her help and advice. We're coming back for a few nights at the Bela Vista, Vina, watch out.

In London, my friends at The Ritz are always there with a huge bathtub and a welcome; I thank everyone, especially Terry Holmes. John Murray in Westport introduced me to Edwardian International through their Heathrow hotel—next time I hope I get to spend the night!

Special thanks to John Lampl and Lilla Santullo at British Airways who always endeavor to make my work load a little bit better. You'll read all about it later, but I have found the best route to China and it is transatlantic! They say BA is the world's favorite airline. Mine too.

My biggest thank yous have to go to my girl-friends in Hong Kong and all that they provide me with: inside information, love and moral support and great dinners. Diane, Lynn, Sheila, Sian, Jane—you're the best. And you make Hong Kong the best.

INTRODUCTIONS

Welcome to Hong Kong, the crossroads of the world. All of the best things in life are here for your pleasure, and often at bargain prices. It's just a case of knowing where to look. Hong Kong is the world's best shopping center. There are world-class shopping malls. There are big-name boutiques that populate Kowloon and downtown Central.

Tourists come for the combination of hotels, local color, and shopping. And, hopefully, bargains.

Every commodity in the world is here in Hong Kong; shoppers never have to travel far to find bargains. The best part of all is that if one shop doesn't have what you want, the next one will...or the next.

Of course, half the fun of shopping in Hong Kong is bargaining. Everyone knows the price is negotiable, and it's a poor sport who doesn't go in prepared to argue.

I have known Suzy Gershman for many years now and know she is an expert in finding the best bargains in town. Sometimes I think she knows this town better than many of the locals. I live here, but when Suzy comes to town and we sit down to visit, I invariably ask her for the latest shopping secrets.

When we sit down together, we often find other common interests as well. It's interesting to me that now that Suzy has changed publishers and brought us a new and slightly different *Born to Shop: Hong Kong*, I too have been refining and modifying the Diane Look. Yes, there will always be demand for the dresses that made me famous, but I've been working hard to expand my line and my image.

So it seems particularly fitting that I welcome you to new times for Suzy, for me, for shoppers and for Hong Kong. You may not develop an overnight love affair with Hong Kong as I did, but I promise you'll love the shopping opportunities, the choices and the bargains.

Diane Freis
Diane Freis International

It would be my pleasure to welcome you to Hong Kong at any time, but I am especially pleased to welcome you now because we at the Peninsula Hotel are celebrating so much.

The year 1993 has seen the hotel's 65th birthday anniversary. In early 1994 our new tower will open, introducing you to even more Peninsula style. Yes, we will regain a spectacular view of the harbour, there will be a health club, a swimming pool, a spa, and yes, even more shopping.

We are pleased to celebrate these two major events in a back-to-back fashion—the old and the new come together at "The Pen" just as they do on almost every street in Hong Kong. Indeed, Hong Kong has changed tremendously in the last few years. We are proud to be part of that change: as the skylines of Central and Kowloon boast a number of architecturally unique buildings, our new tower will be part of the parade.

The Peninsula Hotel has been a landmark in Kowloon since its opening in 1928; we continue into the next century with a mark of the times—a new silhouette merged with our old traditions.

In all our years of service, The Peninsula has played host to a never ending list of royalty, celebrities, famous personalities, business guests, tourists and yes, shoppers. It's been our tradition to meet guests at the airport with one of our Rolls Royces and to treat them to a stay as luxurious as the ride in a Rolls.

I hope that the next time you plan a visit to Hong Kong you'll stay with us; you'll let us send one of our Brewster green Rolls' to the airport for you and your family.

If you cannot stay with us, perhaps you'll come by for tea in the lobby—an old Hong Kong tradition or dinner at Gaddi's—Hong Kong's most famous restaurant. Come take a look at all our news, stroll through the hotel and by all means, check out our shopping arcade. See the new and the old parts of the hotel and come be part of Hong Kong's constantly changing future.

Our door gods stand ready and waiting to welcome you.

And remember, "The Pen" is mightier than the shopping bag...no matter what anybody tells you to the contrary.

Felix M. Bieger
General Manager
The Peninsula Hotel

DETAILS

Welcome to Hong Kong

Hong Kong is known as the "Gateway to the Orient" because more people use it as their Asian base than any other city. Whether they visit on business or as tourists, they come to Hong Kong and then fan out: south to Bangkok or Singapore, west to China or north toward Korea and Japan. Many will change planes in Japan on arrival in Asia, but they won't actually explore Japan until they are on their way home. Home from Hong Kong, that is.

"Stay an Extra Day" has been the Hong Kong Tourist Association's advertising slogan for several years now: The truth is, when you make yourself at home in Hong Kong these days, you don't need an extra day—you need an extra week. Or more. In fact, Macau has now blossomed to such an extent that you may see yourself coming and going—coming into Hong Kong and going home from Macau.

I now find it virtually impossible to "do" the Far East with a three-day stopover in Hong Kong and then a whirlwind tour of assorted other ports. Shopping aside, there's simply so much going on in Hong Kong and Macau these days, that you may want to enter here. . . and stay put. For quite some time.

Get There Now

Most people I talk to seem to be feeling some time pressure to get to Hong Kong, to enjoy Hong Kong, to make sure they've been part of the big show. They worry, that just maybe, things will change once the Chinese officially take over.

Frankly, I've seen so many changes in Hong Kong already that I don't expect anything radical to happen on July 1, 1997. But not knowing what will happen has indeed put the pressure on many tourists—especially Americans—who are now planning ahead to make sure they get to Hong Kong before that date.

All this travel means promotional rates at hotels and airlines, tour groups galore and a certain excitement in the air that makes you think: "Hong Kong. Now!"

Reference Points

For the purposes of my definition, "Hong Kong" encompasses the island itself, of course, but also Kowloon, the New Territories and a few hundred islands. To me it's all Hong Kong. In 1997 the British will return both the island of Hong Kong, the city of Kowloon and all of the New Territories to mainland China. In just a few years, all that we refer to as Hong Kong will technically be considered part of the People's Republic of China (PRC). But that's another story.

Shopping in Hong Kong is concentrated heavily in two areas: Central, on the Hong Kong side, and Tsim Sha Tsui, in Kowloon. Central is very upscale, civilized, businesslike and modern. Tsim Sha Tsui is more gritty and more active in a frenetic way. There is more fashion in Central, but there are more deals to be had in Tsim Sha Tsui. Study a map or two before you go so you have your reference points in order.

Most of the factory outlets are outside of the main shopping areas, in towns like Lai Chi Kok and Kwun Tong. These are all part of the Kowloon peninsula. And, of course, if you are a truly intrepid shopper, you can really have fun and go out into the New Territories where there are more outlets, a few markets and some good shopping sprees to be had.

Both sides of the harbor are divided into distinct neighborhoods, each with its own personality. As you get to be an Old China Hand, you'll get to know the characteristics of each and pride yourself on choosing the less touristy. Hong Kong is bigger than you think and has a lot more to offer than just shopping.

The Mostly Free Port of Hong Kong

Hong Kong did not become a shopper's mecca over a long span of time or because of the industrialization of the world. It was *created* to be a shopping paradise, for very real economic reasons. "Hong Kong isn't a city, it's a shopping mart," one observant soul said back in the late 1800s. Hong Kong is a capitalist's dream: There is duty on only a handful of commodities, and no duty on outgoing goods.

Because Hong Kong is an almost free port, most goods come in without taxation. For example, take your basic Chanel suit. Made in France, the suit costs a certain number of *francs* in France. When it's shipped to the U.S., the price goes up because of shipping costs, and because the U.S. government levies high taxes against items that are competitive with U.S.-made goods. Hong Kong does not have the same protective government policies—thus you may find a bargain.

The real strategy is to buy items that have been made in Hong Kong that will cost more in the U.S. once customs and duties have been applied, stateside.

Note that few European designer items cost less in Hong Kong than in the U.S. or the country of origin (there are exceptions; especially at Hermès!), but for those who don't care about price, you have the opportunity to buy goods that simply are not even sold in the U.S. Some haven't made their American debut, others are items simply not sold in the U.S., and still others don't pass FDA regulations. I bought Chanel eyeliners in colors totally unseen in the U.S. due to FDA rules. And I haven't broken out in hives yet!

A Short History of Hong Kong Trade

If you've read or seen *Shōgun* or *Tai-Pan*, you're going to be one step ahead of me on this, but here goes. The Hong Kong area has always been a hotbed of commerce, because China silk came out of either Canton or Shanghai. Let's step back in time to the middle 1600s. You remember the Portuguese and their "black ship"? The black ship brought goods from Europe in exchange for silk from China. This was a great big fat business, and the Portuguese wanted it all to themselves. So did the British, the Spaniards, the French and, later, the Americans.

The only problem was, the big British ships couldn't get into the shallow waters of Macau (the Portuguese port), which is somewhat closer to Canton. Happily they soon discovered that the perfect port was on the island of Hong Kong. So for no other reason than deep water, Hong Kong became the "in" place.

Queen Victoria howled with laughter when in 1842 Hong Kong was given to the British as a prize of war. And it really was a laughing matter. You see, not only were silks and woolens being traded, there also was a thriving business in opium. The first Opium War ended with the British winning and getting Hong Kong, in perpetuity. The second and third times they won, they got the rights to Kowloon and then certain mainland territories for ninety-nine years. Back then, ninety-nine years sounded like a darn long time. However, on June 30, 1997, that ninety-nine-year lease is up, and those territories will go back to China on July 1. Britain has graciously thrown in Hong Kong Island.

The Yin and Yang of Shopping

In the old days, shopping fever swept Hong Kong, and a certain energy of excess permeated the air. That was the 1980s. Things are different now: Some days you'll hit a lode and it will be just like your wildest dreams (if you are a first-timer), or just like the old days (if you are a repeat visitor). Other days, you'll find nothing; you'll walk Granville Road and mutter to yourself, "Same old junk, jeez....".

You can walk from fancy shop to more fancy shop in the malls and look at sky-high prices and feel like a worm. Nothing you can afford; who buys this stuff anyway, you start to wonder. Then suddenly you whip out your price chart from home and discover those Hermès scarves cost $50 less than in the U.S. and 50£ less than in London!

I've been on the streets enough to know two important yin and yang facts:

- The good stuff is often hidden. Either it's put away or it goes to those who have custom work done and know how to go after real value.
- You have to go back to the same places constantly and hope to get lucky. Or you have to hit it just right. It's just like shopping at Loehmann's (where you have come to accept the hit-or-miss philosophy).

It is virtually impossible to go to Hong Kong and not find anything to buy, but the days of deals galore may be over. Savvy shoppers are off to Bangkok with empty suitcases.

The best value in Hong Kong is represented by the tailor who custom-makes you a suit for the same price as an off-the-rack suit in the U.S., by the jeweler who creates one-of-a-kind jewelry for you at better-than-at-home prices and by the street vendors who are selling their usual junk at prices so low you don't even care that they won't bargain. That hand-knit cotton designer sweater with the intricate floral pattern that I bought for $22 was a steal. An old-fashioned, down-and-dirty, God-I-Love-Hong-Kong kind of steal. Ditto the Gap shirt for $10 and the Baby Gap sweater for $8.

You can still get a namebrand-style wristwatch for $15. And that Hermès-style handbag for $45 looks awfully good. And by the way, those double-strand, matinee-length pearls I have cost only $40. Yes, it is impressive. Confusing but impressive.

If you are British and used to high prices on everything from home-brand goods to American labels (like Gap), you will wonder what I'm even talking about—prices may simply make you giggle. The biggest problem British shoppers will have is that most of the designer goods sold on the streets have American labels and aside from the Gap, British people simply don't know what they are getting. Try explaining to Sophie who Perry Ellis is. Will Bumble ever really understand what a Barney's label means?

When a Buy Is a Good-Bye

A true-blue shopper has been known to lose her head now and again. And no place on earth is more conducive to losing one's head than Hong

Kong. You can see so many great "bargains" that you end up buying many items just because the price is cheap, not because you need or want them. Or you can fall into the reverse trap, seeing nothing to buy, getting frustrated and buying the wrong things. When you get home, you realize that you've tied up a fair amount of money in rather silly purchases. I've made so many mistakes, in fact, that I've had to have a long and careful talk with myself to come up with an out-of-town shopping philosophy that lays down the ground rules.

Shopping in a foreign country is much more romantic than shopping at home, there's no question about it. And face it, most people expect to shop in Hong Kong. Even non-shoppers want to shop when away from home; they, too, love Hong Kong. But if you make a mistake while shopping in another American city, you can usually return the merchandise and get a credit with just a small amount of hassle. On a foreign trip, returns can be a major problem and usually aren't worth the effort. So, to keep mistakes to a minimum, I've got a few rules of the game:

- Don't buy cameras and electronics in Hong Kong. Period. End of story. If you don't believe me, read my saga (page 56).
- Take a careful and thorough survey of your closet (including china and linen) and your children's closets before you leave town. Know what you've got so you can know what you need. While you don't have to need something in order to buy it, knowing that you need it (and will be saving money by buying it abroad) will help your conscience a lot.
- If you *need* an item of clothing to complete an ensemble, bring a piece of the outfit with you. (At the very least, very carefully cut a small swatch of fabric from the inside of the hem or a seam.)

- If you are planning on having an item made to fill a hole in your wardrobe, bring the other parts of the ensemble with you. If you expect to be 100% satisfied with anything you have custom-made in Hong Kong, you have to put 100% effort into your side of the deal. Show your tailor the suit that the blouse is supposed to go with.

- Figure the price accurately. Despite rumor to the contrary, the Hong Kong dollar *does* fluctuate! Since the Hong Kong dollar and the U.S. dollar stay fairly consistent in value, sterling fluctuates like mad, in comparison.

- Figure in the duty. U.S. citizens are currently allowed $400 duty-free. If you are traveling with your family, figure out your family total. Children, even infants, still get the $400 allowance. If you have more than $400 worth of merchandise, you pay a flat 10% on the next $1,000; after that you pay according to various duty rates.

- Calculate what your bargain will cost you in aggravation. Will you have to schlepp the item all over the world with you? If it takes up a lot of suitcase room, if it's heavy, if it's cumbersome, if it's breakable and at risk every time you pack and unpack or check your suitcase, if it has to be hand-held—it might not be worth the cheap price tag. Estimate your time, trouble and level of tolerance per item. Sure, it may be inexpensive, but if it's an ordeal to bring it home, is it really a good buy? Let me tell you just how heavy a fax machine can be....

- Likewise, if you have to insure and ship it, is it still a bargain? How will you feel if the item never makes it to your door?

- Do your research on prices at home first. I spent several hours choosing and shipping lamps from a factory-outlet source only to discover an American discounter who, once the price of the shipping was taken into account, charged the same price.

- I am ambivalent about the value of counterfeit merchandise and cannot advise you whether to buy it or to walk away from it. If you suspect an item to be a fake, you must evaluate if this is a good buy or a good-bye. Remember that fakes most certainly do not have the quality of craftsmanship that originals have. You may also be asked to forfeit the item at Customs or pay duty on the value of the real object. But you may have a lot of fun with your fakes.

- My rule of thumb on a good buy is that 50% (or more) off the U.S. or British price is a valuable saving. I think that a saving of less than 20% is marginal, and probably not worth the effort (of course, it depends on the item and how it will come back into the country with you, etc.). If the saving is between 20% and 50%, judge according to personal desire and the ratio of the previous points. If the saving is 50% or better, buy several and whoop with joy. That's a good buy!

The Bed N Bath Rule of Shopping/Part I

I had one goal firmly in mind on a recent trip to Hong Kong: Victorian-style whitework duvet cover and shams. What better place to buy a duvet cover or two? Need a spare while one's in the wash, right? They should be cheap in Hong Kong, right? Two for the price of one—let's be practical—right? Wrong.

I scoured the streets of Hong Kong, of Kowloon, of Stanley. Duvet covers—and not even in styles I would kill for—cost in the $200–$300 (U.S.) range! I kept searching throughout the trip, but without success. Upon return to suburbia, I bopped right into the local branch of Bed N Bath and found, live from Shanghai, a set including queen-sized duvet cover, dust ruffle and two pillow shams for $149.

The moral of the story: You may find Chinese-made products are cheaper at home than in Hong Kong.

The Bed N Bath Rule of Shopping/Part 2

A few days after returning from Hong Kong, I received in the mail a catalog from the I. Magnin department store, in California. In this small but densely-packed fanfare of merchandise was a very good selection of the same items found in any international duty-free store. The $470 Gucci watch that seemed like a bargain in the duty-free in Hong Kong cost only $495 from I. Magnin.

If possible, try to get your hands on prices and pictures of the kind of merchandise that interests you, so you can decide if there really are savings to be had. The Magnin catalogue had goodies from Fendi, Chanel, Gucci, Ferragamo, etc. Call toll-free for your own copy: (800) 227-1125.

Ian Cook, British photographer and traveling companion extraordinaire, came prepared with a huge list of designer goods available in London, everything from a La Perla bodysuit to Trivial Pursuit. The variations in price range were staggering: Some items cost one-third their London price; some were within five pounds of the London price; others cost less in London than Hong Kong. And London is not an inexpensive city.

Be Prepared

Be prepared with prices from home. But also be prepared for a very different world. Unless you are used to traveling in the Far East, you may find Hong Kong extremely different from anything you've ever seen before. Depending on how sheltered your life has been, you may even go into culture shock. We don't preach about politics or the poor, but we do suggest that you be mentally prepared for what you are about to experience. There are a few particularly important cultural details:

- Chinese street vendors and retailers may be rude to Anglos. We try not to generalize about a thing like this, but you'll soon discover it is a common thread of conversation among tourists and expats alike. There is a two-class system at work. Face it.
- The world works best with "tea money"—tip everyone and anyone if you want favors, information or even a smile. Yep, those rickshaw drivers want money if you plan to take their picture.
- As a tourist, you will never get the cheapest price possible, so forget it. Speak Cantonese perfectly? Great, you're on your way to a better price.
- You are a rich American (or Brit) and will never miss what you overpay, according to many vendors. Take heart, prices are highest for Germans and then Swiss. Americans rank about fourth or fifth on the local list of rich catches. Some vendors want to make enough money to immigrate before 1997—watch out!

Translation, Please

Hong Kong is an easy city to negotiate once you know the system. Spend some time with maps before you go and you will hit the streets running. Don't be afraid of the language barrier:

Most Chinese retailers in Hong Kong understand some English, either written or spoken. Carry your hotel's card with you, with addresses in Chinese in case you end up in the New Territories or at outlying factory outlets and need directions home. Outside of the main shopping districts, there may be fewer people who speak or understand English, but there are plenty of folks who are willing to try to help you out.

If you are asking directions of someone in the street, write down your destination, in English. Your pronunciation of a location can be so mangled that you will not be understood. Also pay attention to the signs in the MTR and make sure they match your maps exactly, as many places will sound alike in your brain. Tsuen Wan and Sheung Wan are nowhere near the same place, but you may pronounce them in rather similar tones. Don't go by ear; go by spelling and make sure every letter matches!

Booking Hong Kong/1

Why pay for a ton of guidebooks when you can get most of what you need to know for free? The Hong Kong Tourist Association has booklets on everything; write to the one near you or pick up a packet full of brochures (published by the HKTA) as you exit passport control at Hong Kong International Airport. If you visit HKTA's main counter at Jardine House, 1 Connaught Place, Central, on the 35th floor, or at the Star Ferry on the Kowloon side, you can pick up a more complete selection.

The HKTA publishes three pamphlets that I consider a must: *The Official Guide to Shopping, Eating Out and Services in Hong Kong* gives you the address of every HKTA member shop by area and by category. While they do not recommend one shop over another, they at least have elicited a promise from their member shops to be honest. If they are not, you have the HKTA on your side. Look for their listings of factory outlets that are members of the association. Addresses are given in both English and Chinese. The *Official Hong Kong Guide* is published monthly and contains general information about the city. The HKTA also publishes a weekly newspaper. It contains news of events and shows, along with the usual ads for shops.

Inside the free packet you got at the airport find the A-O-A *Map Directory*. Maps show both building and street locations. Since so many addresses include the building name, street and area, it makes finding an address simple. For example, if you are looking for the Gucci shop in the Landmark on Des Voeux Road in Central, simply locate Des Voeux Road in Central on the map and find the Landmark Building. You then know the cross streets.

Hong Kong Factory Bargains (sold in bookstores, not published by the HKTA) is an old-time standard for locals, although the author says she may not continue her annual revisions. The last update I bought was the ninth edition; check to see if the tenth is available. If you are planning to be in the city for an extended period of time or are simply determined to hit all of the factory outlets (no matter how exhausting this may be), this is a useful book to have. Addresses are given in Chinese and English. I don't always agree with the write-ups, but the directions in each section are fabulous, there are maps and a local guide offers a voice I can't match. Don't quit, Dana!

Booking Hong Kong/2

Publishing must be inexpensive in Hong Kong since all the hotels publish their own magazines—in glorious color, no less. The pictures and advertising serve to give you a quick glimpse at the whole scene; Hong Kong *Tatler*, similar to the British version before Tina Brown left her mark, will fill you in on the social scene. The ads alone will pinpoint the best shops and malls. There are also numerous trade journals sold at newsstands; they are usually expensive and won't be of much use unless you are in a particular trade.

Hotel Tips

Many tour companies and large hotel chains offer shopping packages for Hong Kong, but few of these include the kind of five-star hotels we depend on. If you're a sucker for luxury, don't fight it—but shop it around so you can get the most for your money. Hong Kong has a good base of hotel rooms and when things aren't too busy, there are big-time deals to be made. Promotional rates can be as low as $109 a night at the Omni (Kowloon) and $149 a night at the Hilton (Central). While the Peninsula is the most expensive hotel in town, they may have celebratory prices when they open their new tower. Don't be afraid to ask for a deal!

Some secrets that might make booking your hotel easier:

- Always ask the hotels if they are offering weekend or five-day rates. Almost all hotels discount rooms during the off-season, or when there is not a lot of business in town. Hong Kong has so many conventions, and so many new hotels, that you should be able to get a deal almost any time except for Chinese New Year.

- The Hong Kong Tourist Association publishes a brochure called *Hong Kong Hotel Guide*. Write to their head office in Chicago for a copy (HKTA, Suite 2400, 333 North Michigan Avenue, Chicago, IL 60601). This publication provides a comprehensive list of all the possibilities, including addresses, phone numbers, room rates, fax numbers and services offered.

- Check the big chains for promotional rates. Often you can prepay in U.S. dollars and save. Consider putting together your own group, and booking yourself as a tour package. Every hotel has a special department to deal with groups, and offers incentives. Watch advertisements in your local newspaper's Sunday travel section or buy the *New York Times* for a few Sundays. From November through March, expect some pretty good deals.

- Ask about inclusive packages that may include breakfast, airport transfers and other items that are usually charged as extra.

Shopping Hotels of Hong Kong

Central

THE HONGKONG HILTON HOTEL

The Hongkong Hilton Hotel is one of the colony's best-established insider's secrets: old-timers and locals know this is THE hotel to book despite the fact that there are newer kids on the block...or around the corner. The first luxury hotel in Hong Kong, the Hilton has just finished a huge renovation so that it can compete in the glitz market with the other power hotels of Central. Not that it needed to. When you tell locals that you are staying at the Hilton, you suddenly put yourself in another category of visitor—one who knows.

The hotel is a huge tower right in the heart of Central, one block from the Peak Tram and two blocks from the Star Ferry. It's next door to the Bank of China landmark building designed by I.M. Pei; there's a gigantic swimming pool, health club, several floors of shopping and half the rooms in the hotel come with dramatic harbor views. You pay more for a view, but it's worth it!

The Hilton also has its own Chinese junk, the *Wan Fu*. You do not need to be a hotel guest to book any of the harbor cruises; they go out for lunch, drinks or dinner. Speaking of lunch, be sure to check out our favorite shopper's lunch spot in town—Sketti's—which is in the lobby of the Hilton (see page 40). The Hilton Grill is the scene of most Central power lunches.

For reservations in the U.S., call 800-HILTONS.

THE HONGKONG HILTON HOTEL
2 Queen's Road Central, Hong Kong (MTR: Central)

Kowloon

THE REGENT HOTEL
Still considered to be one of the most scenic locations in Hong Kong, the Regent occupies the tip of Kowloon Peninsula; the views from the lobby bar at night are nothing short of spectacular.

Aaron and I once got upgraded to a suite that had a whirlpool bath situated against a huge glass wall so you could luxuriate in the tub and watch the Star Ferry float across the harbor. The room also had its own sauna, and a wall of glass to maximize the view. But view is not all the Regent is about: They have the town's best hotel shopping mall, which has replaced the one at the Peninsula Hotel as the chicest address. Every big-name European designer has a shop here, but other big names abound—from Diane Freis to Donna Karan! If that isn't enough, there's also a less fancy mall (New World Shopping Centre) attached to the Regent's three-level mall, and the underground road of dreams that is coming soon—the mall which connects the Regent and the Pen.

Guests in some rooms get Hermès bath goodies while other rooms have only Regent logo bath suds. Harbor-view rooms are smaller than out-side-view rooms, but then again, they do have the view. The Lobby Lounge and the Harbourview Cafe are must stops for eating, especially if you aren't staying at the hotel but want to check out the digs.

Part of what's so interesting about this hotel is that it is both formal and casual at the same time. The pool is great, but the hot tub is what you'll come away raving about. Indeed, I can't consider a trip to Hong Kong to be a success until I've spent some time in the Regent's hot tub. (The cover photo of this book was shot there.) Harbor-view rooms are smaller and more expensive than pool-views, but go ahead, splurge. When dawn breaks over the harbor and you sit in your bed in the Regent and stare at the skyline of Central bathed in pink light, you'll know the meaning of life. A harbor-view double costs about $300 a night.

For U.S. reservations, call 800-545-4000.

THE REGENT HOTEL
Salisbury Road, Kowloon (MTR: Tsim Sha Tsui)

THE PENINSULA HOTEL
The Pen, as it is called, is the most famous hotel in Hong Kong and continues in its friendly competition with the Regent, as the two vie for international titles as the best hotel in town. The only way to decide is to stay in both of them—preferably during the same stay—so you can see how uniquely different the two properties are. (This is not as nuts as it sounds, especially if you are going to Macau for a few days.)

Once the health club, pool and view are in place, the Pen will certainly have a new story to tell. We're marking our calendars for the opening, but we didn't suffer too much with old English elegance galore, private little box doors for morning newspapers and tons of bath goodies, replenished regularly.

The Pen prides itself on its Old-World charm and classy elegance; the crowd is much more dressed up than at the Regent. The lobby, where tea is the most famous beverage, is the best place for spotting rich, beautiful local women, called *tai-tais*. Gaddi's is the single most famous French restaurant in town.

Now then, in case you're tacky and care only about the bottom line, here's the dish you've been waiting for. Yes, the Pen is more expensive than the Regent and yes, they pride themselves on this fact. A deluxe harbor-view room will cost close to $400 a night.

For U.S. reservations, call 800-262-9467.

THE PENINSULA HOTEL
Salisbury Road, Kowloon (MTR: Tsim Sha Tsui)

THE KOWLOON HOTEL

If you want the best location in town but don't feel up to springing for a five-star hotel, perhaps you should consider the Kowloon Hotel, whose secret is the simple fact that it is owned by the Peninsula Group. It is a four-star hotel and more in keeping with an American-style big hotel than a palace, but it's got advantages. You're next door to the Pen, and the hotel is built in a slim tower, so some view rooms are available. Best of all, a suite here costs the same as a regular room at the Pen or the Regent. A harbor-view double costs about $150 a night.

For U.S. reservations, call 800-262-9467.

THE KOWLOON HOTEL
19-21 Nathan Road, Kowloon (MTR: Tsim Sha Tsui)

OMNI THE HONG KONG HOTEL

Harbour City has three hotels built in and around its office and shopping complex; I like this one the best, because it is the closest to Ocean Terminal and has a mezzanine that is devoted to antiques shops. The lobby design is modern chic, and the rooms overlook either the harbor or the shopping. The other hotels also run by Omni are the Omni Marco Polo Hotel and the Omni Prince Hotel.

A lot of groups book here and the place can be swarming with tourists, but the prices are unbeatable for this kind of location. Promotional rates are $109 a night!

For U.S. reservations, call 800-448-8355.

OMNI THE HONG KONG HOTEL
Harbour City, 2 Canton Road, Kowloon (MTR: Tsim Sha Tsui)

Getting There

When it comes to booking your plane tickets, have I got news for you: Transatlantic is the way to go! If you live on the East Coast of the U.S., of course. Or even as far west as Texas.

The day I found out that Hong Kong was a mere ten-hour flight from London is the day I converted. A few months after my discovery, I noted that several airlines, led by Singapore Airlines, began advertising their transatlantic routes.

British Airways doesn't have to advertise; they've got the London-to-Hong Kong and the New York-to-London business sewn up already. They've been voted best airline in the world by *Business Traveller*. They are just about the only airline in the world that isn't hurting.

Now then, let me state the simple facts: New York is technically *closer* to Hong Kong—if the crow was flying transatlantic. It's only a matter of a few hundred miles (about 500), but it's a scientific fact. So don't act like I'm nuts when I tell you my secrets. As it happens, only big-time spenders have heretofore used the transatlantic route because they go via Concorde to London and then on to Hong Kong. But you can make it all work for you without splurging on the Concorde.

Also note it doesn't really matter which way you go, if you are coming from Chicago, Dallas-Fort Worth, Orlando, Raleigh-Durham or Atlanta, BUT you may find you have less jet lag if you fly through London. (I'd also much rather layover in London than Tokyo any day of the week.)

I have now experimented with this route several times and can tell you that this is so much easier than any other route you will never go via the West Coast again. (Unless you live there.)

Now then, I'm not finished on the subject of British Airways on my transatlantic tricks. The deal of the century happens to be an around-the-world ticket on British Airways. I'm giving prices now just for you to compare—obviously prices change with the seasons and the tides, but this is to give you the big picture. OK: an around-the-world, coach ticket on British Airways is good for one year and needs to be bought 14 days prior to departure: it costs $2,570. A business-class ticket on British Airways, which takes you from New York to London, and London to Hong Kong, and then straight home or anywhere else you want to go, is $3,618 with fourteen-day advance purchase. To put that in perspective, please note that a business-class ticket London–Hong Kong round trip is approximately $3,000. Do you smell a bargain, or what?!!

It gets better. A first-class, around-the-world ticket is $5,020, and a Concorde ticket—you fly Concorde from New York to London only—comes with an add-on price: $863 for first-class passengers; $1,719 for business-class passengers.

Before I get into the specifics of the Hong Kong information, you should know that British Airways has added lots of deals for the U.K. and European portions of the ticket and since the ticket can be used over the space of a continuing year, you can book yourself one hell of a deal. You must always travel in one direction, but you can make side-trips, which few other round-the-world tickets allow you to do. You even get deals to various Hawaiian islands (free) as you go 'round.

And now, to get you to Hong Kong: British Airways has two flights a day from London to Hong Kong. If you take the Concorde from New York to London, you can transfer directly to the evening flight to Hong Kong and be there faster than you can say "Tsim Sha Tsui". Since I can't afford the Concorde (and I'm afraid of it, to boot), I've also looked at other British Airways options. I prefer the overnight flight from New York to London with a swift London layover (and a bath) and then the midday flight to Hong Kong, which allows me to sleep on the plane and arrive in Hong Kong ready to shop by midday.

While the around-the-world ticket is the single biggest bargain you will get in or out of Hong Kong, you can do a New York-to-London, London-to-Hong Kong combo ticket and save money.

Book yourself a British Airways economy seat from New York to London; this is only a five-and-a-half-hour flight and you'll sleep, and it's a breeze anyway. Book at a special promotional rate and you can get it as low as $400 round trip. Then book the London-to-Hong Kong leg in business class or economy, depending on your strength. The business-class ticket does cost $3,000, as already mentioned, and isn't as good an overall buy as the around-the-world ticket, but it does give you the advantage of coming and going via London and laying over there so that you only have European jet lag and are not totally disoriented (if you'll pardon the expression). See page 25 for London Layover tips.

Ticket Deals

Flights on all airplanes to Hong Kong, especially from the West Coast, are packed. One of the reasons for this is that there are lots of business people flying these routes. With China opening up, there are even more of them. Add to that the fact that there are wholesalers who buy blocks of tickets, knowing they will be able to resell them to travel agents and tour groups, and you can see why it may be hard to get the flights you want.

Because they buy in bulk, wholesalers often get a better price. These ticket brokers pass the savings on to their customers. Enter Lillian Fong.

Lillian and her comrades are ticket brokers for many airlines to many destinations. We have used her for years to book tickets to Hong Kong and Europe, and find that her prices are hard to beat. You can book any class of service; Lillian will tell you the airline and time when you can get the best deal. The seats are legitimate. They have nothing to do with coupons or other questionable practices. Call her and tell her I sent you, since her business is otherwise in wholesale blocks.

Want to go on and into China? Lillian will also assemble tours into China or other Asian destinations. Be sure to ask. It is usually cheaper to book a package, which includes room, breakfast, and all taxes, than to just purchase the airfare. You may also want to book a circle Pacific ticket, which is sometimes a bargain. This is handy for those who want to see a lot of the Orient and still save money. Call or fax Lillian Fong, Pacific Place Travel, 7540A East Garvey, Rosemead, CA 91770. Telephone: (818) 307-3218; fax: (818) 307-3223.

If you are leaving from the West Coast, look into one of aviation's newest treats: a plane that flies nonstop from there to Hong Kong. The flight takes about fourteen hours, but you don't have to layover at Narita. (If you want to get to Narita, it's only ten hours from the West Coast!) You also have less jet lag!

If you are booking from the East Coast and want to travel transatlantic, you already know to call British Airways. You may also want to call and then follow up with some British bucket shops (travel discounters) who have deals on package tour seats and bulk seats, most frequently in coach—but then, a coach seat from London to Hong Kong is not as great a hardship as it is when flying transpacific—so check it out.

I use STA Travel for deals to the Orient; they have offices in both London and New York. They offer different deals from both cities, so it pays to go for the international phone call to London in order to get a full picture of what's available. STA Travel, Priory House, 6 Wright's Lane, London W8 6TA, England. Phone 001-44-71-937-9962. There are other phone numbers for deals to other parts of the world. The New York office can be reached from anywhere in the U.S., toll-free; call 800-777-0112.

Many bucket shops are best for last-minute travel, because they are selling unsold seats. Prices may vary on immediate and advance purchase tickets. (Advance purchase will be more.) Not that too many people go to the Orient on a whim, but these kinds of deals do make that possible.

Other thoughts:

- If flying from the West Coast, look into what is called a Circle Pacific fare. Most American carriers, and many other internationals, offer you this chance to make your own itinerary, but to travel to several cities in the Orient at package-tour prices. You do not join a group; you set your own pace, but you get a break on the price because you fly all legs with the same carrier.

- Don't be afraid of business-class. The trip is a lengthy one; you will be much more comfortable in business-class. Furthermore, there are more business-class seats than any other (you aren't the only person who really doesn't want to do this trip in a coach seat), so there are more deals than you thought. A few years ago I had the shock of a lifetime when we priced out Aaron Gershman's ticket. The business-class child fare was only $200 more than the economy ticket!

If you are committed to economy, seriously consider the transatlantic route (making sure you get a good price), because the flight is more conveniently broken up and is shorter.

Also consider first-class, or at least check it out. Lillian offered me first-class upgrade tickets if I paid the full fare for business-class. There are all sorts of promotions out there—ask.

- Consider around-the-world tickets; price them at all classes of service before you decide how to fly. Lillian doesn't like to book these because they don't pay a good commission (other travel agents feel the same way) but the truth is that if you call British Airways (800-247-9297) and ask for an around-the-world ticket, they will put it together for you...in a flash. True, you will not fly British Airways on every leg of the trip. (Drat.) You'll fly British Airways and United, and you'll save a bundle! (See page 20).

- Package tours often offer you the best deals, especially if they include airport transfers and some extras. Check them out, especially when you can stay at luxury hotels.

Around-the-World Hotel Deals

Although the savings on around-the-world tickets are known by a handful of businessmen, few people know that you can get around-the-world hotel deals from Hong Kong's Big Two: The Regent—Four Seasons has hotels in New York, London, Hong Kong and Beverly Hills; the Peninsula has hotels in New York, Hong Kong and Beverly Hills, and is a member of Leading Hotels of the World, so you can team up with The Ritz in London. If you book a through trip with them, you get promotional perks.

London Layovers

Now that I'm a pro at going to Hong Kong via the transatlantic route, I have a few tips to pass on to avoid jet lag and maximize the pleasure of your trip.

• Go straight through from New York to Hong Kong without spending a night in London. Do get out of the airport for daylight (needed to combat jet lag) and fresh air. Even though there is great shopping in Terminal 4, I suggest you plan for the early morning arrival to London and have time to leave the airport. You can take a later arrival and just stay in the airport transfer lounge, or go shopping, but I think that's boring...and more tiring. Get your mind and your tush going—getting there is half the fun, remember?

LONDON: Book a day-rate room at either your Hong Kong hotel's London hotel or another hotel (I always book the Ritz!). Have a bath and a big English breakfast and go for a walk. Getting out of the airport and getting some fresh air is essential. Since your luggage has been checked straight through to Hong Kong, you can hop on the tube in Terminal 4 (British Airways' private terminal) and get off at Green Park or Picadilly without changing trains. (Green Park is across the street from the Ritz.)

You can spend a few hours or the day in London, depending on which flight you pick for the Hong Kong leg. Regardless, you'll be refreshed and ready to travel—and to sleep a little bit. Do note that if you are too well-acclimated to London time, you will not want to sleep on the London-to-Hong Kong leg, which will cause jet lag once you arrive in Hong Kong. Ian (who lives in London) likes to eat and watch the movies, and then we're there; this is OK if you take the night flight from London, because you arrive in Hong Kong at nightfall. If you take the mid-day flight, plan to sleep en route to Hong Kong in order to avoid jet lag on arrival.

WINDSOR: Windsor is about seven miles from Heathrow and makes the perfect layover stop. There's a Forte Grand hotel right on High Street, so you can surround yourself with the joys of Windsor, Eton and Britain, walk around town and do it all without the hustle of London. Furthermore, if you arrange it ahead of time, the CASTLE HOTEL will send a car for you, or you can make a deal with your taxi driver so the rate is about half the going price. Call 800-225-5843 in the U.S. If you are already at the airport in Heathrow and realize that you need to get out, call 0345-404-040 for information on the Castle Hotel in Windsor or others. The direct phone to the Castle Hotel is 011-44-753-851-011. From Britain, dial 0753-851-011.

HEATHROW: If you don't want to go into town or anywhere else, book yourself into the Edwardian International—one of Edwardian's many London hotels, this one is conveniently located near Terminal 4 at Heathrow. Created to look like the Disney version of an Olde English Hotel, the hotel offers a fabulous (low) day rate and even better, it has a swimming pool, hot tub, sauna, health club, etc., for the use of guests. You can even book a massage. Exercise is a must in fighting jet lag; when you see this pool (it's almost a lagoon), you will flip. If you feel like splurging, book a suite with a four-poster bed. Curiously enough, some of the suites are decorated in chinoiserie to get you in the mood for Hong Kong. This is also the perfect layover on the way home: you spend the night and catch the flight to New York the following morning. From the U.S., call 800-447-1957 for reservations or information.

- Plan to layover and spend a night in Britain on the way home from Hong Kong if you are not going around-the-world. Your British Airways flight will arrive around 5 A.M., so you'll have plenty of time to exhaust yourself at any of the above locations —or Cliveden, the country estate about ten miles away.

  Cliveden is one of the most famous country homes-turned-hotel in all of England. It dates back to 1660, sits on the banks of the River Thames and breathes fantasy and escape from every nook and cranny. This is the ultimate way to unwind from the Orient and to beat jet lag—they have huge bathrooms, many of which have fireplaces in them! They do not like nonresidential breakfast guests, so you may as well come for the night, get some sleep and get acclimated so that by the time you reach New York the next day, jet lag is minimal.

  Cliveden is a member of Leading Hotels of the World; for U.S. reservations, call 800-223-6800. Dial directly 011-44-628-668-561; fax 628-661-837. In Britain: 0628-668-561.

- Do layover in London on the return, either at an airport hotel (Edwardian International!), the Castle Hotel in Windsor, or in town— you'll have the luggage with you, but you'll get a chance to break up the jet lag.

One Final British Word

Gatwick. That's my final word. Do not let anyone talk you into going to Hong Kong from Britain via Gatwick! The reason is that all those flights to Hong Kong get there via India. This makes the flight longer. If you are doing this in economy-class (and we have done it!), you will not appreciate the extra tar time...or the bug spray.

While the bus ride from Gatwick to Heathrow at dawn is absolutely lovely, you do not want to make this trip if you can help it.

Arriving Hong Kong

Hong Kong's Kai Tak International Airport is almost in downtown Kowloon; you're just a few minutes away from the Regent and the Pen. The controversial new airport on Lantau Island won't open until 1997—so we'll worry about that later. Right now, Kai Tak is a breeze.

Get from the airport to your hotel in the swank car your hotel will send for you (you pay; it's added to your bill) or via bus or taxi. While public transport is simple and inexpensive, part of the fun of being in Hong Kong is settling into that Rolls or Daimler or Mercedes Benz that the hotel has provided. Expect to pay $30–$40 (it varies from hotel to hotel) each way for the luxury, but do try to find it in your budget.

While one certainly doesn't pick a hotel based on the cost of the luxury car service, do note that hotels in Central charge more because of the Cross-Harbour Tunnel. The Peninsula, merely a block further from the airport than the Regent, charges about $15 more for its car—each way! And no, riding in a Rolls isn't any more fun than riding in a Daimler.

The Airbus is the bus service operating between the airport and major hotels. Fares run about $8 H.K. to Tsim Sha Tsui hotels and $12 H.K. to Central. There is no Airbus for Causeway Bay. Buses run every fifteen to twenty minutes from 7 A.M. until 11 P.M. Check to make certain that your hotel is on the list.

Taxi stands are near the arrival lounge. A large sign will give you approximate fares to different areas of Hong Kong and Kowloon. If you are confused, look for the transportation desk. Taxis usually charge a flat rate: about $40 H.K. to hotels in Kowloon, $80 H.K. to Central. It's certainly less expensive than the Rolls—a little more than $10 (U.S.) gets you to the Hilton.

Getting Around

Hong Kong is an easy city to navigate because public transportation is excellent. It's a good city for walking, true, but you'll also want to enjoy ferries, *kaidos* (bigger ferries), trams, double-decker buses and the MTR. If you're going someplace adventurous, get the address written out in Chinese from your hotel concierge...just in case.

Hong Kong is still a British Crown Colony; English is a second language. Most cab drivers speak and understand English. Always travel with a map, in case you need to point to where you want to go, or if you are merely wandering around and simply want to get your bearings. Also have matches from your hotel in your pocket with the address written in Chinese—that way you can always get home.

Mass transportation in Hong Kong is superb. Most rides on the MTR take under twenty minutes; you can cross the harbor in about five minutes. Crossing the harbor by car or cab during rush hour is hardest, but doing it on the Star Ferry or the MTR is a breeze. If you intend to sightsee, pick up the HKTA brochure *Places of Interest by Public Transportation* to get exact directions

and bus routes throughout Hong Kong Island and
Kowloon.

MTR

Before I get into any long explanation about
the system, I want you to remember one basic
rule: When looking up a listing in this book, the
MTR stop at Central will get you to most locations
in Hong Kong; the stop at Tsim Sha Tsui will get
you to most locations in Kowloon. Unless otherwise noted in the addresses given, these are the
MTR stops you want. Simple enough.

Now then, the Mass Transit Railway (MTR) is
half the fun of getting to great shopping. Look for
the symbol, ✱, which marks the MTR station.
Three lines connect the New Territories to industrial Kwun Tong, to business Central, to shopping
Tsim Sha Tsui, to the residential eastern part of
the island; each station is color-coded in case you
can't read (English or Chinese).

The longest trip takes less than sixty minutes,
and the cost of the ticket is based on distance.
You buy your ticket at the station vending
machines by looking for your destination and
punching in the price code. You will need exact
change, which you can get from a change machine
nearby. There are also ticket windows where you
can buy multiple tickets.

If you are visiting Hong Kong from overseas,
the best value is a $20 H.K. tourist MTR ticket,
which can be obtained from any HKTA office, MTR
station, select Hang Seng banks or MTR Travel
Services Centres. You must buy your ticket within
two weeks of your arrival and show your passport
at the time you purchase it. The smallest denomi-
nation, stored-value ticket is $50 H.K. (Seniors
can get $20 H.K. tickets.)

Since the MTR is always crowded, you'll be hap-
piest if you horde your $1 and $5 H.K. coins for use
in the machines. One-stop journeys usually cost $3
H.K. (less than fifty cents U.S.) and $6 H.K. can get

you just about anyplace in the midst of things on either side of the harbor. Your ticket comes out of the machine into your hand; insert it into the turnstile and then retrieve it as you go through.

Remember to keep your ticket after you enter the turnstile, because you will have to reinsert it to exit. If you get off at the wrong stop and owe more money, an alarm will sound and you'll have to go over to a window to pay up. Unless you have a stored-value ticket, the turnstile will eat your ticket upon exit and you will be denied that pretty souvenir you were counting on.

The MTR runs between 6 A.M. and 1 A.M. If you need to get somewhere earlier or later, take a taxi.

Taxis

Taxis in Hong Kong are cheap, cheap, cheap, so go ahead and splurge. I make it a matter of principle to never take a taxi through the Cross-Harbour Tunnel, but you may even want to splurge for that.

The meter starts at $9 H.K. and sometimes you simply pay the minimum fare. After that the charge is $1 H.K. per quarter kilometer. Taking the Cross-Harbour Tunnel will cost an extra $10 H.K. each way, making the total additional fees you pay $20 H.K. (See why I am against this flagrant waste of $3 U.S.?) There are surcharges for luggage, waiting time and radio calls.

If a taxi is in Central and has a sign saying "Kowloon," it means that the driver wants a fare going back to Kowloon and will not charge the extra $10 H.K. tunnel fee. Shift changes occur at 4 P.M., and it is sometimes hard to find a cab then. If a taxi doesn't stop for you on a busy road, it is probably because he is not allowed to. Look for a nearby taxi stand where you can pick up a cab. Hotels are always good places to find a taxi. Even if you are not staying at that particular hotel, the doorman will help you. Tip him $5 H.K.

We recently tried to take a taxi from the Regent to Aberdeen for our dinner at Jumbo. Once we got through the tunnel and over to Wan Chai, the driver suddenly didn't know where he was going and asked us to take another taxi—he said he was a Kowloon taxi. Hmmmmm.

On another expedition, I ran the meter to the New Territories and then made a deal with the driver to wait for me, take me to three more stops and return me to the Regent for a price slightly above the return trip. It was not an easy negotiation, but I was spared having to find a taxi in the middle of the New Territories.

Trains

The Kowloon–Canton Railway (KCR) services the areas between Hung Hom and the Chinese border. Since you can't get into China without a visa, chances are you aren't going that far. But do hop on board, because you should take this chance to get out into the New Territories and see some of the real world.

If you're thinking about riding the iron rooster and all that, forget it. The KCR is modern, clean and just like any big-city commuter train. The stations are modern poured concrete and while some of the passengers may be worthy subjects for a photographer, the train itself is not a romantic experience. But it's cheap, it's fun and it feels exotic just because there aren't that many tourists.

Ferries

The most famous of all Hong Kong ferries is the Star Ferry, with service from Kowloon to Central and back. The eight-minute ride is one of the most scenic in the world. You can see the splendor of Hong Kong Island's architecture and the sprawl of Kowloon's shore. The green-and-white ferries have been connecting the island to the peninsula since 1898.

Billed as the least-expensive tourist attraction in the world, the Star Ferry is a small piece of magic for less than fifteen cents a ride. First-class costs $1.20 H.K.; tourist-class is $1 H.K. The difference is minimal except at rush hour, when the upper deck is less crowded. The difference is maximized if you want to take pictures, since you get a much better view from the upper deck, where the first-class passengers loll. The Central/Tsim Sha Tsui service runs from 6:30 A.M. to 11:30 P.M.

There is also a ferry connecting Tsim Sha Tsui with Wan Chai and the new convention facilities. This service operates between 7:30 A.M. and 11 P.M. and costs $2 H.K.

Trams

Watch out crossing the streets of Central, or you are likely to be run over by a double-decker tram. Island trams have been operating for more than eighty-five years, from the far western Kennedy Town to Shau Kei Wan in the east. They travel in a straight line, except for a detour around Happy Valley. Fares are $1 H.K. for adults; pay as you enter. Many trams do not go the full distance east to west, so note destination signs before getting on. Antique trams are available for tours and charters, as are the regular ones.

The Peak Tram has been in operation for more than 100 years. It is a must for any visitor to Hong Kong—unless you are afraid of heights. You can catch the tram behind the Hilton Hotel, on Garden Road. A free shuttle bus will take you from the Star Ferry or Central MTR station (Chater Garden exit) to the Peak Tram terminal. The tram runs to the Peak every ten minutes starting at 7 A.M. and ending at midnight. The trip takes eight minutes. At the top you hike around to various viewing points, or peek in on some of the expensive mansions and high-rises. The best time to make this trip is just before dusk; you can see the island scenery on the trip up, walk around and watch the spectacular sunset, then ride down as all the city lights are twinkling.

There's a restaurant and coffee shop on top of the Peak called simply the Peak Tower Restaurants. There's a big Sunday buffet breakfast which is a must-do; on a clear day you can see forever. Afternoon tea is served on weekends and holidays only.

Rickshaws

The few remaining rickshaws are lined up just outside of the Star Ferry terminal on Hong Kong Island. No new rickshaw licenses have been granted since 1972, and the gentlemen who still hold their licenses have been pulling rickshaws for some years. Rarely, if ever, do people actually go for a ride around Central. Most people just want to have their pictures taken. The cost for a ride or picture is negotiable. The going high rate is $50 H.K.; sometimes you can put $20–$30 H.K. in the driver's hand for a few snaps.

Car Rental

Avis, Budget and Hertz have offices in Hong Kong if you want to drive. Ha! It is far better to hire a car and driver directly from your hotel. Prices vary with the hotel but are usually least expensive if you go for the Mercedes rather than the Rolls. Rates are about $50 an hour, although the Pen only rents out their Rolls Royces by the hour and you'll pay about $90. Remember that you can also make a deal with a taxi driver for several hours or even a day.

Legends and Landmarks

If you think Hong Kong is most famous for its shopping, think again. The international word is that the number one attraction in the town is the quality of the eats! There are certain places in town that are so famous you just have to try them in order to complete your Hong Kong experience; here's some tips that may help you get organized and maybe save a little.

JUMBO FLOATING RESTAURANT

My first thought about Jumbo is that only tourists go here and I am above it all. It took me years to get up the nerve to come here and now that I've done it, I feel like a fool. Why did I wait so long? I can't wait to come back and bring my son! If ever there was a fantasy place to bring your kids, this is it. Jumbo, as you may already know, is the most famous of the floating restaurants in Aberdeen Harbour. It twinkles out there on the water, waiting to entertain you.

Jumbo is best seen at night when all the lights are aglow, but you can go for lunch and take advantage of the various souvenir vendors who set up shop in junks and on the pier that provides service from Aberdeen Harbour to the floating restaurant. (There's more shopping when you get into the restaurant, but all these prices are marked in yen.)

The place is enormous; menus feature pictures, so you just point to what you want. This is not intimate dining, but you will eat it up with chopsticks because it's so very silly. You can dress up in a mandarin's outfit and have your photo taken; dinner for two with beer is about $40. The food is American-style Chinese (bland Cantonese), so the kids will eat. For reservations, call 553-9111.

JUMBO FLOATING RESTAURANT
   Shum Wan, Aberdeen (MTR: None)

GADDI'S

From Jumbo to Gaddi's is surely going from the ridiculous to the sublime: Gaddi's is known to tourists and locals alike as the best French restaurant in town; serious foodies wouldn't consider a trip to Hong Kong complete without a visit.

Lunch and dinner are both popular; lunch is less expensive. However, we have indeed found a deal: The house offers a set dinner menu of five courses, each with its own wine, at a flat price of about $125 a person. Considering that wine is included and you are getting the gourmet treat of the city, this is actually a bargain meal.

The dinner is for a minimum of two people. We got terrine of lobster, quail chop filled with *foie gras*, lamb tenderloins, baked cheese dish, chilled pear soup, caramelized hazelnut savarin, coffee and petit fours along with five different glasses of wine—and birthday cake.

This is the most expensive and fancy restaurant in Hong Kong; going here is truly an event (dress the part). Add to that the silver candelabra, the piano player and the stuff that memories are made of, and you can splurge and decide to eat Chinese take-out every other day of the year. The maitre d' is named Rolf; call 366-6251 for reservations.

GADDI'S
The Peninsula Hotel, Salisbury Road, Kowloon

THE HILTON GRILL
For decades, Central's big power eatery has been the Grill—not only business, but many show-business deals are hatched over lunch here, when the room is thick with power brokers.

The trick is to come for dinner when few people are muttering into their cellular phones. The continental menu is a rich mixture of Western styles with a touch of the Orient and is known around town for its inventive combinations. But to us, the most important feature of the dinner is dessert—leave room because you will never get over the experience of seeing a sign of the Chinese zodiac drawn in chocolate, raspberry and vanilla crème as it floats across your plate.

There is a fixed-price dinner menu, but because of the extraordinary combinations the kitchen is famous for, it's far more fun to come with several people, order different things, and taste all around. We brought Willie and Jane; we tried Iranian Royal Caviar "Snow" (a potatoes-and-caviar combo that is incredible), phyllo tart with crab, mushroom cannelloni with black truffles and more—and that was just for starters. For reservations, call 523-3111.

THE HILTON GRILL

The Hongkong Hilton Hotel, 2 Queen's Road Central, Hong Kong

LA PLUME

La Plume is one of two restaurants in the Regent Hotel that we try to visit each trip to Hong Kong. It's here that Aaron Gershman, then age ten, sipped his first glass of champagne. It's also here that I frequently entertain Diane Freis, because she is a strict vegetarian and La Plume has a special vegetarian menu already printed—no need to be self-conscious or ask favors of the chef.

The best thing about La Plume, without question, is the view. After that, you get a formal restaurant with a fancy menu and prices to match. They are currently in transition in terms of style, so watch this space. The point is, you come here on a first night or final night in town and you come for the splendor of the experience. Here's looking at you, Hong Kong.

For reservations, call 721-1211.

LA PLUME

The Regent Hotel, Salisbury Road, Kowloon

LAI CHING HEEN

This is the second Regent Hotel restaurant we frequent and it too has a tradition behind it. Every trip Peter Chan takes us to dinner here for either the first night or the last night in town. You don't get the same view of Central that comes with dinner at La Plume (the two restaurants are in different parts of the hotel), but you do get a view of Causeway Bay. Last time we were there, we also got to watch a full moon rise over Causeway Bay. Talk about perfect! But I digress.

It's the food, not the view, that draws people from all around the world in droves. Even *Gourmet Magazine* and big-time food writers agree that this is the best Chinese restaurant in Hong Kong. Peter always does the ordering in Chinese, so I'm not much help on house specialties. They are known for their fresh seafood and wide selection of dishes. During hairy crab season (October–November) there was no hairy crab on the menu; nonetheless they went out and bought them for us and cooked 'em right up. Then the waiters gave lessons in how to dismantle the crabs.

The place is fancy, yet casual—people are dressed all sorts of ways; lunch and dinner are served. Aaron broke one of the jade chopsticks and no one said a word. This is surely the place to go to impress anyone on a first visit or to make sure you have good joss for the rest of your trip.

For reservations, call 721-1211.

LAI CHING HEEN
The Regent Hotel, Salisbury Road, Kowloon

LAN KWAI FONG

This is not the name of a single restaurant, but a small street which in itself is a landmark in Central. Looking more like a Disney set than anything else, the short one-block stretch of cute storefronts features several casual restaurants, many of which become discos later in the evening. Locals like to discuss which is their favorite restaurant or which is more "in" at the moment: Willie and Jane say CALIFORNIA is the best one, Liam votes for MECCA 97 for dinner and bellydancing. There are other choices as well. Reservations are always a good idea; they are essential on a Friday or Saturday night.

MECCA 97
9 Lan Kwai Fong, Hong Kong, 877-9779

Snack and Shop

It's quite easy to get a snack while shopping in Hong Kong. It's simply a question of how adventurous you are. *Dai pai dong* is the Chinese name for the zillions of street vendors who cook food from carts in street markets or corners.

If this kind of adventure is not your cup of tea, you should know that there are tons of franchised American fast-food joints in Hong Kong. You'll have no trouble finding McDonald's or Kentucky Fried Chicken anywhere you turn. One of our best evenings in town was dinner in a local diner where there were no other *gweilo*s and then dessert from Haagen Daz!

For lunch, I like to eat in hotels so I can look around, get a feel of the crowd and the action, and still get table service and a little peace and quiet. Also, my sister, Dr. Debbie, advises that anyone who is worried about getting sick from street food should stick to hotel fare. Dr. Debbie happens to eat from street stands all the time, but if you are one of those people who worries, hotels can solve your problems.

You can have all the magnificence of the Regent and its glorious view from the coffee shop, Harbourview Cafe, where you can get a hot dog for $4. Honest. The smoked chicken salad at $10 is to die for. When you order iced tea, it comes with a small pitcher of sugar water. The coffee shop is downstairs from the lobby; walk toward the wall of glass, past check-in, and go down the stairs to your left.

The Peninsula Hotel, which used to be a must for tea, is always a must for me when I eat dinner alone—I can have spaghetti and a Coke, tax and tip included, for $15. Meals are served right in the lobby. Be sure to look up to marvel at the columns and the ceiling.

The Mandarin Oriental, in Central, serves a high tea that can be a complete meal; the Mandarin Coffee Shop is a fabulous quick stop for shoppers who are working the fancy malls or the Pedder Building nearby. Enter from the back end of the hotel on Chater Road.

A regular lunch haunt of Ian's and mine is Sketti's, which is alongside the Hilton lobby on the Bank of China side—this is another quick stop for shoppers and is also great for people on their way to the Peak Tram or the Museum of Tea Ware in Flagstaff House. Their specialty is gourmet pizza; they also have a wide selection of foreign beers. Two can share a pizza easily.

You might also want to try:

LUK YU TEAHOUSE

It's not the teahouse of the August Moon, but this place could be a movie set. Order dim sum from a menu in Chinese only (good luck); try not to take pictures since that's what all the other tourists are doing. Go early for lunch (locals eat at 1 P.M.; be there by noon to get a table and be prepared to eat quickly) or at teatime—when you can get a table easily. We pop in without a reservation between 11:30 A.M. and noon and can get a table if we promise to eat quickly, which suits us just fine. Dim sum are served until 5 P.M. A perfect location in Central makes this a good stop for shoppers; it's halfway to Hollywood Road. Cash only. For reservations, call 523-5464.

LUK YU TEAHOUSE
24 Stanley Street, Hong Kong (MTR: Central)

YAT CHAU HEALTH RESTAURANT

This "health-food restaurant" is an experience you will dine out on for years—the food we tasted was pretty much like American-style Chinese food, but the menu is something else and the three penis wine was the hit of our last trip. Yes, you read right. And Ian is still talking about it.

The gimmick is that you see a doctor when you enter, the doctor diagnoses you and then you choose your menu according to your personal needs. Based on ancient Chinese foods and medicines, the practice is sound to those who believe. The examination is free; lunch or dinner can get pricey if you pick dishes with civet cat, ginseng or even more exotic ingredients. Our rather bland meal was about $40, which included the $10 for a single glass of three penis wine. Credit cards accepted. The English-speaking doctor is not in-house on Saturday. Conveniently located between Western and Central, a few blocks short of Western Market. Check a map and choose your MTR stop according to what else you will do that day. Credit cards accepted.

OK, so we know you're dying to know: What's the three penis wine for? Backache, of course. Ian's had a bad back since a car accident several years ago. Did it do any good? Well, no. But then he didn't drink every drop. If you are traveling with preteens or older children, they will eat this place up. And never stop talking about it.

YAT CHAU HEALTH RESTAURANT

262 Des Voeux Road, Central (MTR: Central or Shueng Wan)

THE VERANDAH

The Verandah is in Repulse Bay; the point here is that you combine a morning's shopping spree in Stanley Market with an upmarket lunch in this modern residential complex with its designer stores and snazzy colonial-style restaurant. Repulse Bay is about five minutes from Stanley; a taxi will take you, although you can easily get here by bus.

The lunch crowd is business folk, so you don't want to come in your blue jeans, but if you want to see how the two-martini lunch crowd in Hong

Kong lives, then splurge for this treat. Do allow time to wander the patio-style mall, which houses a branch of almost every designer shop in town. Phone 812-2722.

THE VERANDAH
    109 Repulse Bay Road, Repulse Bay, Hong Kong

Store Hours

Shops open late in the morning and stay open until late in the evening. The majority of specialty stores open at 10 A.M. and close at 6:30 P.M. However, these are just general guidelines; depending on the area, some stores open whenever they feel like it.

Mall stores are open during regular business hours on Sunday. Most shops in the main shopping areas of Tsim Sha Tsui and Causeway Bay are open seven days a week. Those in Central close on Sunday.

Major public holidays are honored in many shops. Everything closes on Chinese New Year; some stores are closed for two days, others for two weeks. Do not plan to be in Hong Kong and do any shopping at this time. The stores that remain open charge a premium. The stores where you want to shop will all be closed.

Store hours are affected by the following public holidays: January 1 (New Year's Day); January/February (Chinese New Year); March/April (Good Friday, Easter Sunday and Monday); June (Dragon Boat Festival); August 25 (Liberation Day); December 25 (Christmas); and December 26 (Boxing Day). On public holidays banks and offices close, and there is a higher risk of shops closing as well. Factory outlets will definitely not be open. Many holiday dates change from year to year. For specific dates contact the HKTA before you plan your trip.

If you are planning a tour of the factory outlets, remember that lunch hour is anywhere from noon to 2 P.M., although 1 P.M. to 2 P.M. is most common. Outlet shops will close for one hour, along with the factory. You might as well plan to have lunch then too.

Department store hours differ from store to store. The larger ones, like Lane Crawford and Chinese Arts & Crafts, maintain regular business hours, 10 A.M. to 5 or 6 P.M. The Japanese department stores in Causeway Bay open between 10 and 10:30 A.M. and close between 9 and 9:30 P.M. They're all closed on different days, however, which can be confusing. Don't assume because one department store is closed, they all are.

Market hours are pretty standard. There's no point in arriving in Stanley before 9 A.M. Even 9:30 is slow; many vendors are still opening up. The Jade Market opens at 10 A.M. every day and closes around 3 P.M.; this includes Sunday. The weekend street market on Reclamation is a local market so it opens earlier; there's plenty going on at 9 A.M.

Christmas in Hong Kong

Christmas decorations go up in Kowloon (it's hard to spot the neon for all the neon) in mid-November as the stores begin their Christmas promotions. Among the best deals in town is the fact that many of the department stores offer free shipping to either the U.K. or anyplace in the world. . . depending on the store.

Marks & Spencer sends Christmas hampers to any address in the U.K. for free, as long as the hamper costs 40£ or more. Chinese Arts & Crafts stores will ship items as long as they cost $350 or more (U.S., not H.K.!).

Christmas permeates the air; even street markets sell decorations—plastic wreaths, silk flowers, ornaments, etc. If you're familiar with the fabulous Christmas ornaments they sell at Pottery Barn stores in the U.S., you'll be thrilled to find some of these Victorian-style embroidered goodies in stores in Hong Kong.

Better yet, Hong Kong is the perfect place to load up on inexpensive presents—what can you find at home that's fabulous for less than $1? (Or 1£?) Not much! Go to the Jade Market and you'll find plenty.

Even when I'm in Hong Kong in July, I start thinking about Christmas.

Made in Hong Kong

There is a caveat about those famous words, "Made in Hong Kong." Just because an item is made there does not mean you will find it in local stores or outlets. Many garments are shipped directly to the overseas stores, with only dust left behind in the warehouse.

Toys, which are made in Hong Kong, are sent out to be packaged and therefore are imported back into Hong Kong at prices pretty close to those at home. Don't expect any great deals. There are some savings on Nintendo (see page 147).

Whenever I look in my closet and see all the "Made in Hong Kong" labels, I wish I had bought those items in Hong Kong (on Granville Road in a bin, of course),—yet the chances of making a match-up are pretty slim.

European-Made Bargains

There are few European-made bargains in Hong Kong. OK, there may be several if you run into a big sale period. But for the most part, it is wrong to assume that Hong Kong prices are cheaper than U.S. or U.K. prices. My rule is that you don't buy European designer merchandise in Hong Kong unless you are equipped with a price list from home. Expect prices to be high; be ready to pounce when a bargain shows itself.

Hermès scarves and enamel bracelets cost less than in the U.S. and the U.K.; Chanel makeup also costs less, although all Chanel items are not necessarily less. Ian compared prices on an extensive list of designer goods and found them to be generally similar in London and Hong Kong—and London is usually more expensive on designer goods than the U.S.

Hong Kong on Sale

Hong Kong has two traditional sale periods: the end of August and shortly before Chinese New Year (January or February).

Aside from European merchandise, everything else goes on sale during this same period. You'll find a lot of no-name merchandise that didn't interest you when it cost $50 (U.S.), but is looking a lot better now that it's marked down to $30.

The best thing about the sales in Hong Kong is that this is your best time to get regular retail merchandise at its lowest price. The real bargains in Hong Kong are not in retail stores; the real bargains in Hong Kong may not be in perfect condition. So if you insist on brand-new, clean, undamaged goods, you should feel safe buying them on sale. If you have teens or are on a limited clothing budget, shop Hong Kong during the sale periods. Check the *South China Morning Post* ads for special sale announcements.

Remember, the best buys in Hong Kong are not in retail shops—so, to us, whether you are there for a sale period or not is meaningless.

Typhoon Retailing

During the summer (from May to September), Hong Kong falls prey to typhoons. To protect the population best, the Royal Observatory now ranks the typhoons on a scale from 1 to 10. While each number has some significance in terms of the velocity of the wind, we will translate this to you only in terms of shopping habits.

No. 3 typhoon: The Star Ferry might stop running.

No. 8 typhoon: All stores are supposed to close; everyone is supposed to go home or seek shelter. Offices will not be open during a No. 8. However, hotel stores will stay open and may even jack up their prices.

Tourists are told to stay inside the hotel during a No. 8. The hotels circulate a brochure telling you what to do: Close the drapes, stay away from the windows, etc. You can stay in your room all day reading a book, or you can drink Singapore Slings at the bar. Or you could do what any normal person would do: Go shopping. If you stay indoors, you'll find every shop in the hotel is doing a booming business.

Seconds for Sale

We hear that the first words a manufacturer learns in Chinese are "no problem," which is all he says when faced with samples that aren't quite right. What happens to these samples or all the items that just don't quite cut the mustard? They frequently go for sale in the shelves and streets of Hong Kong.

In the industry, this merchandise is called seconds, irregulars or imperfects. In Hong Kong, this merchandise is sold on the streets or in factory-outlet stores and may not be marked with tape or tags to tell you it is less than perfect.

Depending on the brand, the "inferior" merchandise may not have anything wrong with it. With name-brand goods in particular, the quality controls are so incredibly strict that when a unit does not pass inspection, it still may *appear* to be perfect. Possibly only the maker could find the defect.

"Damages" almost always have something wrong with them, but often it's fixable, or something that doesn't upset you considering how good the bargain is.

Here are some of the flaws that may send a unit to the seconds or damages bin; watch for them in your inspection of lower-priced name goods:

- a dye lot that does not match other dye lots
- stripes that are not printed straight or do not match at seams
- prints that are off-register
- bubbles in glass or plastic
- uneven finish
- unmatched patterns at seams
- zipper set in poorly or broken zipper
- puckered stitching
- belt loops that don't match

Remember, seconds are not sale merchandise that hasn't sold; they are stepchildren. Most stores will not admit that they sell seconds. If you are shopping in a seconds resource or a factory outlet, remember to check for damages or slight imperfections. Some imperfections are more than slight.

Factory-Outlet Shopping

Since manufacturing is the business Hong Kong is in, it didn't take the head honchos long to figure out a brilliant piece of merchandising: factory outlets. Factory outlets have become so popular in Hong Kong that they are an established part of the retail structure. In fact, there are about half a dozen local publications that report on the goings-in, -out, and -on of the factory-outlet trade.

Some manufacturers have done so well in the factory-outlet business that they now produce their goods solely for their tourist and local clients—they don't even export! While most of the outlets listed in the various guides are fun to visit, many of them are rip-offs. Or, to put it more kindly, are in business just to be in business.

Fakes for Sale

New York's streets are teeming with vendors selling faux Chanel earrings, T-shirts and scarves. These goods are easily differentiated from the real thing. While Hong Kong doesn't have a lot of fake Chanel on the streets (it's hidden), there are many items for sale—especially at markets—that appear to be real. But they aren't!

I bought Ian a canvas-and-leather book bag from a street market for the high (for Hong Kong) price of $20 U.S. It had a big and perfect Gap label on the front. While Ian doesn't normally like logos or flashy names, this was a handy camera bag and he loved it. Until it started to fall apart 36 hours later. Both buckles and one leather strap broke so quickly (in three different incidents) that I am convinced that real Gap labels were sewn on rather ordinary canvas bags. Let the buyer beware.

The Building System

Most of us are used to finding stores on street level, with fancy glass storefronts and large numbers identifying their addresses. There are many such stores in Hong Kong, but many more are operated high up, out of office buildings. You may arrive at an address and see only a cement building. Before you think that the address is wrong, go into the lobby and look at the directory. The store or business will probably be listed with a floor and room number next to it.

Because of this practice of "office shopping," the addresses in Hong Kong usually refer to a particular building. When getting the address of a particular shop, you are likely to be told that it is in the Sands Building, instead of being told that it is at 17 Hankow Road. Luckily many maps are marked with the actual buildings and their addresses. Cab drivers are so used to the system that you can usually give them the name of the building and they will take you right there.

If you are not using one of our tours to plan your shopping expedition, work carefully with a map so that you determine all the shops in one building at one time. Remember that it is not unusual for a business to have a shop on each side of the harbor, so decide if you are going to be in Hong Kong or Kowloon before you make plans. Use the A-O-A *Map Directory* to locate a building before you head off.

The Beijing Rule of Shopping

The Beijing Rule of Shopping is the Asian version of our Moscow Rule of Shopping:

Now: The average shopper, in pursuit of the ideal bargain, does not buy an item he wants on first seeing it, not being convinced that he won't find it elsewhere for less money. This is human nature. A shopper wants to see everything available, then return for the purchase of choice. This is a normal thought process, especially in Hong Kong, where every merchant seems to have exactly the same merchandise. If you live in Beijing, however, you know that you must buy something the minute you see it, because if you hesi-

tate it will be gone. Hence the name of our international law. If you live in Hong Kong, you know
the guys from Beijing can come over the hills any-
time soon and take it all away. So you buy it when
you can.

When you are on a trip, you probably will not
have time to compare prices and then return to a
certain shop. You will never be able to backtrack
cities—and if you could, the item might be gone
by the time you got back. What to do? The same
thing they do in Beijing: Buy it when you see it,
with the understanding that you may never see it
again. But since you are not shopping in Beijing
and you may see it again, weigh these questions
carefully before you go ahead:

1) Is this a touristy type of item that I am bound
   to find all over town? Are there scads of
   shops selling this kind of stuff, or is this
   something few other vendors seem to have?
2) Is this an item I can't live without, even if I
   am overpaying?
3) Is this a reputable shop, and can I trust what
   they tell me about the quality of this merchandise and the availability of such items?
4) Is the quality of this particular item so spectacular that it is unlikely it could be matched
   anywhere else or at this price?

The Beijing Rule of Shopping breaks down
totally if you are an antiques or bric-a-brac shopper, since you never know if you can find another
of an old or used item, if it would be in the same
condition or if the price would be higher or lower.
It's very hard to price collectibles, so consider
doing a lot of shopping for an item before you
buy anything. This is easy in Hong Kong, where
there are a zillion markets that sell much the
same type of merchandise in the collectibles area.
(This includes the entire Hollywood Road area.)
At a certain point, you just have to buy what you
love and not worry about the price. Understand

that you always will get taken; it's just a matter of for how much.

The Tiananmen Square Rule of Shopping

This is a very simple and very important rule for all shoppers in Hong Kong: When things get violent—run.

You think I'm kidding? I wish!

I had a very difficult experience in one of those electronics stores on Nathan Road (see page 56), during which much drama was enacted—there was yelling and screaming, and laying on of hands and attempts to physically threaten and bully me. When I told Ian of the encounter he looked at me as if I was utterly stupid and said simply "Why didn't you just run?"

Indeed.

If you are shopping for cameras, watches or high-ticket electronics, you must go through a very elaborate bargaining process before you ever get to the price you might pay if you were going to buy. This makes comparison shopping very difficult and, when you are nearing a decent price, puts you in a vulnerable position. Beware.

Vendors know how to make it even more difficult by putting the screws to you. For example, you want a camera. You have done your homework and know that the camera you want costs $275 from 47th Street Photo in New York. You decide to go to a few shops in Hong Kong to find out how prices compare and what's available before you make the big purchase. You walk into Shop A, which you have chosen at random, since there are several million such shops within shouting distance. The marked price on the camera is $300. You begin to bargain, because you know that $275 is the U.S. price. You finally get the price down to $250. You think this is a pretty good price, but you want to try some other shops. You thank the vendor and say you want to think about it. He says, "If you buy it right now, I'll make it $225. No one else would take this loss, but I've spent all this time with you already, and my time is valuable. If you come back later, the price will be $250."

Now you are in hot water. Is this a con job to get you to commit, or must you take advantage of a great bargain when it comes your way and get on with living life? Well, I can't decide this one for you, because there are many values at stake here—which include the fun of the chase, your time and the camera. I can tell you that I was cheated on the purchase of a fax machine in a very elaborate con and that there are times when the bargaining and the shopping aren't fun and you have to listen to that tiny voice within you, especially if it whispers, "Run."

If you are verbally or physically threatened in the bargaining process, leave at once.

If you are frightened, if things don't seem kosher, run.

Please note that it is unlikely that these tactics will be practiced in any store that features a red junk on it and the HKTA label of membership.

Who Ya Gonna Trust?

Trust being such a desirable commodity (since it's also so elusive), I've developed a few simple guidelines for those who are concerned and don't know whom to trust in Hong Kong.

1) The Chinese System of Trust: The Chinese know that you can't trust anyone except family. As a result, nepotism reigns supreme. Rich people in Hong Kong (whether Anglo or Chinese) do their business within a small cadre of those they trust, most of whom are interrelated. On high-ticket items, they never take risks on outsiders or unknown vendors.

2) The HKTA System of Trust: The HKTA is the Hong Kong Tourist Association. They are a heavy-duty presence in Hong Kong and are uniformly referred to as the HKTA. Because rip-offs are so common in Hong Kong, the HKTA put together a merchants' association. They make merchants swear to be honest when they join. In exchange, the merchants get a little red Chinese-junk sticker (it's about 8 inches high) to put in their window, signifying that they are approved by the HKTA and therefore honest.

This is nice in theory, but let's face it, honesty can't be policed. However, if you have problems in one of the HKTA-approved shops, you have recourse. If you have a problem, call the HKTA. They have set up a special shopper's hotline for consumers with questions or complaints. Call the main number (524-4191) and ask for the Membership Department. If the shop is not a member of the association, there's little that can be done.

3) The Godfather System of Trust: This is really simple—trust no one.

Watch Out

This is the saga of the Chanel watch I didn't buy.

Jill said she wanted a fake Chanel watch. She also specified she didn't want me to spend more than $10 for it, since she had already bought one in Hong Kong for $10.

When I was approached on Nathan Road by a young man who whispered "Copy watch, lady?" I immediately brightened.

"How about Chanel?"

"Sure."

He then asked me to follow. Apprehension set in after we ascended the second set of back staircases in a rickety, poured-concrete shopping mall above Nathan Road. When the guide led me down a deserted hallway and opened the door to a broom closet filled with Chinese youths, I thought it was over. Time stopped. Who needed a watch in the Twilight Zone?

In the broom closet was a hot-water heater and three chairs, as well as five youths, one of whom had a walkie-talkie.

"Have a seat."

"No thanks."

I looked at photographs of two different Chanel-style watches; I asked to see them in person. Prices were discussed: $100 per watch. The young man with the walkie-talkie spoke into it.

Time passed. A hundred years. Maybe a thousand years. Finally the door opened: A young man walked in, his shirt stuffed with packages. The door shut behind him, and he opened his shirt to reveal five watches, including the two Chanel models I had asked to see.

The watches were almost perfect fakes, and said "Chanel" on the face, but the gold on the chain-and-"leather" strap was too yellow; $100 was out of the question. I offered $35. The door opened.

"Don't waste my time," said my host. I was dismissed.

Sorry, Jill....

Scams

Hong Kong is the original Scam City. If you think you are street smart, you can still learn a trick or two in Hong Kong. If you know you are naive, get smart now.

The wise man asks, "How can you tell if you are being cheated in Hong Kong?"

The philosopher answers, "How can you tell how much you are being cheated in Hong Kong?"

We list only shops we have done business with, and, we hope, any retail establishment listed in this book would never seriously consider cheating you. But we don't guarantee it, and it doesn't hurt to be on the ball. Markets and street vendors are much more likely to con you than established retail outlets. Whatever the source, there are a few basic steps you can take to protect yourself when making a purchase:

- Feel the goods and carefully inspect any item wrapped in plastic. For example: You go to a store and see the sample silk blouse and decide to buy it. As you are paying, a seemingly identical silk blouse, perfectly wrapped in sealed plastic, is put in your shopping bag. You're no dummy, so you say, "Is that the same blouse?" You even check the size. You are assured that everything is correct and you have just been given a factory-perfect blouse that is clean, unlike the much-handled sample you chose. You smile with contentment. Fool. Open the plastic. There is a good chance that the blouse you have been given is exactly like the sample in every way—except that the silk is of an inferior quality. Feel the goods. Not everyone will cheat you. But many will try.

- Pick the skins for shoes or leathergoods that are being custom-made, and make it clear that you expect the skins you pick to be the skins in your garment. Have them marked with your initials. If you go for a fitting, before the linings are added, check your skins to make certain they are the same.

- Jade is very difficult to buy. A true test requires scientific measurement of hardness, specific density and light refraction. Good luck, sailor. If it's not incredibly expensive and guaranteed, walk away.

- Never trust anyone, no matter how much you

think you can trust him. Never underestimate the possibility of a scam. Murphy's Law of Hong Kong: If you can be taken, you will be.

The Big Chill

This is a true story. The names have not been changed to protect the guilty. These are the fax, ma'am...just the fax. Dumb de dumb dumb, dumb.

OK. So I decided to buy a British fax for the London *Born to Shop* office. I had been thinking about this for several months, was quite familiar with different models of fax machines from the U.S. and was versed in equivalent British prices. Ian and I had discussed our needs ad nauseam. I know that fax machines are much cheaper in the U.S. than in Hong Kong, but Hong Kong seemed to be much cheaper than London, and I needed the proper voltage for the U.K.

Meanwhile, over the years of reporting this book, I have always told people to avoid the camera and electronics stores on Nathan Road. I passed on the street talk, the rumors and the stories. I never spent much time in these stores and never bought anything from one, so I thought I owed it to these stores, myself and my readers to get the low-down on these places. When a specific store on Nathan Road was recommended by a travel magazine, I dutifully wrote down the name and address.

Then one night it happened: Ian went to dinner with Willie and Jane. I hit the streets. I priced fax machines in eleven shops before arriving at the address I had written down. For the most part, these eleven shops had the same merchandise, the same machines and the same prices. Some salesmen were rude to me, others would only play the game so far. There were no bargains; there was nothing to write home about. I was told in all cases that the fax machines I was inspecting were for use in Great Britain.

When I got to VICTORY, 3 Nathan Road, the electronics store recommended in the magazine article, the scene changed dramatically. The salesman was friendly, anxious to please and anxious to make a sale. Not too anxious, but not indifferent or rude as many others salesmen had been.

He immediately traded me up to a better machine; that was OK, because I was familiar with the machines and he was indeed giving me correct information about the characteristics and differences. He quoted me a price of about $8,800 H.K. for the Toshiba fax. I priced a number of other things in the store and then began to negotiate on the fax. It was fast and furious. The price eventually went to $5,000 H.K., if I paid half in U.S. cash.

I asked to see the box, the machinery unwrapped, the warranty, the plug (I was buying British, remember), all the parts, etc. I asked if the fax could be returned. No problem. If I would get a full refund, part cash, part credit card. No problem. I decided to leave and come back with Ian the next day.

As I stood up and walked toward the door to leave, two other salesmen from the shop (and it's a small shop) came up beside me, each put a hand on my arm to prevent me from leaving. Yes, I was slightly frightened. Meanwhile, my salesman begins to shout at me.

"You asked to see all these parts; I took them out for you. You asked to see the warranty, I got it for you. I did everything you ask but jump through a hoop and you are not fair to take my time like this and then leave."

Now then: Important message—a little voice inside me said, "The guy is right."

One voice said, "Run," and yet another said, "Hold on, Suze, calm down. Give the guy a chance.

You said you'd buy it if it met your specifications."

There it is, folks. I hung myself with my Western mentality, my good-girl training. I never remembered I was in Hong Kong, I never remembered I was swimming with sharks or that the rules are different.

I went back and sat down and went over the facts again. I asked for a contract to be written stating I could return the fax within 30 days. I meant 30 hours, but the salesman kept saying there was a 30-day return period. The rules of the game were spelled out in my handwriting and signed by both of us.

I bought the fax. It was an excellent price for a British fax. I was too nervous to be ebullient. Yes, it was a good price but the shouting, the threats and the hands-on approach bothered me. I felt as if I had been cheated, although I didn't know how I was cheated or why I felt that way. "At least I can return it tomorrow," I said to myself as I fell asleep.

The next morning, I showed the fax to Ian. Ian is a much more cautious person than I am; he does not make a big purchase quickly. Although we had been talking about a fax for months, he was shocked that I had bought one in one night.

He unpacked the box. He looked at the plug (which I had inspected) and the writing underneath (which meant nothing to me).

"It's an American or Canadian machine with 110 voltage," he announced, his lips making this flat line that they make when he is annoyed.

"But it has a British plug," I said.

We examined the plug closely. It had been added to the original plug.

I'd been had.

Although I wanted to take Ian with me for the return, I decided that I had gotten myself into this alone and should return the machine alone; I did not need the presence of a man in order to be taken seriously.

Right.

As it turned out, I doubt the presence of the police would have helped these guys take me seriously. My salesman didn't work there; there was no manager; there was no return policy. When I reached for the phone to call the police, I was physically threatened. The phone was ripped from my hand and I was pushed toward the door.

I fought back. I suggested I be given the proper machine with 220 voltage. "No problem; you pay $1,600 H.K. more." I suggested an exchange—no problem. But the prices on the same items I had priced the day before were suddenly tripled.

When it became apparent to me that I had lost, I decided to at least go out in style. The store was filled with Western tourists; I assumed many of them would speak English. I raised my voice and announced the insults and complaints and how I was cheated.

No one looked up. No one took note. They kept on shopping and buying.

But that's not the end of the story.

It happens to be illegal to use a 110-voltage fax with a step transformer in Britain, so there was no question of Ian trying the machine in London. It was my machine. Well, my husband had been after me for a year to get my own fax and not use his. Hmmm, this isn't what I had in mind, but I did indeed own a new fax.

I brought my fax home with me—hand-carrying it halfway around-the-world. I declared it and paid duty on it. I plugged it in.

Pop. Noise and then burning smell.

I called Toshiba's 800 number. After much discussion, during which Toshiba explained to me that the warranty was a fake and that goods bought in Hong Kong were not normally covered, they agreed to take back my machine and repair or replace it. I shipped it off to them in Irvine, California, via UPS. It came back ten days later and works just great.

I would fax a complaint about Victory to the HKTA, but the shop is not a member. There was no red junk in the window. The moral of the story? Don't buy anything expensive from a store that doesn't display a red junk in the window.

The hero here is Toshiba.

The winner is you, but only if you heed this story as a warning and avoid ALL camera and electronics stores in Hong Kong, especially those on Nathan Road.

I learned so much that I can't really feel like a victim, so I guess the loser is Ian, who never did get a fax machine for London. Maybe next trip.

Mail Bonding

One of the best ways to get back at the system is to mail yourself some packages from Hong Kong. The post offices are wonderful, clean and efficient. The postal rates are fair enough. Know the Customs laws as you ship; mark your item as a gift with value under $50 and do not address it to yourself. Your cat will do just fine. Air mail takes about a week; surface (by boat) takes about six weeks.

You can get wrapping supplies in many stores, or just use jiffy bags. Breakables must be properly packed, but if you're just sending home a blouse or two, this may be a great system for you.

There are many post offices: Shoppers can easily get to the one next door to the Hilton in Central. There's a main post office near the Star Ferry in Central; another is up Nathan Road in Kowloon.

Ask your concierge what he would charge to mail a package to you—it could be very little.

Shipping

Shipping from Hong Kong is easy and it's safe. Container shipping is not inexpensive, but freight is moderate. Whether the item is as cumbersome as a giant Foo dog, as small as a few ginger jars or as fragile as dinner plates, you can arrange to ship it home. All it takes is a little time and a little more money.

Remember that Hong Kong is an island and that shipping is a way of life, as it has been there for centuries. The British are used to bringing things in from overseas. People with money who live in Hong Kong automatically expect to pay the price of shipping something in—especially items of Western design. Importing is a way of life for expats; exporting is a way of life for big businesses. Shipping in and out of Hong Kong is therefore very easy.

If you anticipate buying an item that needs shipping, do your homework before you leave the U.S. You may need a family member to claim the item at Customs if you will still be out of the country, or you may even need a Customs agent (see page 64). You will also want to know enough about shipping costs to be able to make a smart decision about the expense added to your purchase. To make shipping pay, the item, including the additional cost of shipping, duty and insurance (and Customs agent, etc., if need be) should still cost *less* than it would at home, or should be so totally unavailable at home that any price makes it a worthwhile purchase. If it's truly unavailable (and isn't an antique or a one-of-a-kind art item) at home, ask yourself why. There may be a good reason—such as it's illegal to bring such an item into the country! If you are indeed looking for a certain type of thing, be very familiar with American prices. If it's an item of furniture, even an antique, can a decorator get it for you with a 20% rather than 40% markup? Have you checked out all the savings angles first? Are you certain the item is genuine and is worth the price of the shipping? There are many furniture fakes in Hong Kong.

There are basically two types of shipping: surface and air. Air can be broken into two categories: unaccompanied baggage and regular air freight.

Surface mail (by ship in a transpacific transaction) is the cheapest. Surface mail may mean through the regular mail channels—that is, a small package of perfume would be sent through parcel post—or it may require your filling an entire shipping container, or at least paying the price of an entire container. Surface mail may take three months; we find two is the norm. If you are doing heavy-duty shipping, look in the back of the *South China Morning Post* for shippers wanting to fill containers.

If you're shipping by container but can't fill a container, you might want to save even more money by using groupage services. Your goods will be held until a shipping container is filled. The container will then go to the U.S., to one of only four ports of entry (Los Angeles, New York, San Francisco or New Orleans), where you can meet the container at the dock, be there when your items are unpacked and then pay the duties due. A full container is approximately 1,500 cubic feet of space (or 8'6" × 8'6" × 20') and will not be delivered to your door (no matter how much you smile).

If you are shipping antiques, discuss the possibilities with Glenn Vessa at Honeychurch (see page 89) and ask about his sources and recommendations.

There are international overnight air package services, like Federal Express, UPS, DHL, etc., that deliver within a day or two. This area is growing just the way overnight U.S. services expanded in the past three years, so check out the latest possibilities. Crossing the dateline can make "overnight" deliveries seem longer or shorter. Local Hong Kong office numbers for several shippers are listed below:

FEDERAL EXPRESS: 730-3333
UPS: 735-3535
DHL: 765-8111

The U.S. Mail has international express mail, which is a three-day service from U.S. post offices. Hong Kong post offices offer a similar program. Ask at the counter.

If you want to price a few local freight offices, try:

- Unaccompanied Baggage Ltd.
  Counter 330, Departure Hall
  Hong Kong International Airport, Kowloon
  phone: 769-8275

- Michelle International Transport Co. Ltd.

  20 Connaught Road West
  Room 1002
  Western District, Hong Kong
  phone: 548-7617

Shop Ships and More

You can have items shipped directly from shops for you. Many Hong Kong stores, especially tailors, will ship your purchases to the U.S. Most people we know who have done this are surprised when their goods arrive by UPS. Ask about the shop's shipping policies before you decide to ship—some stores will charge you for their trouble (a flat fee), then add the actual shipping rate and an insurance fee.

Try to pay for the purchase with a credit card; that way if it never arrives you'll have an easier time getting a credit or a refund. Be sure to ask when the store will be able to ship the goods out. We planned to send home some perfume so as not to have to lug it around for a month's worth of touring. The shopkeeper told us she was so backed up on her shipping that it would take her at least six weeks to mail our order. Then it would take several weeks or months for the package to arrive by surface mail. We took it with us.

The U.S. Postal Service automatically sends all incoming foreign-mail shipments to Customs for examination. If no duty is being charged, the package goes back to the post office and will be delivered to you. If duty is required, the Customs officer attaches a yellow slip to your package, and your mail carrier will collect the money due when the package is delivered to you. If you feel the duty charge is inappropriate, you may file a protest, or you don't have to accept the package. If you don't accept it, you have thirty days to file your objection so the shipment can be detained until the matter is settled.

Be sure to keep all paperwork. If you use a freight office, keep the bill of lading. If the shop sends your package, keep all receipts.

Ask about the policy on breakage from any shop that ships for you.

Know the zip code where you are shipping to in the U.S.

Insure for replacement value, not Hong Kong value.

Insurance

Insurance usually is sold per package by your shipper. Do not assume that it is included in the price of delivery, because it isn't. There are several different types of insurance and deductibles, or all-risk (with no deductible); you'll have to make a personal choice based on the value of what you are shipping. Remember to include the price of the shipping when figuring the value of the item for insurance purposes.

U.S. Customs and Duties

To make your reentry into the U.S. as smooth as possible, follow these tips:

- Know the rules and stick to them!
- Don't try to smuggle anything.
- Be polite and cooperative (until the point when they ask you to strip, anyway....)
- Have receipts handy. If you have no receipts whatsoever, you will immediately become more suspicious to an already suspicious agent.

Remember:

- You are currently allowed to bring in $400 worth of merchandise per person, duty-free. Before you leave the U.S., verify this amount with one of the U.S. Customs offices. It is about to change, so ask your local office before you leave town. Each member of the family is entitled to the deduction; this includes infants (but not pets).
- You pay a flat 10% duty on the next $1,000 worth of merchandise. This is extremely simple and is worth doing. We're talking about the very small sum of $100 to make life easy—and crime-free.
- Duties thereafter are on a product-type basis. (For instance, there are hefty levies on hand embroidery!)
- The head of the family can make a joint declaration for all family members. The "head of the family" need not be male. Whoever is the head of the family should take the responsibility for answering any questions the Customs officers may ask. Answer questions honestly, firmly and politely.
- You count into your $400 per person everything you obtain while abroad—this includes toothpaste (if you bring the unfinished tube back with you), gifts given to you, items bought in duty-free shops, gifts for others, the items that other people asked you to bring home for them and—get this—even alterations.

- Have the Customs registration slips for things you already own in your wallet or easily available. If you wear a Cartier watch, for example, whether it was bought in the U.S. or in Europe ten years ago, should you be questioned about it, produce the registration slip. If you cannot prove that you took a foreign-made item out of the country with you, you may be forced to pay duty on it!

- Take two Polaroid pictures of everything you buy—one for your records and one for the shipper. It's very hard to prove damages on an antique piece without a picture. It's also good to have a picture of what you bought, because human memory is so frail that you will imagine you bought something very different after you haven't seen it for three days.

- The unsolicited gifts you mailed from abroad do not count in the $400-per-person rate. If the value of the gift is more than $50, you pay duty when the package comes into the country. Remember, it's only one unsolicited gift per person.

- Do not attempt to bring in any illegal food items—dairy products, meats, fruits or vegetables. Liquor-filled chocolates are a no-no for some reason, but coffee is OK. Generally speaking, if it's alive, it's *verboten*. We don't need to tell you it's tacky to bring in drugs and narcotics.

- Antiques must be at least 100 years old to be duty-free. Provenance papers will help. Any bona fide work of art is duty-free, whether it was painted fifty years ago or just yesterday; the artist need not be famous.

- Dress for success. People who look like hippies get stopped at Customs more than average folks. Women who look like a million dollars, who are dragging their fur coats, who have first-class baggage tags on their luggage and who carry Gucci handbags, but declare they have bought nothing, are equally suspicious.

- The amount of cigarettes and liquor you can bring back duty-free is under state government regulation and varies with your port of entry. Usually, if you arrive by common carrier, you may bring in duty-free one liter of alcoholic beverages. You may bring in an additional five liters on which you must pay duty—at $10.50 per gallon on distilled spirits—so obviously you don't want to go over your allowance unless you are carrying some invaluable wine or champagne. If you drive across borders, the regulations may vary, but it's unlikely you will drive home from Hong Kong. (If you do, please write and tell all.)

  You may also bring back 100 cigars and one carton of cigarettes without import duty, but there will be state and local taxes on the smokes. You cannot trade your cigar-cigarette-liquor quota against your $400 personal allowance, so that even if all you bought while abroad was ten gallons of champagne (to bathe in, no doubt), you probably will not have paid $400, but will still have to pay duty and taxes. Also please note that you must be 21 or over to get the liquor allowance, but you may be any age for the puffables—thus an infant gets the same tobacco allowance as an adult. No cigars from Cuba, please.

- Environmental and endangered species no-nos are a big problem in Hong Kong, so U.S. Customs agents will be watching carefully.

1) Ivory cannot legally be imported into the U.S. unless it is antique and comes with papers.
2) Tortoise shell is also forbidden, no matter where it comes from (unless, that is, it comes from a plastic tortoise).
3) If you are planning on taking your personal

computer with you (to keep track of your budget, perhaps), make sure you register it before taking it out of the country. If you buy a computer abroad, you must declare it when you come in.

British Customs and Duties

The legal allowance is less than 50£. Good luck.

CHAPTER TWO

MONEY MATTERS

Paying Up

Whether you use cash, traveler's check or credit card, you are probably paying for your purchase in a currency different from American dollars or pounds sterling. For the most part, I suggest using a credit card.

Plastic is easy to use, provides you with a record of your purchases (for Customs as well as for your books) and makes returns a lot easier. Credit-card companies, because they are often associated with banks, may give the best exchange rates. The price you pay, as posted in dollars, or sterling, or whatever your hometown currency is, is translated on the day of your purchase. Let's say the Hong Kong dollar is trading at $7.80 to $1 (U.S.). Your hotel may only offer an exchange rate of $7.40 when you convert your money. American Express will probably give you a higher rate of exchange.

The bad news about credit cards is that you can overspend easily, and you may come home to a stack of bills. But one extra benefit of a credit card is that you often get delayed billing, so that you may have a month or two to raise some petty cash.

If possible, travel with more than one credit card. Some stores will only take MasterCard or Visa. Others will accept only American Express. Some prefer one to the other, but will accept either. Very often you can negotiate a discount for not using plastic at all.

Traveler's checks are a must for safety's sake. Shop around a bit; compare the various companies that issue checks, and make sure your checks are insured against loss or theft. While I like and use American Express traveler's checks, they are not the only game in town. Ask around. At different times of the year, during special promotions, American Express checks may be offered free of a service charge by the banks. This is a good time to stock up. If you are a very good customer, your bank should offer this service to you anyway. Call and ask.

Thomas Cook has offices all over Hong Kong; they are a favorite of Ian's. Peter Chan says if you exchange money at HongKong and Shanghai Banking Corp. Ltd. (any branch) or Hang Seng Bank Ltd., you will get the day's rate as listed in the *South China Morning Post.*

Cash and Carry

While cash has many benefits, and often greases the wheels of bargaining, it puts you in the most vulnerable position in cases of exchanges, rip-offs or returns. Once you have paid cash for an item—especially a camera or an electronic goodie which is going to be pricey—you can kiss that money good-bye.

Remember, credit-card companies may help you out if you dispute a charge; once you pay cash you will never see it again. Especially in Hong Kong.

Personal Checks

Always travel with your checkbook. End of story. Yes, even to a foreign country. Period.

You see, in many places in the world (and Hong Kong is one of them), retailers are very happy to take your check. In fact, they may prefer it to a credit card.

Let's face it, Hong Kong is a place in transition. Most successful retailers (and business people) have bank accounts elsewhere, so that if they have to run in 1997, they will have money stashed away. Although they have banks all over the world, many like to have an American bank account. Your check will be accepted in Hong Kong, then processed through an American account.

Whether or not the people you do business with do all their banking transactions in Hong Kong is beside the point: Being able to write a check is incredibly convenient. When we make our regular pilgrimage to W.W. Chan (our tailor), we can easily order several suits. To pay for additional traveler's checks seems silly. They know this at the tailor's and take personal checks as an additional customer service.

British cheques are likewise easily accepted, especially while Hong Kong is a British Crown Colony.

Fluctuating Dollars

There is no question that the dollar dances, so don't let anyone tell you that the Hong Kong dollar remains constant at 7.8 to the U.S. dollar. True, it generally hovers around 7.8, but this is not a hard-and-fast rule. If you happen to be in Hong Kong during a time when the U.S. dollar is weak and the Hong Kong stock market is going strong (as it has been recently), you may find that the official rate is 7.6 or 7.7, and that your hotel will give you no more than 7.3. Prices in this book were calculated at a flat rate of $7 (H.K.) per $1 (U.S.), and $14 (H.K.) per 1£, according to rates prevailing at the time we did our research.

When you are shopping, it's very easy to divide prices by 8 in order to get a ballpark exchange rate between U.S. and Hong Kong dollars. But if you pay for your purchases in cash, in order to be fair to your cash flow, you must divide by the number you received in exchange, not by the bank rate. We often find it is safer to divide by 7 when the American dollar is weak.

Fluctuating Pounds

The Hong Kong dollar is in some way pegged to the U.S. dollar in bank vaults around the world. Despite British government, the currency goes with the dollar, not the pound. This means that the pound-to-H.K. dollar ratio swings even more dramatically than the H.K. dollar-to-U.S. dollar ratio.

Currency Exchange

As we've already mentioned, currency exchange rates vary tremendously. The rate announced in the paper (the *South China Morning Post*) every day is the official bank exchange rate, and does not apply to tourists. Even by trading your money at a bank, you will not get the rate of exchange that's announced in the papers.

- You will get a better rate of exchange for a traveler's check than for cash because there is less paperwork involved for banks, hotels, etc.
- Hotels generally give the least favorable rate of exchange, but we find some flexibility here. You are limited by where you are staying, however. Many hotels will not change traveler's checks for non-patrons. Hotel shops will often negotiate on the rate of exchange. It is important to know that day's

bank rate before you start shopping. When in doubt, use your calculator to double-check.

- Don't change money (or a lot of it, anyway) at airport vendors, because they will have the worst rates in town—even higher than your hotel.

- If you want to change Hong Kong dollars back to U.S. dollars when you leave, remember that you will pay a higher rate for them. You are now "buying" dollars rather than "selling" them. Therefore, never change more money than you think you will need, unless you are planning to stockpile for another trip.

- Have some foreign currency on hand for arrivals. After a lengthy flight you will not want to have to stand in line at some airport booth to get your cab fare. If you are being met by a car from your hotel you will not have a bill to pay, but you are going to want to tip the bellboys. (Don't tip the driver; it's included in the hefty price you pay the hotel for sending the car!) Your home bank or local currency exchange office can sell you small amounts of foreign currency. Kiosks at the airport usually have foreign currency as well. No matter how much of a premium you pay for this money, the convenience will be worth it. I like to arrive anywhere in the world with at least $50 worth of that country's currency.

- Keep track of the exchange rate you pay each time. If you are going to several countries or must make several money-changing trips to the cashier, write the sums down. When you get home and wonder what you did with all the money you used to have, it will be easier to trace your cash. When you are budgeting, adjust to the rate you paid for the money, not the rate you read in the newspaper. Do not be embarrassed if you are confused by rates and various denominations. Learn as much as you can, and ask for help. Take time to count your change and understand what has been placed in your hand. The people you are dealing with already know you are a tourist, so feel satisfied that you understand each financial transaction.

- Don't be embarrassed to clarify a transaction—say, "Are we talking U.S. dollars here or Hong Kong dollars?"

- Determine mental comparative rates for quick price reactions. Know the conversion rate for $50 and $100 so that in an instant you can make a judgment. Then, if you're still interested in an item, slow down and figure out the accurate price.

- When you check your credit-card slip before leaving the store, make sure to circle the "H.K." in front of the "$" sign. Since both currencies use the "$" symbol, you want to make very certain that your credit-card company does not bill you in U.S. dollars. When your credit-card bill arrives, double-check once again. I got a letter from a reader who thought a store in this book had cheated her; when we sorted through the whole thing she was simply confused between U.S. dollars and H.K. dollars as written on her charge slip.

Banking in Hong Kong

If you are an architecture freak, as I am, or just generally curious, you can't help but notice that two of Central's most famous landmark buildings are banks. One is I.M. Pei's Bank of China (next door to the Hilton), the other is the HongKong and Shanghai Bank, a block from the Hilton, toward Central.

We've spent a good bit of time exploring these

buildings, just because they are so extraordinary, and finally decided to open local bank accounts. Morally opposed to the Bank of China, we went for the HongKong and Shanghai Bank.

You might not find that it is prudent, either time-wise or money-wise, to have a Hong Kong bank account. If you do business in Hong Kong, however, or are ever paid in Hong Kong dollars, you will find that a savings account only pays 1% interest, but you are allowed to withdraw your funds locally in H.K. dollars or at branches in New York, London and elsewhere. You have your choice of currency. And your bank passbook will make a wonderful souvenir. Your ATM card from home may also allow you to withdraw cash at any local branch bank or ATM machine, so you don't have to change money at your hotel (as long as there's money in your local account). There are 74,000 ATMs for HongKong and Shanghai Bank alone, so I am never very far from my money. Instructions on the screens are in English.

Bargaining as a Way of Life

When you walk into a store in New York, Paris or London, you ask the price of an item, whip out your credit card or cash, and say "Thank you very much." No bargaining, no haggling.

Not so in Hong Kong, where life is based on bargaining. Hong Kong society revolves around the art of the bargain. You want to buy a mango at the corner stand? Buy two and offer a little less than double; you will probably be successful.

Bargaining does not take place on buses, in the MTR or in taxis (unless you are going for a long drive, or are hiring the car for a day). Hotel rooms are a flat rate. Your tailor has a flat fee. After that, you're on your own.

We must warn you that when times are tough in Hong Kong, vendors are less likely to bargain with tourists. I've fought with vendors in Stanley over $5 H.K. and not won out. I once left a fancy store in the Pen because they would not take $10 U.S. off a high-priced item.

The problem with bargaining is that you can get so wrapped up in the drama that you lose sight of what you wanted to buy or the amounts you are fighting over.

Nowhere is bargaining more important, however, than in the various markets (see page 157). Here, it is open season on tourists and you are expected to bargain fiercely to get the best deal. Unless you come from a similar background, you will very likely become exhausted and give up. Once you give up, it's guaranteed that you have just gotten the bad end of the bargain. In fierce bargaining you will know that you are getting near the fair price when the shop owner becomes less gracious and more grudgingly quiet.

If you are hoping to bargain successfully, we have a few tips for you to follow:

- Do not try to bargain while wearing expensive jewelry or clothing. We always go to the market in jeans and a T-shirt, or old slacks and a nondescript sweater.
- If you are bargaining for an expensive item like a carpet, camera or piece of jewelry, have some background knowledge. If you can find a fault with the product and emphasize that you are doing the merchant a favor by relieving him of inferior goods, you will be in a stronger bargaining position.
- Never chat with the shopkeeper, argue or show that you are passionately interested in the item. The more businesslike and disinterested you appear to be, the less quickly the merchant will think that the cash is in his pocket.
- Always try to bargain alone. If you are with your spouse or friend, take the white hat/

black hat positions. If you are the one looking at the item, have your friend talk about
how he/she saw the same thing in New York
and it was less money, better looking and
easier to buy.

- Ask to see the inside of the item (watch,
camera or electronic device). Most shopkeepers won't want to bother. If they do, look
like you know what you are examining and
make clucking noises as if something is
wrong. If the shopkeeper says "What?" just
shrug knowingly. The trick is to be on the
offensive, not the defensive.

- You must have a lot of time available to bargain well. Wearing down the opponent is the
key to success. If you're not ready to sit there
and squabble, pay the asking price and get
out.

- Know your hometown price for the same
item. Whip out a newspaper ad if need be.

- Decide how much you are willing to pay, or
what you think is fair. Put this amount of
money (exactly) in your palm before you start
the dance. After a while, offer that amount
on a take it or leave it basis.

- As a last resort in bargaining, walk away. But
don't ever walk away from something you
can't live without. If you're just bluffing the
shopkeeper will know, and you will lose
ground in the bargaining. If you are serious
about walking away, the shopkeeper will
more than likely offer you a final deal, with
the understanding that if you do walk away
the price will not go that low again. Don't be
too surprised if the price the shopkeeper
offers you as you start away is much lower
than where the bargaining had broken off. If
the item is so special that you can't live without it, pay that price. If not, then be prepared
to do without.

A Word About Non-Bargaining: No one likes to bargain more than I do. Shopping just isn't fun if I can't haggle. Yet as I get older, I find myself feeling that the people I am buying from may need the fifty cents difference more than I do. I mention this—out of guilt, I guess—because more and more, I pay the asking price, or very close to it. And I can sleep at night.

Don't worry if you find that you can't play the game. Enjoy what you buy at the price you paid for it and don't look back.

Charitable Contributions

If you go to a Buddhist temple and want to partake in any of the rituals, you are welcome to do so. Provided you pay. See that box with a slot across the top? Insert money. Sometimes you will be given prices for items; frequently you just make a contribution and then help yourself to the candles, joss sticks or paper items. Someone in the temple may indeed give you lessons in temple etiquette or banging of drums.

Want to take pictures inside a temple? Please pay for the right with a donation.

My favorite ritual is to buy a kite-shaped piece of paper with a big yellow picture on a flap and pink streamers. Take a pen and write out your message. Then walk to the stove in the corner and burn your piece of paper. The ashes, carrying your message, go up the chimney to Buddha.

Amen.

Tipping Tips

Tipping rituals in Hong Kong are complicated because you pay a service charge at your hotel. Yet I find every time I check in or out of a hotel, the $100 H.K. bills seem to disappear.

Here's the system I go by:

- We do not tip the driver of the Rolls or the Daimler that the hotel has sent;
- We do not tip the front-desk person who shows us to the room;
- We tip $10 H.K. per suitcase when the luggage arrives in the room;
- We tip $50 H.K. to the person who performs the welcoming tea ceremony upon arrival in the room;
- We tip $5 H.K. for each taxi hailed at a hotel (any hotel);
- We tip taxi drivers by rounding up to the next convenient figure, not by any science or percentage;
- We do not add on extra tips for room service or meals signed for at the hotel, nor do we leave extra at the table;
- We tip the floor boys $100 H.K. when we check out;
- If the concierge staff has been helpful, I leave an envelope with $100 H.K.–$200 H.K. (depending on how helpful). I use the free hotel stationery that's in the drawer (I take home the rest) and write across the front: "With Thanks for Your Help—Suzy Gershman, Room 841;"
- We tip the same $10 H.K. per item on the baggage as we check out;
- I do not tip the driver of the hotel car on arrival at the airport for departure to London. (Ian tips the driver while I make faces or yell at him for tipping.) I think that $40 for a ride to the airport is plenty, thank you, but Ian is British and very polite;
- Tip the hotel baggage representative at the curb at the airport if he takes charge of your luggage and really helps out. The guy from the Pen who was there waiting for us last trip was fabulous. We gave him 5£. (All our Hong Kong dollars had been spent.)

Returns, Repairs and Rip-Offs

The problem with returns, repairs and rip-offs is that they take more time than cash to fix, and your time is what's valuable. Try not to buy merchandise abroad that you think may have to be returned. However, should you have a problem, see to it at once.

If you are already home when you realize there is a problem, send a fax or telex rather than a letter (too slow). Don't phone (no record of your complaint). Notify your credit-card company so that your bill is adjusted and the charge is held.

When you return the item, send it by registered mail to ensure that you have the signature of the person who received it. You must have receipts to prove you have mailed the item. You will have to do a Customs declaration anyway, if the package is of any bulk. Let the store manager or owner know when you expect it to arrive.

If the problem is serious, contact the Hong Kong Tourist Association and send them carbon copies of your correspondence. They are the authorized, government-sponsored body of the tourism industry in Hong Kong, and they have a special section set up just to deal with customer inquiries or complaints. From the U.S., call 011-852-801-7278, 9 A.M. to 5 P.M., weekdays; 9 A.M. to 1 P.M., Saturday. If you wish to write, the address is: Hong Kong Tourist Association, Jardine House, 1 Connaught Road, Central, Hong Kong. They will intercede on your behalf if the store is a member of their association (most are). If the store is not a member, they will pass the complaint over to the Consumer Council, a division of the city government. Hong Kong is very consumer-oriented, and does not want dissatisfied tourists. If you have a legitimate complaint, don't hesitate to pursue it.

Sometimes with better-quality merchandise you can exchange it in an American store. This is highly unusual, since many stores are franchise operations, but it is worth a try before you start negotiating halfway around the world. If you are making a return, you must have your sales slip to prove what you paid. Don't expect a cash refund, and be happy if you get a store credit, another size or color.

American outlets should repair Asian-bought European merchandise, provided it's genuine. There may or may not be a fee for this; it may be negotiable. The bigger problem is whether your "international guarantee" will be honored in the U.S. Before you leave the store, check to make sure that your guarantee contains a complete description of the item, including model and serial number, plus purchase date, name and address of the shop and official stamp. If you are buying a name-brand watch or electronic device, be sure that the store is an authorized representative.

Guarantees that do not have all these items are not worth the paper they are written on. Be sure that you are not receiving a local guarantee or retailer guarantee instead of a worldwide/international guarantee. If you have been misled, first contact the head office of the store, then send your paperwork to the HKTA and your credit-card company to notify them of your dispute. You must do all of this in writing.

The last resort is, in fact, your charge card. The American Express Card, and some versions of bank cards, offer purchase protection plans. Remember to save all receipts. Some plans extend the warranty of any purchase up to one extra year. Some companies ask you to sign up for the program; some plans are only for customers with "gold" cards. Check with your individual credit-card company to find out the rules before you go.

If you discover a problem before you leave town, return to the store for battle. Only you can decide if this is going to be worth your time and trouble. I found my attempt to return the fax machine I got conned into buying to be fascinating, but a total waste of my time and adrenaline.

Ask for the store manager when you attempt to make a return; be prepared for the fact that at a sleazy store they will deny that there is a manager and tell you that you must make returns through the salesman you patronized. He is nowhere to be seen, of course.

If you have paid cash for your item, consider yourself seriously had.

Exit Tax and Duty-Free Dollars

While you're figuring out what to do with your spare Hong Kong dollars (how about a final spree on Granville Road?), make sure that you have tucked aside $150 H.K. *in cash*. You will need this for your exit tax, per person. There is no tax for children under twelve. The tax must be paid in local currency, not foreign; credit cards are not accepted. Verify the amount with your hotel concierge, since it can change and then you won't have change.

If you are planning on spending your last Hong Kong dollars at the duty-free stores in the airport, you may be surprised to note that prices are pretty much the same as in Hong Kong proper and there are very few bargains.

CHAPTER THREE

SHOPPING NEIGHBORHOODS

A Word About Neighborhoods

When I refer to Hong Kong in this book, I generally mean the entire territory and area that includes the island of Hong Kong. However, the whole territory encompasses more than Hong Kong Island—it also incorporates Kowloon, the New Territories and many islands as well. These areas can be broken down into accessible neighborhoods, many of which will appeal to tourists. Locally they are called districts, and in most cases I have named a specific shopping district after its proper district, but not always.

When people give you an address for a shop "in Hong Kong," you'll soon realize that addresses here are a combination of street, neighborhood and district. An address such as "121 Ice House Street, Central, Hong Kong," would be on Hong Kong Island, in the Central District. An address reading "6 Nathan Road, Tsim Sha Tsui, Kowloon," would be on Kowloon Peninsula, in the district of Tsim Sha Tsui.

As far as basic tourist shopping is concerned, Hong Kong and Kowloon are the most popular areas. But I will certainly send you to the New Territories, although this is a schlep you have to be in the mood for; I'll also tell you how to get into some factory districts.

The more I visit Hong Kong, the more I'm comfortable with getting away from the tourists and the commercial main streets of Central and Kowloon; I'd define a successful visit to Hong Kong as one in which you've spent at least a little bit of time in the real-people neighborhoods.

Getting Around the Neighborhoods

The MTR will get you most places you want to be, or at least into the main neighborhoods and basic shopping areas. Unless I specifically note otherwise in the address listing, the MTR stop at Central will get you to most locations in Hong Kong; the MTR stop at Tsim Sha Tsui services most Kowloon shopping areas. There's also excellent bus service, and ferries to outlying islands where you can just roam around upon arrival. Getting to specific addresses in the New Territories can be difficult without a car; consider hiring a taxi or a car (with driver) from your hotel.

A Word About Addresses

Although we have already warned you that the address you will be given is most often the name of the building and not the street address, I want to stress that when street addresses are written out, they may designate a specific door or portion of a building. So you may see different addresses for the same buildings, like the Landmark, Swire House or Prince's Building. Don't freak out, go nuts or assume it's an error. Simply check your trusty map. If an office building takes up a city block, as many do, the shops can claim different street addresses on all four sides! Don't panic. Once you are in the proper neighborhood, simply ask someone on the street for the right building.

The same is true when cruising the boutiques in a shopping center like the Landmark: Often the shop's address will be simply the name of the building. At other times, the address may be more specific, and include the shop number or other helpful information. The easiest way to find what you're looking for is to check the directory on the main floor. Some show a schematic layout of all the shops; others, especially in the more outlet-oriented buildings, just list the names of the stores and corresponding floor numbers.

Hong Kong Island Neighborhoods

The island of Hong Kong actually makes up only a portion of what most tourists refer to as "Hong Kong." While government, business and "downtown" functions take place on the island, much of the local population lives elsewhere. The island is divided by a ridge of hills, including the famous Peak. The rich and famous live in villas lining the roadway up the Peak; the almost rich and famous (as well as the upper-middle class) live in what's called the Mid-Levels, the area of the hills above Central but below the Peak. To get to most other portions of the island you either go through a tunnel under the hills toward Aberdeen, or take the tram or MTR along the shoreline to the housing estates, where more middle-class people live in housing blocks and "mansion" developments.

Central

Central is what we used to call "downtown" when I was growing up. It's the main business and shopping part of town: It's the core of Hong Kong island. The Star Ferry terminal is located in Central. The Pedder Building (outlets galore!) is in Central. The Landmark is located in Central. The Hongkong Hilton Hotel is in Central. The antiques shopping area—Hollywood Road—is in Central. The Lanes are in Central. Our favorite teahouse (Luk Yu) is in Central. And yes, most of the architectural wonders of Hong Kong are in Central. The MTR stop is called Central.

Hong Kong Island

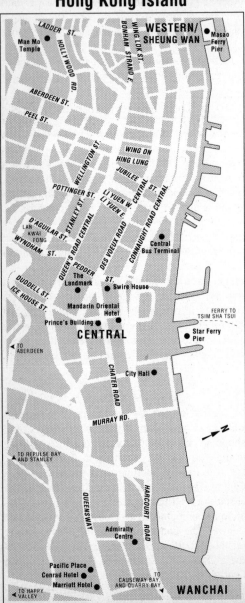

Man Mo Temple
LADDER ST.
HOLLYWOOD RD.
WING LOK ST.
BONHAM STRAND E.
WESTERN/
SHEUNG WAN
Macao Ferry Pier
ABERDEEN ST.
PEEL ST.
WING ON
HING LUNG
JUBILEE
CENTRAL ST.
WELLINGTON ST.
POTTINGER ST.
STANLEY ST.
LI YUEN W.
LI YUEN E.
DES VOEUX ROAD
CONNAUGHT ROAD CENTRAL
Central Bus Terminal
D'AGUILAR ST.
LAN KWAI FONG
WYNDHAM ST.
QUEEN'S ROAD CENTRAL
QUEEN'S ROAD PEDDER ST.
The Landmark
Swire House
DUDDELL ST.
ICE HOUSE ST.
FERRY TO TSIM SHA TSUI
Mandarin Oriental Hotel
Prince's Building
CENTRAL
Star Ferry Pier
TO ABERDEEN
CHATER ROAD
City Hall
MURRAY RD.
TO REPULSE BAY AND STANLEY
QUEENSWAY
HARCOURT ROAD
Admiralty Centre
Pacific Place
Conrad Hotel
Marriott Hotel
TO CAUSEWAY BAY AND QUARRY BAY
WANCHAI
TO HAPPY VALLEY

Shopping in Central is mostly glitzy, but wait, you round a corner and voilá—it's the Lanes: real-people galore. You walk up Pottinger to Hollywood Road and, again—the real thing. Central seems to house the ridiculous and the sublime within the same city block; it's your opportunity to mix Westernized shopping with Eastern lifestyles.

The LANDMARK, a shopping mall of mythic proportions, houses five floors of shopping including stores in the basement, at street level, on a mezzanine above the street shops and up in two towers that rise above the main floors of shopping. European designers have their shops here or across the street in Swire House, the Prince's Building or the Mandarin Oriental Hotel.

The LANES are two little alleys half a block away from each other—they are lined with storefronts and then filled in with stalls so you have to look behind the stalls and poke into nooks and crannies to get the full flavor. One lane specializes in handbags (most imitations of famous brands and styles; few of good quality); the other, underwear. There are some fabric stores as well as the usual vendors selling electronic souvenirs that blink and beep and T-shirts warning that 1997 is just around the corner.

The PEDDER BUILDING (see page 115) is a must: This one building is conveniently located across the street from the Landmark and in every shopper's direct path. There are enough outlets here to empty your wallet and keep you satisfied, even if you have no more time for stores.

HOLLYWOOD ROAD: Although it's in Central, I consider this street more of its own neighborhood (see page 88).

Western

Take the MTR to Sheung Wan to get to Western, which is a lot more Chinese, in both appearance and attitude, than Central, despite the decidedly touristy flavor in the renovation of Western Market. Here you'll feel less like a sightseer and more like a visitor to the Far East. Welcome to the shops with snakes in cages, to little restaurants where you're not sure if the snacks are snacks or snakes. There's an electronics district in Western, there are old-fashioned Chinese medicine shops, there's our favorite health-food restaurant Yat Chau (the doctor is in) and the ferry terminal for heading off to Macau.

Going west from Central, the area begins shortly after Central Market, at Possession Street, and continues to Kennedy Town, where most of the local working people live. Western includes the famous Man Wa Lane, where you can purchase your own personalized chop (see page 274), the Shun Tak Centre (off to Macau) and Bonham Strand East, which is full of Chinese herbalists. The farther west you wander, the more exotic the area becomes.

My best way of "doing" Western is to combine it with a trip to Hollywood Road; if you walk downhill from Hollywood Road, you'll automatically end up in Western. Then you can take in the WESTERN MARKET before walking back to Central or hopping in the MTR station right there at Shun Tak.

Hollywood Road

Up above Central, and technically within the Central district, Hollywood Road is a shopping neighborhood unto itself. You can reach it from either the Central or Sheung Wan MTR stops. It's within walking distance, if you're wearing sensible shoes and have the feet of a mountain goat; you can also tell your taxi driver "Bo Fye Gong" (meaning "white flower") and be dropped off in the core of the antiques area, in what used to be the neighborhood where the white prostitutes plied their trade.

Hollywood Road is Hong Kong's antiques neighborhood. Because of the escalator which is being installed (don't ask) and the ever rising rents in Hong Kong, the area has changed tremendously and will continue to do so. There are antiques stores elsewhere, but Hollywood Road is still a great place to get to know. Once the escalator is completed, it will conveniently stop at Hollywood Road so you can ride up (or down) the hill in style.

Hollywood Road isn't hard to get to, but it is not necessarily on the way to anywhere else you're going, so it's essential that you specifically plan your day or half day to include this outing. The idea is to walk the three blocks of Hollywood Road from Wyndham to the Man Mo Temple. Then you'll hit Cat Street and the flea market before descending into Western. (See page 87.)

If you're making this a walking tour, simply remember: up Wyndham or Pottinger; down Ladder. At the top of Wyndham Street, hang a right— Wyndham turns and becomes Hollywood Road. From Hollywood Road you can walk along, browsing the shops until you get to Cat Street (Upper Lascar Row), which is one level below Hollywood Road, and begin your descent. Not only is this the downhill stretch, but there is shopping along the way. If you are a real sport, you'll continue walking downhill toward the harbor, right into the Western District.

As charming as this area is, we warn you up front that much of what is in these shops must be considered imitation, or at least faux. If you are looking to do anything more serious than a browse, I suggest you make your first stop HONEYCHURCH ANTIQUES (No. 29), where the expat American owners Glenn and Lucille Vessa are bright, honest and always willing to help. They know who's who and what's what in their world of dealers and will tell you about their stock and everyone else's. Their look is an eclectic blend of antiques from around the Orient (kind of Country chinoiserie); however, they know who has the more formal pieces. In fact, they know who has everything.

If you are spending big bucks, it is imperative that you buy from a reputable shop. Ask Glenn and Lucille for guidance.

You may also want to poke in at C.P. CHING (No. 21); SCHOENI (No. 27); GALLERY ONE (No. 33; it doesn't look like much, but has beads that are to die for), HOBBS & BISHOPS (No. 28), P.C. LU (No. 26).

YAU SANG CHEONG (No. 39) is an artist-supply shop in the middle of all this—they do make chops (see page 274), and will carve your name (or whatever) in one hour.

The most visually arresting "store" on the street has a quasi-fleamarket feel and the name LOW PRICE SHOP written in scrawl across the door. Bird cages, beads, old clothes, new snuff bottles all spill out onto the sidewalk at No. 47, where prices range from dirt cheap—about $3 (U.S.) for an American bestseller paperback, used but recent—to outrageous. Most of the so-called antiques are not so old and the prices can be rather high. Old-looking postcards and photos (newly made, my friend) are sold here and make very popular souvenirs. Despite the fact that the place is of questionable authority, it's still a heap (and I mean heap) of fun. Great photo opportunity.

Many dealers sell what look like reproductions to me (although they swear this is the real stuff), and I get that empty feeling in the pit of my stomach as I work these stores, trying to discern real treasures from imagined finds. I must also tell you that Glenn Vessa gave me a blue-and-white ceramics test (after I read and studied four books on the subject) and I flunked outright. I could not accurately ID a piece that was 300 years old. Glenn says knowing what you're doing with ceramics is easy (that's what brain surgeons say about their job as well), but I beg you to be careful.

There are serious porcelain dealers on Hollywood Road, and then Tourist Traps that sell porcelains and then some factories. It all starts to look alike to me and that's why I know you should worry. HWA XIA sells only blue-and-white and looks very important (No. 56); THE PLACE (No. 81A) is very Western-looking in style and sells lots of porcelains, but also other objects and some furniture too.

My best tip is to turn right and walk down one flight of stairs at Shin Hing (an alley). After half of the flight of stairs, look to your left for the ceramics shop LEE TAK CO., where the sign also says "Porcelain at Lowest Prices." We have to agree with the sign, and reluctantly tell you that this is one of our best resources. (Don't tell too many people.) You don't have to worry about whether you are buying an antique or not; these are all brand-new items.

They will only ship huge orders, and their English isn't great. This is ready-made stuff that has not been antiqued, but their blue-and-white has a tinge of gray in the white parts, so it doesn't look as cheap as other versions we have seen. We bought a pair of Foo dogs for the mantel for $25 (the pair); I left behind a series of blue-and-white planters that at $5 each may have been the deal of the century.

The three blocks from Wyndham to the Man Mo Temple has a concentration of shops that will interest you. After you've passed the temple, there are more shops on Hollywood Road, but the real treat is to go down to Cat Street to get to the vendors with their wares spread on blankets. Cat Street is sort of an alley; it stretches west for another two blocks or so. There are also some bona fide shops on Cat Street.

You can find just about anything here: old

sewing machines, hunks of jade, broken Barbie dolls, Mao buttons, old folding sunglasses from the 1930s and pieces of blue-and-white porcelain. When you finish the prowl, walk back the way you came, to Ladder Street.

But wait! Before you head down to Cat Street, please stop by Man Mo. It's one of the best temples in town; you can buy various offerings at the front desk and participate in your own style of Buddhist prayers (see page 78).

Walk down Ladder Street to Hillier Street, and into Western District and the Sheung Wan MTR station to finish off what we think you'll remember as one of the best days of shopping in Hong Kong.

Lan Kwai Fong

Take the MTR to the Central station and you'll find Lan Kwai Fong, which is right in the heart of Central, beneath Hollywood Road in an alley right off D'Aguilar Street. This area is more of an eating neighborhood than a shopping neighborhood. Look carefully or you will miss it.

The place almost looks like a Disney set—this is a must-do just to get a look at a very non-Hong Kong experience and to see how the Chinese yuppies wine and dine.

This is where everyone goes to party and to see and be seen; where everyone wants to know which of the clubs or eateries you think is best so they can judge their own chicness (and yours). There are only a few boutiques; I know the area well because there's a GAT factory-outlet store in one of the buildings here; there are other outlet shops nearby. Jammed on Friday and Saturday nights.

Wan Chai

Heading east from Central (take the MTR to Wan Chai), you will encounter the well-known

"Suzy Wong" district of Wan Chai. Back in the 1950s and 1960s this was the red-light district, frequented by sailors on leave and wealthy businessmen looking for diversion. Not anymore.

Wan Chai these days means Convention Center. It means great location between Central and Causeway Bay and it means expensive real estate. It does not particularly mean shopping, despite a gigantic China Arts & Crafts store.

The Star Ferry provides direct access from Kowloon Peninsula as it travels from Tsim Sha Tsui to Wan Chai Pier. Old Wan Chai has been pushed back from the waterfront, and will continue to be developed. If you want to see some of the original architecture and shops, prowl Queen's Road East and the lanes connecting it to Johnston Road. Shopping in the convention center is decidedly boring, but we've had two positive shopping experiences in Wan Chai: Ian rents his lights, extra lenses and camera equipment from RENT A PRO, right near the MTR exit. (Phone 838-6328; fax 834-8043; reserve your needs with a fax— they will send you a confirming fax.)

Our next adventure was to hop on the tram in front of the Hilton and just ride until it got to an area that looked non-touristy and turned out to be wonderful. It didn't take long. We ended up near the Hopewell Building in Wan Chai at a street market (Fenwick Street) that was fabulous. No other tourists in sight. Great pictures.

Causeway Bay

On the first *Born to Shop* trip to Hong Kong, we all stayed in Causeway Bay and learned its alleys and back roads with great joy. It's the kind of neighborhood that few people take time to explore unless they are staying here. Which is a shame, because some of those back roads and alleys are great fun.

Causeway Bay features one deluxe hotel (the

Excelsior) and many tourist package-style hotels. This area is far more funky than Central. The MTR stop is Causeway Bay. It is bordered by Victoria Park on the east. Part of the bay has been filled in and is now home to the Royal Hong Kong Yacht Club. One of the most colorful parts of Causeway Bay is its typhoon shelter, where sampans and yachts moor side by side. You can have dinner on a sampan while cruising the harbor. Or you can take your children to see (hear) the Noon-Day Gun, which only mad dogs and Englishmen acknowledge.

Shopping here breaks down into three different categories: funky street shopping (a great market and JARDINE'S BAZAAR), Japanese department stores and hip Hong Kong boutiques, where with-it designers (who can't quite afford Central) open shops.

There are four big Japanese department stores: SOGO, DAIMARU, MATSUZAKAYA and MIT-SUKOSHI. We think Sogo is the best, but if you are into Japanese department stores, you'll want to visit each. Note that each one is closed one day of the week; they work on a rotation system. There are a few Japanese department stores in Kowloon, but this is the concentrated area of biggies. SEIBU is in Central.

Continue your shopping spree away from the modern stores and onto Lockhart Road—sort of a main drag down the center of Causeway Bay—for a good look at some lost Chinese arts. This street is crammed with herbal and medicine shops and yep, snake shops. Pick your fave from the cage. Ian thinks it's a great photo op.

And speaking of photo opportunities, I'm always after Ian to shoot the fruits and veggies in the fresh food market right before Jardine's. JAR-DINE'S BAZAAR is alive with action from the early morning into the night. This is the Hong Kong I want you to see. First you get to a produce mar-ket, then it becomes a clothes, fabrics and notions market. There is an indoor meat market, but I only suggest a visit here if you are very strong and not at all squeamish.

Many of the shops in Causeway Bay stay open until 10 P.M., due to the street action. Causeway Bay lacks the expensive sheen of Central, but still has a lot of glitter packed in with the grime. The Excelsior Hotel—the fanciest hotel in the area—has a huge shopping arcade that most would call a mall. There are also a number of newer malls and mini-malls. Most of the stores in these are designer shops, or at least sell an upscale look. The ESPRIT store is one of the newer architectural hotspots, although the store is not so new anymore.

There are also paper shops that sell ceremonial paper money for burning at funerals and street vendors with donuts made of antique "jade." You'll know it's old because it's brown. Hmmmm.

Happy Valley

Happy Valley is situated directly behind Causeway Bay (no MTR—take a taxi) and is well-known for its racetrack, amusement park, and shoe shops. Horse-racing season lasts from September to June, and during this time thousands of fans stream in and out of the area.

I've only tried shopping in Happy Valley once, because this is home to a number of infamous shoe shops and I thought I should give it a whirl. Wrong. Cheap, icky shoes. And no big sizes for my big American feet.

Willie recommends the fruit and vegetable market, but we haven't checked it out yet.

Your taxi to Aberdeen and/or Stanley will pass through Happy Valley via the freeway; when you see the racetrack you can nod knowingly and say, "Ah yes, Happy Valley." This will impress your friends, who will think you know where you are.

Otherwise, you can pass on Happy Valley.

Quarry Bay

I've visited this neighborhood and it was interesting, but frankly, I think you want to pass. With the expansion of the MTR to the end of the island and the opening of the second cross-harbor tunnel connecting Kwun Tong to Quarry Bay, shopping in North Point and Quarry Bay has begun to perk up as a real possibility for tourists. But not for those on a tight time schedule.

I can only send you to Quarry Bay for academic reasons, with the warning that this adventure isn't for the person who is only interested in the world of luxury. This is a trip for the true traveler, who wants to see something fascinating, who understands that you only know a people by seeing how they live and how they shop.

Quarry Bay is where the Chinese yuppies live and shop. Very few tourists come out here. It has very little Old Chinese flavor, and much to remind you of American, Japanese and British shopping traditions. The mansion blocks here are high-rise towers that look so much alike they are painted candy colors, so you know if you live in the pink one with the fuchsia stripe or the pink one with the lavender stripe.

Amidst the residential towers, there are what look like concrete boxes that house several malls, most notably CITYPLAZA II and III—we defy you to figure out what happened to I and to tell which is II and which is III. (See page 190.) They come complete with bowling, ice skating, WHIMSEY-LAND (mechanical rides), food courts and every store known to man. They are sterile and mall-ish.

While you can get here on the MTR (get off at Taikoo Shing), the journey can take about forty minutes from Central. We prefer to go with a car and driver, as part of a day's outing. The drive along the harbor highway is beautiful, and you'll be fascinated by the changing scene as you drive away from Central. You'll also live happily ever after if you never get here.

Aberdeen

Say "Aberdeen" to most tourists and they think of the floating restaurants this waterside community is famous for. Say "Aberdeen" to me and I nod and smile and whisper "WAH TUNG", my favorite pottery and porcelain factory.

The community is a bit out of the way, and there is no MTR stop; you'll need to take a taxi, the No. 7 bus or call Wah Tung for a ride. But for those staying long enough in Hong Kong to relax and go for the gold, it's a place to see some colorful sights and, yes, do a little shopping. OCEAN PARK is at the edge of Aberdeen (if you have the kids with you), but it doesn't compare to Typhoon Lagoon at Walt Disney World, so beware.

Aberdeen is halfway to Stanley, and you can easily combine the two as a day trip. Come in the evening for dinner at JUMBO, and it will be yet another experience.

If you want to be adventurous, take note: Ian and I tried to do an Aberdeen shopping and eating tour with a side trip to Lamma and found it frustrating and confusing. Your taxi driver will automatically assume you want to go where all the tourists go—to the special pier with the shopping stalls that services Jumbo and the other floating restaurants. This is not Aberdeen Harbour proper, nor is it downtown Aberdeen. It's the middle of nowhere Aberdeen.

When we tried to get the *kaido* (local ferry) to Lamma for lunch, we were told there were only two a day—no regular lunch service from Aberdeen. For a better schedule, we were told to go all the way back to Central! Yipes. (You'll want to go to Lamma for dinner anyway; lunch is fine, but dinner is better; see page 111.) We could have rented a sampan to take us over to Lamma and wait for us—this sounded fantastic—but we priced it at about $100 (U.S.!) and decided that we weren't that rich.

So we never saw the ABBA SHOPPING CEN-TRE (but it's a boring mall; I've been there before), or any really scenic parts of Aberdeen. We had to call the Wah Tung van for a direct ride to Wah Tung, which is not a bad way to get there at all. Sooooo, despite the fact that Aberdeen isn't as big as Cleveland, it does have several parts and it can be confusing.

There is one serious shopping adventure awaiting you. Send the husband and kids off in their own taxi to play at Ocean Park while you hop a taxi for china (not China). You may dash off to WAH TUNG CHINA COMPANY in a taxi, but plan on needing a truck to get home—this is *the* place for pottery. There's some 30,000 square feet of breakables here. They claim to have the largest selection in the world, and they ship (see page 60). Hours are 9:30 A.M. to 5:30 P.M. Monday through Saturday, and 11 A.M. to 5 P.M. on Sunday. This happens to be a great Sunday adventure, by the way. You can even call Wah Tung (873-2272) and they'll come and fetch you. This is a fabulous way to shop. The showroom is in a warehouse; follow the signs to the elevator. There are four floors of glorious finds. Pay no mind to the price tags; negotiate for a 30%–40% discount. Tell them I sent you. (They don't know me, but I always tell them I sent myself and they give me a discount.)

Stanley/Repulse Bay/Ocean Park

It seems to be very "in" to bash STANLEY MARKET and say it isn't up to the old standards. That may be true, but it's still a fabulous place and still worth doing even if you only have three days in town. Part of the pleasure is the drive across the island, the view as you go around some of those coastal curves and the entire expe-rience, whether you buy anything or not.

The Stanley Market, in the heart of downtown Stanley (no MTR; take a taxi or the No. 6 bus.), is indeed a Tourist Trap. Who cares? It's fun and it's moderately-priced enough for you to not care. Besides, my Hong Kong shopping friends still claim to find bargains here. So there.

Not only is Stanley Market worth visiting for shopping (see page 159) and the view, but you can make a side trip to Repulse Bay. If you have kids with you, they will adore Stanley Market. You can then take them to the Kentucky Fried Chicken/McDonald's in Repulse Bay. If you have sophisticates with you, head for the luxury shopping in the Repulse Bay mini-mall and lunch at the Verandah (see page 41).

Stanley is exceedingly crowded on the weekends, but delightfully quiet midweek. You can visit Stanley Village, shop and get in a little time at the beach all in one easy trip. Buy a bathing suit at the Stanley Market (about $3) if you decide on this impromptu treat.

Kowloon Neighborhoods

The peninsula of Kowloon was ceded to the British during the Opium Wars, in one of three treaties that created the Royal Crown Colony of Hong Kong. We think it was the best gift Britain ever received; too bad they have to give it back.

Kowloon is packed with shops, hotels, excitement and bargains. You can shop its more than four square miles for days and still feel that you haven't even made a dent. Like Hong Kong Island, Kowloon is the sum of many distinct neighborhoods.

Tsim Sha Tsui

The tip of Kowloon Peninsula is made up of two neighborhoods: Tsim Sha Tsui and Tsim Sha Tsui East. It is home to most of the fine hotels, and the heart of serious tourist shopping in [INS-

Kowloon Peninsula

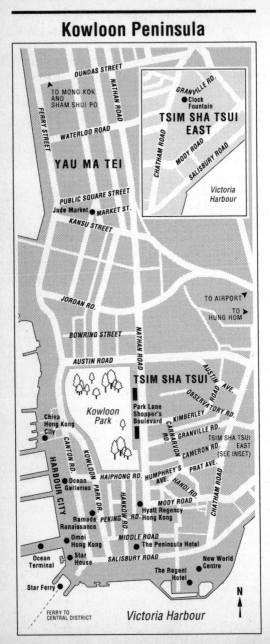

Kowloon. The Tsim Sha Tsui station on the MTR will get you into the heart of things. There's also the Jordan Road station for when you're traveling a bit further into Kowloon.

At the very tip of Tsim Sha Tsui are the Star Ferry Terminal and the Harbour City Complex. This western harbor front includes Ocean Terminal, Ocean Galleries, Ocean Centre, the Omni Marco Polo Hotel, Omni The Hong Kong Hotel and the Omni Prince Hotel. It has miles and miles of enclosed shopping, with no sight of sky.

The heart of Tsim Sha Tsui, however, is Nathan Road, Kowloon's main shopping drag; Ian says it's the equivalent of London's Oxford Street. Nathan Road stretches from the waterfront for quite some distance and works its way into the "real-people" part of Kowloon in no time at all. The most concentrated tourist shopping is in the area called the Golden Mile, which begins on Nathan Road perpendicular to Salisbury Road. Both sides of this busy street are jampacked with stores, arcades, covered alleys and street vendors. There are also some hotels here, each with a shopping mall and enough neon to make Las Vegas look boring.

If you are walking north (away from the harbor), you'll pass what's known as the Golden Mile as you get to the mosque on your left-hand side and then the Park Lane Shopper's Boulevard, also on the left. To your right, across the street from Park Lane, is Burlington Arcade. The next street on your right is Granville Road, which is famous for its jobbers, where brand-name goodies are sold from bins.

Although there are no sure-fire buys, it's still fun to wander here and get deeper into the "real-people" shopping and away from the tourist push. Few tourists wander to Granville Road, which is their loss, because if you hit it big here, you'll find name-brand U.S. goods in the $10-per-item range.

While Nathan Road is the core of Kowloon, my

favorite part of Tsim Sha Tsui is actually a bit off the beaten path, although directly in sight. In the Golden Mile section of Tsim Sha Tsui, there are two streets that run parallel to Nathan Road and are centered between the Golden Mile and Ocean Terminal: Lock Road and Hankow Road. They are essentially right behind the Peninsula Hotel.

If you have adventure in your soul, we ask you to wander this area with your eyes open. It's crammed with shops, neon signs, construction and busy people, and does not get so many tourists because it has the aura of being hidden. At the top of Lock Road, right before you get to Haiphong Road, look to your left, where you'll find a small alley that leads all the way through to Hankow Road. This is called the Haiphong Alley, and it is crammed with vendors. Many of these vendors do not speak English, and will drive a very hard bargain, if they bargain at all. Who cares?

Once you become an Old China Hand, you'll note that prices on Nathan Road are for tourists and you may disdain the whole Golden Mile area. Near Jordan Road the atmosphere is more real. It's also a schlep from the Star Ferry, so in your normal stroll of Tsim Sha Tsui you will not "do" the Jordan Road area. But you'll get here, don't worry. I want to make sure you get to the Temple Street Market, a must for an evening's shopping and entertainment (see page 163). And, of course, you can't miss the Jade Market. So don't worry, you'll get out to Jordan Road.

Harbour City

Although technically still part of Tsim Sha Tsui, I count the western portion of Kowloon as a separate neighborhood, since it is basically one giant shopping mall—or, actually, several giant interconnected shopping malls. I call the whole entire stretch of Canton Road—from the Star Ferry to China Hong Kong City—Harbour City.

This definition includes the buildings across the street on Canton Road, like Silvercord and the Sun Plaza Arcade. Perhaps it would be fairer to call this neighborhood Canton Road, but the truth is, the buildings are almost indistinguishable from each other, many are joined together, and after half a day's shopping you may be hard pressed to name which one you are in or even which side of the street you are on!

Note: If you are arriving from the Hong Kong side, it's easier to get to the Harbour City part of Tsim Sha Tsui by the Star Ferry. You'll be right there when you land. Don't take the MTR.

The denser shopping is on the Ocean Terminal side, where (walking away from the Star Ferry) the buildings, in order, are: Star House, Ocean Terminal, Ocean Galleries, Ocean Centre, World Financial Centre, Omni Prince Hotel and China Hong Kong City, which is a mall-and-towers complex and ferry terminal. This entire stretch of shopping buildings also includes office space and residential towers, as well as some of the well-known tourist hotels in this area: the Omni Marco Polo, Omni The Hong Kong Hotel and the Omni Prince Hotel. Confusing? Not really. Just consider the whole thing Harbour City.

On the right-hand side of Canton Road, beginning at Peking Road, there's the Sun Plaza Arcade and then the Silvercord Building. Silvercord has probably the best CHINESE ARTS & CRAFTS branch, a LACE LANE and computers. Sun Plaza has a few big names (IKEA, MITSUKOSHI), but is not really a good mall, especially for tourists. Most of the stores cater to local yuppies and have European-style home furnishings.

If possible, avoid this entire area on weekends (especially in summer), when locals come not only to shop but to enjoy the air-conditioning. It is crowded! While there are some very nice stores in Harbour City and all of the European designers have their shops here, I think you can give the whole thing a pass and stick to the area behind the Pen and the more authentic local shopping.

Antiques aficionados should check out the mall called THE SILK ROAD (see page 284). Photographers should note there's a FOTOMAX on the street just as you come off the Star Ferry at Star House; ROBERT LAM, the professional lab which Ian uses, is at 116-120 Canton Road, across from the Omni Prince Hotel.

Tsim Sha Tsui East

If you have Hong Kong Harbour to your back, Ocean Terminal to your left, and the Regent to your right, you are looking at the heart of Kowloon, or Tsim Sha Tsui. As the Kowloon Peninsula curves around the harbor and the land juts away from Kowloon and the Regent, the area just east of Tsim Sha Tsui but before Hung Hom and the airport is known as Tsim Sha Tsui East. Because it is waterfront property, it has become known mostly for its string of luxury hotels. And where there are luxury hotels, you know there are shopping opportunities.

Although the MTR does not come over in this direction, the walk to Tsim Sha Tsui station is not unreasonable, even in the noonday sun. You may also get here via a specific routing of the Star Ferry.

The hotels here are anchored by the Shangri-La and the Nikko, directly overlooking the harbor, with the Regal Meridien and a few others right behind them, offering water views from some of the higher floors. The waterfront street continues as Salisbury Road, and you are essentially just down the street from the Peninsula and the Regent. The street between the two rows of hotels is Mody Road, a main shopping street in this unusual neighborhood.

Tsim Sha Tsui East strikes me as an older version of Taikoo Shing: It is a city unto itself and is mobbed on weekends by local shoppers. Tsim Sha Tsui East is separated from Tsim Sha Tsui by a greenbelt of park, complete with an elaborate fountain right behind Auto Plaza (where there's an ESPRIT branch). The various buildings include Auto Plaza, Houston Centre and, of course, the enclosed mall itself, which is Tsim Sha Tsui Centre. There is street-level shopping all along Mody Road, in the various buildings, inside the mall itself (of course) and then on street levels of the buildings behind the Nikko. There is even a branch of WHIMSEYLAND, a kiddie park with small rides and entertainments. In ChinaChem Golden Plaza, right behind the Nikko, there's a DFS store for duty-free cosmetics and the like. WING ON, the Chinese department store, is the anchor of the area. There is also some shopping inside each of the hotels.

Can you visit Hong Kong and/or Kowloon and never get to Tsim Sha Tsui East? You betcha.

Yau Ma Tei

Remember when I was telling you about Jordan Road and the area north of Tsim Sha Tsui? Well, here we go. Take the MTR to Jordan Road. Above Tsim Sha Tsui, if you go north on Nathan Road or Canton Road, is the district of Yau Ma Tei—small and easily overlooked by those who are dazed by neon.

The most famous shopping site in the area is the well-known JADE MARKET at Kansu and Battery streets. Here you can shop from 10 A.M. until 3 P.M. (although many stalls close about 2:30 P.M.), going from stall to stall, negotiating for all the jade that you might fancy (see page 144). There are two different tents filled with vendors. Have fun!

At night you will want to visit the TEMPLE STREET MARKET. As you push your way through the shoulder-to-shoulder crowds you'll have the chance to buy from the carts, have your fortune told, or enjoy an open-air meal. We had a reader write in and say she couldn't find the fun parts, so check out the details (see page 163).

We went to the Jade Market on a Sunday last time and walked there via Reclamation Street, which was filled with stalls heaped with market goods, from fruits and veggies to chicken feet and dried lizards and finally cheap T-shirts and socks. We had a ball.

HUNG HOM/KWUN TONG/SHAM SHUI PO/MONG KOK

You say you want to get down-and-dirty with the real people, see some of the quickly vanishing world of yesteryear, get into a few factories for good shopping and see someone skin a live snake and swallow its gall bladder? Step this way, folks.

Hung Hom

Don't say "ho hum" to Hung Hom, because this area has really cleaned up its act. It is better described by individual factory outlets (this area is fast becoming Westernized and even touristy; see page 124), although there are also "real-people" parts where few tourists explore. The most famous address in Hung Hom is Kaiser Estates, which is not a group of estates or anything royal. It is sort of an industrial development of factories and factory-outlet stores and it's getting fancier every day—when you look at JBH/FASHIONS OF SEVENTH AVENUE, you'll be seeing a boutique as smart as anything in Central. There's no MTR stop; you'll need to arrange for a taxi, or hotel car and driver.

Kwun Tong

You can take the MTR to Kwun Tong, home to the less-fancy factory outlets, whose addresses and directions you can find in any local shopping guide. This area takes a while to travel to, and you'll probably get lost frequently as you explore, but it is genuine. With Leather Concepts now located in Central, there's not as much reason (for me) to even go to Kwun Tong, but we do recommend it to those who crave adventures in the real world.

Sham Shui Po

For more adventures of a very real kind, hit the food markets in the streets just down from the Sham Shui Po MTR station, where Kwelin Street crosses Ki Lung Street. You can walk around this city block to see live fish wriggling in red plastic bins, heaps of bok choy and cages of bound bamboo sheltering fowl of every type. Watch more carefully to see the true details of market life. This is not for young children or the squeamish.

Sham Shui Po is also headquarters to the wholesale computer world, where video games can be bargained for and will cost anywhere from 25% to 75% less than U.S. prices. Head for GOLDEN ARCADE SHOPPING CENTRE, at 44B Fuk Wah Street; you'll see it from the MTR station.

Mong Kok

Mong Kok is for real people. This area is clustered around Upper Nathan Road, where the tourists thin out fast. The Mong Kok Market at Tung Choi Street is an afternoon market also called the Ladies' Market, and my friend Jane says it's pretty good. I tried it a few years ago and thought it was boring. But that's after the Temple Street market, so call me jaded. (Pun intended!)

But Mong Kok has other features—like the bird market and the exotics market, one street over, which may break your heart. Ian and I were all but in tears as we saw all the endangered critters in cages. But I digress. At least the birds are great fun. I don't even like birds and I can still tell you that not only are they fabulous, but I consider my antique bird cage (from Honeychurch Antiques, of course) a brilliant souvenir of my last trip. After you've seen the men walking their birds, you'll want a bird cage too.

To get there: Depart the MTR at Mong Kok station and find Hong Lok Street, which is more of an alley on the south side of Argyle Street. It's two blocks west of Nathan Road (if your back is to the harbor, then west is to your left).

Now then, my friend Jane, who has lived in Hong Kong for ten years, says that some of her shopping friends swear they have found bargains and occasional designer finds by poking around the stalls on Fa Yuen Street in Mong Kok.

When I study my shopping bags from Granville Road, I note that some of the jobbers who sell U.S. name clothing on Granville also have a store on Fa Yuen Street. This market is not the same as the Ladies' Market, but is another shopping opportunity two blocks away and it is a day-time shopping adventure that can be piggy-backed with the Ladies' Market, which opens around 4 P.M.

You must be prepared to rummage at Fa Yuen, but it's not overrun by tourists. If your back is to the harbor, turn right from Nathan Road at Dundas Street. This area is south of the bird market.

New Territories Neighborhoods

There's some question as to where Kowloon and the New Territories merge and what the proper names for these areas are. If you see an address written with N.T. after it, that means New Territories.

The New Territories I visit are out there in the boonies, but they have shopping opportunities that are not to be missed. The best days to visit the New Territories are Friday (big market day) or Sunday. The best things about the New Territories are the scenery and the rural nature of some of the trip—you'll see hills and be able to imagine what China is like.

Luen Wo

This is not the best market in the area and may not be worth the trip for you. It's a very authentic market and there aren't many tourists; you also get to ride the KCR to Fanling, and then a taxi or bus (No. 78) and come very close to the China border—but don't come for the shopping alone.

There's an indoor core market with meats and things you don't want to know about (or look at), surrounded by a city block of stalls selling fruits and vegetables. Then there's overflow into a parking lot with more fruits and veggies. It's scenic, it's real, it's not Disneyland.

While you can catch a bus from the KCR train station, we thought the $2 cab fare was fair enough and the Sunday bus schedule seemed too slow for us.

We stopped in Sha Tin on the way back to take in the 10,000 Buddhas. No shopping.

Sek Kong

If you are lucky, you will be able to latch onto a bus tour to Sek Kong, or if you are brave enough (it's easy and doesn't require bravery, you just think it does), you will take public transportation—bus No. 51 will get you there. If you are luckier still, you have friends (or a rich uncle) who will bankroll a taxi or car-*cum*-driver to take you on a delicious half day or day trip of shopping fun. I made an ad hoc deal with my taxi driver after I did the first leg of the trip—for $400 H.K. he waited for me and took me to several outlets after I shopped the market, then to Kowloon City (he waited) and then back to the Regent. It was worth every penny.

Sek Kong is way out there, but it is gorgeous, fun and funky. Market day is Friday—don't miss it! This is the single best new experience I had on my last trip to Hong Kong, and I wish I could share it with everyone.

Sometimes there are bus tours that take shoppers to Sek Kong; they run regularly at Christmas time, but the idea is such a good one that it's worth asking your concierge to investigate for you. The service Jane told me about is run by CITYBUS LTD.; call their hotline at 647-4864 to see if they have a trip that suits your schedule. The one Jane told me about made several stops in Central, departing the Star Ferry at 8 A.M. and then leaving Sek Kong at 1 P.M. (figure 2 P.M. arrival back in Central). This is a luxury air-conditioned coach; you pay on the bus. Fare is about $5 for an adult; children under 12 are half price.

The drive is beautiful, from the harbor at Tolo to the hills and fields and huts. You truly get a feeling of freedom and adventure, and hills and China. And then the market is great—it's in a park or a field or something and it just sort of sprawls out with people setting up shop at tables, on blankets and in open spaces. Everything is dirt cheap but may be fake; the Gap book bag I bought for Ian fell apart almost instantly. I suspect now that real Gap labels were sewed to inferior goods. Hmmmm.

I saw Ralph Lauren/Polo shirts for $45 H.K. Blue-and-white pottery began at $25 H.K. Are you beginning to get the picture? There were tons of Christmas decorations and ribbons and things when I visited during the first week in November; seasonal artificial flowers are always sold. The "Gap" backpacks were $10 U.S., but the infamous book bag was $20.

SUM NGAI BRASSWARES

This is one of several outlets you will pass on your way out to the market in Sek Kong. If you're on a bus tour, well, too bad. If you have a car or a taxi, be sure to stop here. Although there are a few outlets in a row here, this is the only one I think is worth your time.

The store is rather large and takes credit cards.

They specialize in very average brass tourist and housewares items; a lot of their clientele are local women who are finishing their homes. However, there are some great gift items here and fabulous souvenirs for about $10 U.S. I went crazy for these brass medallions embossed with logos and emblems of local merchants, the bowling league, the firefighters, the hospital union. I thought they were great gifts for the person who has everything.

SUM NGAI BRASSWARES
195 Kam Shueng Road, Kam Tin, N.T.

Outer Island Neighborhoods

The more I visit Hong Kong, the more I need to get away from the touristy places and the malls, and find the true spirit of China. Or at least, Hong Kong. Often this means a day trip to an island. I haven't gotten to them all yet; in fact, there are hundreds of islands that are part of the territory. I haven't even gotten to all of the big ones. But I'm working on it.

Since shopping and eating are two of the best things to do in Hong Kong, I'm hitting the islands with the best combinations of those two things first.

The great thing about the outer islands—all technically part of the New Territories—is that they make fabulous little side trips. Since being on the water is so much a part of the Hong Kong experience, being able to take local ferries and *kai-dos* will add to the pleasures of your visit. Shopping, eating and simply wandering these islands can make a perfect day trip; some hightail it to Lantau, especially for the beaches. I prefer to wander little village streets and poke into the shops.

Lamma

Lamma doesn't have any shops that I've noticed, but there are a few vendors here and there to add to the colorful scene. They sell things like waxed parasols, plastic back-scratchers and straw hats, but hey, isn't that what you came here to buy anyway?

Actually, you go to Lamma to eat at one of the harbor-front dives where the food is fresh and the clientele is local. Since cars aren't allowed on Lamma island, take the ferry from Central and make a day out of the whole thing. Walk across the island and see the scenery (and the cement factory), or come for the real fun at night, when the lights are twinkling on the tiny boardwalk and everyone is pigging out.

There are two main towns on Lamma, but the place you want to be is Sok Kwu Wan, with its view of the harbor (and the cement factory) and its stretch of outdoor cafes. It's the second stop on the *kaido* from Aberdeen; there is direct service from Central.

Cheung Chau

Don't go to Cheung Chau for the famous Bun Festival; do go when no one else wants to go, so you have the full non-touristy glory of the place all to yourself. Take the ferry from Central. Like Lamma, this island has also banned cars, so all you can do is walk the garden paths. There are temples, shops (lots of porcelain shops) and restaurants—who could ask for anything more? Oh yes, there's also a market along the Praya (beach front) in Cheung Chau Village.

Factory Outlets by Neighborhood

I know, I know, in your fantasies of Hong Kong silk blouses grow on trees and cost only $30 each. I'm sorry to have to be the one to tell you, but it is in fact a complete fantasy. You can get silk blouses for $30 (and less), but you may not like the quality of them. You can also pay over $100.

Even if you shop in a factory outlet. And yes, I am talking U.S. money here.

A drop-dead-chic, top-of-the-line quality silk blouse easily costs $100. But you can get by for less.

To do so you will have to work the street markets, Granville Road and the infamous factory outlets. Factory outlets have become big business. There are, in fact, hundreds of factory outlets in Hong Kong. It is a trend in Hong Kong's manufacturing business to have your own. They are located in nice neighborhoods, out-of-the-way neighborhoods, scary neighborhoods and chic neighborhoods. Finding all of them is easy (there are many local guides and an HKTA brochure); getting to all of them in a short amount of time is impossible. But don't panic; many of them are not worth getting to.

If there's a good deal to be had, it will more than likely be advertised the local paper, the *South China Morning Post*. There is an entire page devoted to this sort of advertising; look here first for news of special sales or bargains.

If you see something in the paper that sparks your interest, go for it. Otherwise, I suggest you pick your outlets carefully because so much time can be spent looking for a bargain that effort invested begins to outweigh money saved. I must also warn you that many outlets aren't as good as they used to be, that many outlets manufacture fake bargains and simply that many outlets aren't cheap. (You may do better at Loehmann's!)

Ian recently bought his wife an Anne Klein II silk blouse for $125. I fail to find a bargain anywhere in that; I'm sure it would cost less at an American discounter. True, it was a gorgeous blouse and the best of many we looked at in several outlets, but it was no "street bargain."

Furthermore, an Anne Klein label may not be such a status symbol in Britain. Sure, a woman can judge the quality of the garment for herself, but the cachet of an expensive label can be lost on someone who doesn't know what you pay to get such a label.

The moral of this story? Know your prices at home before you assume there are savings in outlets; if you are buying a gift for someone, make sure they can understand its true value. Your friends and family at home might not grasp the fact that quality costs a lot of money, even in Hong Kong.

Also take note of addresses. Don't expect to find a great deal in a factory-outlet shop that has a tony address. Outlets attached to real factories still offer the most certain guarantee of authenticity, and your best bet for a real bargain.

There are some outlets which are fun; some which are easy to get to; some which are worth doing. We can't tell you to track down all the wild and weird ones, especially because after your trip to the Sek Kong Market in the New Territories you'll be broke anyway. Outlet shopping these days becomes a matter of choices and neighborhoods; time, convenience and personal shopping style. If you don't like funky shopping, forget most of the outlets. (But not all of them!)

Choose by neighborhood and you'll never be angry that you schlepped halfway around the world to find a dump.

Be sure that you are not planning your factory-outlet visits on a public holiday, and especially not during the Chinese New Year, when everything will be closed up tight. Remember that factories and their outlets close during lunch, usually from 1 P.M. to 2 P.M. If you can't get enough of the outlets, don't forget that there is a local guide that lists only outlets.

Ambiance in the outlets varies widely. Some good outlets are in the factories themselves, and are exciting to visit. Other outlets are funky but have good-quality merchandise mixed in with seconds. More and more outlets are quite elegant, have large, modern showrooms, and accept credit cards; nevertheless, they offer quality merchandise at discount prices.

One thing to remember about shopping in an outlet is that there are no returns or credits. Once you leave the store, the merchandise is yours, even if you find a huge hole in the sleeve when you return to your hotel room. Always check the merchandise for dye lots and damages before you buy it. Always try on an item; verify sizes. Most outlets will have some place for you to try on items. Sizes are not always marked correctly. As with the rest of Hong Kong shopping, the motto is "Buyer Beware." When possible, shop with a credit card that has an automatic purchase protection plan so you can get a refund in case of disaster.

Central

Central is the main retail shopping, banking and business hub of Hong Kong. The rents are very high. Get the message? Because more and more tourists are looking for factory outlets that are convenient, more and more manufacturers are complying by opening branches in Central. However, you cannot expect to get a fabulous bargain in a shop where the overhead is outrageous. Especially if the floor is clean.

I like the Central outlets for convenience. It sure beats an hour on the MTR and getting lost in Kwun Tong. But you will pay the price for this convenience. For many, time is money.

THE PEDDER BUILDING

My friend Willie is an architect and he asks everyone to take a look at the Pedder Building as one of the last examples of old-fashioned Hong Kong architecture. Frankly, I think the Pedder Building is just shy of being a dump. But it does have a lot of convenient outlets.

But buyer beware: Many of the shops located within the building are not discounters. Many of them that claim to be outlets still have very high prices. Like that Anne Klein II blouse I was telling you about. But then, I bought a silk skirt at Anne Klein for $30, so you never know.

Because places come and go and we all do have different tastes, the best advice I can give you is to start at the top of this building and simply work your way down. Go up in the elevator then continue downward via the staircase. There are stairs on both ends of each hall; do not be frightened.

My personal favorite resources are listed below. There is a DAVID SHEEKWAN boutique in the building, but it's not an outlet. Stop by to see the gorgeous interior and the drop-dead-chic clothes because I happen to know where the outlet is. J.R. PEDDERS is another shop in the building—it's chic and wonderful and everything you want it to be. . . except cheap.

THE PEDDER BUILDING
12 Pedder Street, Hong Kong

SHOPPER'S WORLD SAFARI

This is what a factory outlet should look like. It was one of the first, and may be one of the last. It is small, crowded and packed with people and merchandise. Men's shirts are in bins along the wall in the back of the shop; the rest is women's sportswear and most of it recognizable. And affordable. Like $25 for a knit dress.

Hours at the Pedder Building are Monday through Sunday, 9:30 A.M. to 6:30 P.M.

SHOPPER'S WORLD SAFARI
Pedder Building, 12 Pedder Street, Hong Kong

TAKPAC

A smart, modern outlet in the Pedder Building that features Anne Klein II with some deals and some non-deals. There are lots of choices to make in lots of colors. Some of the merchandise matches up to what you see in U.S. stores, some of it may be in colors cut especially for the outlet. There is a sale rack in the rear to the right, sort of hidden from view as you enter. A lot of the clothing is small; there were no size 14s when I asked. Prices may not be any better than at a good sale in the U.S. The selection is clean, bright and attractive; shopping here is satisfying if you don't mind the high prices. This certainly isn't the down-and-dirty Hong Kong outlet shopping that can be found elsewhere. Hours are Monday through Saturday, 9:30 A.M. to 6:30 P.M.

TAKPAC
    Pedder Building, 12 Pedder Street, Hong Kong

WINTEX
    One of the tonier outlets in Central, Wintex carries a combo of big-name labels and names you've never heard of, but sure-fire quality nonetheless. All the clothing is spanking clean; much of it is still in plastic. Prices average around $100 for a blouse, which we don't consider to be much of a bargain. Ian got a Barney's silk blouse for $50 that was the steal of the day. I paid $130 for a cashmere sweater in a hard-to-find color. The cashmere selection is large, and while not dirt-cheap, it is reasonably-priced. This is another one of those outlets for people who don't like dirty places and insist on high quality. Hours are Monday through Friday, 9 A.M. to 6 P.M., and Saturday until 5 P.M.

WINTEX
    Pedder Building, 12 Pedder Street, Hong Kong

LEATHER CONCEPTS
    While there is a bigger and better Leather Concepts outlet in their factory in the New Territories, this shop is so convenient that I suggest you forget the big schlep and blow your wad right here. Note that while the door says Leather Concepts, your credit card receipt will not say that, so when you get the bill you may temporarily freak out. (I did.)

So what did I buy? Well, let's see, what didn't I buy? I got a red leather-and-suede woven car coat for $200 and a Bottega Veneta-style woven purse for $80. I quit then but could have gone for men's leather jackets, belts and various women's styles in coats, skirts, trousers, handbags, etc. Each item is top quality, high fashion, stunning, to-die-for, and of did-you-get-that-in-Italy? quality.

Hours are Monday through Saturday, 9 A.M. to 6 P.M.

LEATHER CONCEPTS
Pedder Building (Room 406), 12 Pedder Street, Hong Kong

Other Central Addresses

ÇA VA
Ça Va carries export merchandise, not seconds. They are rumored to own rights to big-name U.S. merchandise, which they sell here at a discount. Ça Va manufactures a full line of clothing, mostly in silks and gabardines, but it also has cotton-knit clothing and novelty sweaters.

Ça Va is open Monday through Friday from 10:30 A.M. to 6 P.M., and Saturday from 10:30 A.M. to 5 P.M.

ÇA VA
Central Building (Room 1552), 3 Pedder Street, Hong Kong

JENNIE
It's in a newish location, in a clean modern building in Central, so it's easy to pop in. It's also easy to skip this one: I was not knocked out, despite Jennie's reputation as one of the best resources in town.

The merchandise includes sweaters, silk blouses, pleated silk skirts, gabardine blazers and cotton knits of all varieties. The average price of anything is $50 and up. There are no labels that I recognize, but the merchandise is very well-made and appears to be of very high quality. Mostly this outlet was simply too upscale and too fancy for me (can you believe it?)—I could have spent a fortune here easily, but I simply want to pay less. Hours are Monday through Saturday, 10 A.M. to 6 P.M.

JENNIE

Well On Commercial Building (4th floor), 60 Wellington Street, Hong Kong

GAT

GAT has several outlets in Hong Kong; this one is on the food street Lan Kwai Fong and is conveniently located for Central shoppers. It's also half a block from Jennie, so you can hit two birds with one credit card. GAT appears to be the distributor for the Kenar label.

Hours are Monday through Saturday, 9 A.M. to 6 P.M.

GAT

8–11 Lan Kwai Fong (10th floor), Hong Kong

Kowloon

Tsim Sha Tsui and Tsim Sha Tsui East are the focal areas where Kowloon Peninsula's "retail" outlet shops are located. These outlets, usually found in commercial buildings, cater to the tourist trade, while still trying to pass on a bargain or two. We must warn you that looking for an address is frustrating, however. Many buildings are old, and their numbers have been worn away or buried under shop signs. For this reason, we give building names in our listings. The name of any building seems to be more clearly marked than the street address is. Travel with the A-O-A *Map Directory.* You can match up buildings by name and location on their block to find the right doorway. We give as specific directions as possible, but even we still get lost. Credit cards are accepted at these shops unless otherwise noted. You can take the MTR to the Tsim Sha Tsui stop for the following stores, unless otherwise noted.

SANDS BUILDING

The Sands Building is not a factory outlet building, although you might think so from all the listings. It is an office building, located right in the heart of the action, towering above the Chung Kiu Department Store. (Don't miss Chung Kiu, if you like Chinese department stores.) The entrance to the Sands Building is to the right of the store. Go to the back to find the elevators to the shops:

SANDS BUILDING
17 Hankow Road, Kowloon

ORIENTAL PACIFIC

O.P. is an old hand at the outlet business, and I'm happy to report they still have good prices, especially on cashmere.

O.P. is a real find as a basic resource for sweaters galore. There's nothing flashy about it, but the shop is quite large, with sweater bins and racks lining three of the four walls. Displays are arranged by quality. Summer cottons are in one area, children's clothing in another, cashmeres on the wall nearest to the cash register. Sizes all tend to be marked large, but there is stock in the back; just ask.

Stories of serious bargains are legion; cashmeres begin around $100 and go up. There are sale items in cardboard boxes; some woven men's business shirts were available on our last visit. Who knows what you'll turn up?

Hours are Monday through Saturday, 9 A.M. to 6 P.M.

ORIENTAL PACIFIC
Sands Building (6th floor), 17 Hankow Road, Kowloon

TOP KNITTERS

Top Knitters produces knitwear for some of the major, major, major designers. If you are up on designs, you will recognize them. This is one of those feast-or-famine outlets; we wish you good hunting. Don't expect cheap. I've been here when the selection was so tacky I could have cried. I've been here and bought Andrea Jovine goods that I still wear and adore. They seem to feature the good, the bad and the ugly on a regular rotation.

Hours are Monday through Friday, 9 A.M. to 6 P.M., Saturday till 5 P.M.

TOP KNITTERS

Sands Building (10th floor), 17 Hankow Road, Kowloon

DORFIT

Dorfit is a small version of Oriental Pacific. There are sweaters piled all over the room. Some are a little seedy, but if you ignore these and concentrate on the cashmeres and cottons, you will love it here too. Dorfit carries everything from men's and women's cashmere basics, to novelty knits, cotton sweaters and kids' knits.

Dorfit's main shop is on Peking Road behind the Pen, but this one is convenient if you are shopping the Sands Building.

Hours are Monday through Saturday, 9 A.M. to 6 P.M.

DORFIT

Sands Building (11th floor), 17 Hankow Road, Kowloon

ÇA VA

This is a branch of the sweater and silk separates outlet already mentioned (page 118). It's conveniently located one block from the Sands Building as you exit the Star Ferry.

ÇA VA

Star House, Salisbury Road, Kowloon

GREAT OUTDOOR CLOTHING COMPANY

It was Michele in New York who sent us after Microlite, the perfect travel fiber because it's lightweight and warm. We found it and anything else we could want at this outlet for outerwear. There's a selection of activewear and sports outerwear in this huge store with very fair prices. Men, women and children will do well.

Please note the hours since this store is in a mall, but does not observe regular mall hours. The store opens at 11 A.M. and closes at 7 P.M. seven days a week.

GREAT OUTDOOR CLOTHING COMPANY

Harbour City/Ocean Galleries (Store 229), Canton Road, Kowloon

SHIRT STOP

This outlet has become so popular that it has multiplied and spawned many others around town. We shop in Kowloon because it's convenient. Shirt Stop specializes in men's shirts, most especially from a major French designer with three initials. They are very up front about displaying the merchandise, labels intact and all. Other designer goods have the labels mostly cut out, but it is still possible to read them. Much of the merchandise is unisex. There can be items other than shirts and sweaters; we lucked into gorgeous terry robes on our last trip. Shirt Stop is a good place to stock up on everyday shirts at good prices. A button-down cotton runs $20 or less. There are also sweaters in wool and cashmere for sale. The heavy knits are less expensive and a better value than the cashmeres.

Hours are Monday through Saturday, 9 A.M. to 6 P.M.

SHIRT STOP

Hyatt Regency Hong Kong (basement), 67 Nathan Road, Kowloon

Granville Road

Granville Road: My heart beats faster at the very words. Granville Road is not only my first and last stop on any shopping spree to Hong Kong but it is the barometer of my faith. When Ian wants to grant me a treat, he simply says, "How about a stroll on Granville Road?"

We have been on Granville Road when bargains are dried up and when they are flowing; when it's good, this is as close to shopping heaven as you will get. Granville Road is the home to jobbers who have bins and racks filled with American goodies. Most are about $10 an item.

We're not going to name a lot of stores because that's actually more confusing than helpful. Just start at the MCDONALD'S one block into Granville Road from Nathan Road and walk east until the street ends. Please note that these stores do not take credit cards. Many will take U.S. dollars but will peg the rate of exchange where they want it—which may be better than you'll get at your hotel, anyway. There is one place to change money toward the end of the stretch across from the Ramada. Bring cash and maybe a trailer.

The last time we were there we saw labels from the Gap, the Limited, Victoria's Secret, Harvé Benard, Mexx, Eddie Bauer, Banana Republic and Calvin Klein.

Just go from store to store; don't worry about names and addresses. I always buy from VALUE (No. 32), SAMPLE NOOK (No. 30), GX WAREHOUSE (No. 26), FACTOR FASHION CO. (No. 26A), STOCK SHOP (No. 32A) and PARK LAI FASHIONS (No. 46).

Note that several of these stores have branches on Fa Yuen Street in Mong Kok (see page 107), an area recommended by my friend Jane.

Kowloon City

DD WAREHOUSE

Speaking of Jane, here's another one of her tips. This is the find of the century. DD Warehouse is the outlet for David Sheekwan. And David Sheekwan is one of the hottest designers in town.

The outlet is in a clean modern building in a factory neighborhood near the airport (take a taxi); this is near Kowloon City, but is technically an area called To Kwa Wan, which no one (and I mean no one) has ever heard of.

Fear not: The shop is as fancy as the Sheekwan boutique in Central. And they take credit cards. Besides, we got the "in" here because Willie's sister owns part of the business or all of the business or knows some big cheese here. I didn't ask too many questions; I've never met Willie's sister.

Prices are not street cheap, but neither is the merchandise. The sweater I bought for $40 is my favorite new item this season, it's got a fabulous Euro-Japanese drape and a simple but utterly chic look, just like all the suits and sportswear items here. You can buy an entire wardrobe; tons of working woman's suits.

If you choose to get to only one wild and crazy outlet in a semi-far-flung area, this just may be it.

Hours are Monday through Friday 9:30 A.M. to 5:30 P.M.; Saturday from 9:30 A.M. to 4:30 P.M. Saturdays.

DD WAREHOUSE
11 Yuk Yat Street, To Kwa Wan, Kowloon

Hung Hom

Once you are out of Tsim Sha Tsui, you have entered the world of true factory outlets. Hung Hom is the neighborhood closest to Tsim Sha Tsui, and was the first to make factory outlet shopping an event. Kaiser Estates Phases I, II and III are the mainstays of Hung Hom, although there are three other buildings where outlets have popped up as well.

Getting to Hung Hom is best done by taxi from Kowloon. Ask to be let out in front of Kaiser Estates Phase I, as the majority of the shops are located either in Kaiser Estates or in the Winner Building across the street. If you are compelled to come by bus, routes 5C, 8 and 25 leave from the Kowloon Star Ferry Terminal. Get off at Ma Tau Wei Road, just after Station Lane. Walk to Man Yue Street for Kaiser Estates. To return, backtrack and catch the bus on the other side of Ma Tau Wei Road marked "Star Ferry." Taxis come and go on a regular basis in front of Kaiser Estates Phase I. Better yet, consider coming with a car and driver if you want to check out the scene and then move on.

ÇA VA

We don't want you to miss this branch of Ça Va, if you didn't visit it in Central or Kowloon. Ça Va is well-known for silks. You can buy shirts, still in the plastic wrap, for under $50. Ian bought men's silk shirts for $25 each. If you come at the right time of year, there is a good selection. Sample sale times are January to February, June and July to August. You will get your best buys then. Hours are Monday through Friday, 10:30 A.M. to 6 P.M.; Saturday to 5 P.M.

ÇA VA

34 Man Yue Street (ground floor), Hung Hom, Kowloon (MTR: None)

MORELLE

This store has been around for a while and was never one of my favorites because I thought it had sort of boring, typical Hong Kong silk blouses. This trip, something in the window caught Ian's eye and we combed this store top to bottom. He bought his wife several silk shirts, and I have to admit that I was impressed. The blouses are basics, but they are well-made and are perfect with suits or dressy trouser looks. There's also a good range of fashion colors. There were some silk parkas and anoraks that I would have happily bought if I had a spare $200.

MORELLE
Winner Building (ground floor), 32 Man Yue Street, Hung Hom, Kowloon (MTR: None)

HANGREEN FASHION

My friend Susan Granger pronounces this outlet "the cheapest and the best." Since it's next to the Diane Freis outlet, it's also very convenient. The scene here is tons of washed silk for men and women. Ian was knocked out by the choices. I flipped for silk parkas. I worry that stonewashed silk will be yesterday's news in terms of fashion, but it's so practical for those of us who travel—and so cheap here—that you almost don't care. Trousers at about $30; tank tops, $10. Think 15£ and up.

Hours are Monday through Saturday, 9 A.M. to 6 P.M. They are now open on Sunday (although Diane Freis is not, and you'll want to get them both) from 10 A.M. to 4 P.M.

HANGREEN FASHION
Kaiser Estates Phase I (10th floor), 41 Man Yue Street, Hung Hom, Kowloon (MTR: None)

JBH/FASHIONS OF SEVENTH AVENUE

This is a hot source for locals, who claim they get very big-name stuff here. I've heard rumors of the magical name Donna Karan, although I have never once with my own eyes seen anything with any kind of Karan label. So don't count on Donna, but remember that this is high-end merchandise; prices are middle of the road to high, but the choices for a working woman can be excellent. Some nice sportswear too. The boutique is on the ground floor in the corner, easy to spot, and it's a modern beauty.

Ian bought Bumble another silk blouse for $50 (yes, she does get a lot of blouses) and I bought a raw silk stretch bodysuit for $40. We could have bought out the store, but we were on our best behavior. Yes, 20£ can buy a blouse.

I have no idea what JBH stands for, but there

are other addresses for this outlet (see below), I've just never been to them. Still, after what I saw (and bought) in Hung Hom, I'd try this source any chance I got.

Hours are Monday through Saturday, 9 A.M. to 6 P.M. Phase III is around the corner from Phase I; the shop is easy to spot on street level.

JBH/FASHIONS OF SEVENTH AVENUE

Kaiser Estates Phase III, corner Hok Yuen Street and Man Lok Street, Hung Hom, Kowloon (MTR: None)

Mirror Tower, 61 Mody Road (ground floor, Shop 10) Tsim Sha Tsui East, Kowloon (MTR: None)

Convention Plaza, 1 Harbour Road (Shop M12), Hong Kong (MTR: Wan Chai)

Sing Pao Center (Shop 12A), 8 Queen's Road, Hong Kong

EDE

Even though we're not sure how to pronounce this name, we can tell you we pronounce the goodies as "swell." This medium-sized outlet has moderately-priced suits and women's clothing with some separates. We bought a Ralph Lauren/Polo, long-sleeved, cream-colored, silk blouse for $45 with label intact; an Ellen Tracy, short-sleeved, silk blouse was also $45 (Both 22£).

Ian bought his wife the most gorgeous pair of creamy, heavy silk pajamas you have ever seen for $100 (50£). That doesn't mean these same deals will be available when you stop by, and don't tell anyone we named names. Just remember that we were thrilled with the resource and can't wait to go back.

Hours are Monday through Saturday, 9:30 A.M. to 6:30 P.M.; closed Sunday.

EDE

Kaiser Estates Phase I (1st floor), 41 Man Yue Street, Hung Hom, Kowloon (MTR: None)

DIANE FREIS FACTORY OUTLET STORE

Diane Freis no longer sells from her factory in the boonies—luckily for us, since this convenient, clean, spacious outlet is on your regular everyday shopping route. I promise that your heart will stop when you see all the choices. Most of the clothes are on racks organized by style and price. There are some bins, and there is a dress-up area with hats and some accessories. This is one of the largest outlet stores in Kaiser Estates; it takes credit cards. Dresses are mostly in the $100 to $200 range; some of them are more than a year old, but that's the beauty of a Diane design: No one can tell. There are special promotional styles and deals: I bought a dress, with sequins no less, for all of $69; Ian bought Lizzie a tea dress for 70£.

I must also tell you that sometimes the prices in Loehmann's are better than in Hong Kong. Right before my last trip to Hong Kong, I bought a new outfit to wear to dinner: $129 (plus tax), but I thought that was fair enough. Loehmann's doesn't always carry Diane Freis, but you can get lucky in the U.S. as well as in Hong Kong.

DIANE FREIS FACTORY OUTLET STORE
Kaiser Estates Phase I (10th floor), 41 Man Yue Street, Hung Hom, Kowloon (MTR: None)

Lai Chi Kok

Now we are talking factory town. This feels like the New Territories, but actually it isn't. Lai Chi Kok is just a tad uptown from the basic Kowloon neighborhoods that tourists frequent. It is safe, the MTR access is great (no need to switch trains; take the red line toward Tsuen Wan and go two stations past Sham Sui Po), and outlets are within walking distance of the MTR station. You don't have to get lost, or go any great distance (it's about ten minutes from Tsim Sha Shui) and all of a sudden, wham, you are in the heart of Hong Kong and the real world. It's a fabulous experience.

Note: When crossing back and forth on Cheung Sha Wan Road and Tung Chau Road, don't be too brave or foolish. The traffic is terrible. Use the lights to cross.

SPLENDID

Splendid is a strong resource for leather garments; note that this is a new address if you have visited before. Same factory, same city but different outlet, so don't get confused. They have moved the outlet into the main office.

Splendid manufactures upscale leather clothing for European stores. Many lines are made specifically for Germany and Italy. The styling is top-of-the-line. Men's jackets come in every size and many styles. Stock up on leather trousers in various colors.

Now then, let's talk about prices. You've come all this way; it's a very foreign neighborhood; you are expecting a bargain. Well, yes and no. These items would easily retail for between $750 and $1,000 (500£) and up in New York or London. But prices are in the mid-hundreds here, and I do mean in U.S. dollars. Men's leather jackets cost $250–$350. That's what they cost. Don't make this trek if you think you're going to get $50 bargains.

Hours are Monday through Saturday, 9:30 A.M. to 6 P.M.

SPLENDID

LeRoy Industrial Building (2nd floor), 15 Cheung Shun Street, Kowloon (MTR: Lai Chi Kok)

AH CHOW PORCELAIN

Ah Chow is in the opposite direction from the MTR station as Splendid, and since they sell merchandise of a completely different nature, it seems fitting enough.

Ah Chow is a very good porcelain resource. Now then, before you get out your street map and start making tracks, take the time to compare a few things. First off, if you're going to the boonies for porcelain, I like Wah Tung better (page 98).

Also, getting here can be a gritty experience — you have to enter through a garage and find the proper lift. You need to have a spirit of adventure and a want to conquer the whole neighborhood. Don't come for this one listing.

That said, I'd like you to know that Ah Chow is indeed great. And worth the trip.

The showroom is crammed with huge jardinieres, waiting to go to a mansion or hotel, and lamps and vases of every size imaginable. Directly ahead from the entry is a room full of sample dishes. If you were a buyer for one of the major department stores, you would go in here and pick one from column A and one from column B. Many of the pieces on the floor have "Sold" signs (in Chinese, of course) on them. We asked; that's how we knew.

If you look at the fine Chinese-style ashtrays, lamps and ceramic goods in American department stores, you will recognize Ah Chow's merchandise. While they will make any pattern you want, or copy anything you want, it is easier to just pick from the overrun stock sitting around the shop.

I shipped a set of ginger jars, and they arrived in perfect condition—wrapped better than a mummy. The shipping cost more than the jars, but who wants to hand-carry china for twenty hours on a plane? Please note that it took a very, very long time for the jars to arrive and that I have gotten letters from readers who have also complained that shipping seemed to take forever. They were happy with the product but anxious during the wait.

The place is a little bit dusty, but this only adds to the charm. Breakables are piled high— don't bring the children! No credit cards are accepted, but traveler's checks are OK.

Hours are Monday through Saturday, 10 A.M. to 7 P.M.

AH CHOW PORCELAIN

Hong Kong Industrial Centre (Block B, 7th floor), 489–491 Castle Peak Road, Kowloon (MTR: Lai Chi Kok)

SANG WOO

Cross Cheung Sha Wan Road to get to Sang Woo. The building is located opposite the Leighton Textile Building, at number 883. Take the elevators to the 6th floor and turn right for Room 604. This is another great leather source with big- (and we mean BIG-) name designers. The outlet is air-conditioned (important in summer), and neatly arranged so you don't have to rummage. The biggest selections are in leather jackets for men. A bomber jacket sells for about $300. Soft leather pants were $200, and a chamois sweatshirt $100. This is upscale styling and prices. Try your luck and hope that a shipment has just arrived. There are also women's clothes.

I feel compelled to tell you that local author Dana Goetz, who writes about the outlets professionally, thinks this outlet has gone downhill fast. Maybe we were lucky on the last visit.

Hours are Monday through Friday, 9:30 A.M. to 5:30 P.M., Saturday to 12:30 P.M.

SANG WOO

Elite Building, 883 Cheung Sha Wan Road, Kowloon (MTR: Lai Chi Kok)

BROADWAY SPORTSWEAR

Broadway Sportswear is located around the corner from Ah Chow. The building has a huge sign on top that says "Broadway," so once you are close you can't miss it. You will be more than pleased that you came. Broadway Sportswear is the single best source for designer raincoats in Hong Kong and Kowloon. This is where I bought my Calvin Klein wool-lined raincoat for $150. It is a man's coat, which is important to note in this outlet as much of the merchandise is for men. Think unisex; think less than 100£.

The inside of Broadway is massive and confusing. Don't make this your last stop when you are already tired, or you will turn around and walk out.

Hours are Monday through Saturday, 9:30 A.M. to 5:30 P.M. Closed for lunch from 1 P.M. to 2 P.M.

BROADWAY SPORTSWEAR
7 Wing Hong Street (ground floor), Kowloon (MTR: Lai Chi Kok)

CHAPTER FOUR

HONG KONG DICTIONARY

An Alphabetical Guide

Antiques

According to the U.S. government, an antique is any item of art, furniture or craft work that is over 100 years old. The reason the U.S. government cares is simple: You pay no duty on genuine antiques.

The problem lies in proving your item is over one hundred years old. There is no governing body in Hong Kong that "officially" proclaims an item to be over 100 years of age. There are many agencies that look and sound official, and have official papers, stamps and seals, but none of them are government-sanctioned. In Hong Kong, anything goes. This is very frustrating for the consumer who is trying to determine a fair value for a piece of art. It's also one of many reasons why you should only buy from a reputable antiques dealer.

True antiques are a hot commodity, and unscrupulous dealers take advantage of that need by issuing authenticity papers for goods that are not old. To make matters worse, Hong Kong does not require its dealers to put prices on their goods. Depending on the dealer's mood, or assessment of your pocketbook, the ginger jar you love could cost $100 H.K or $150 U.S.

Only you can determine if you feel like you're getting a good deal. Pick a reputable dealer, and ask a lot of questions about the piece, its period, etc. If the dealer doesn't know, and doesn't offer to find out, he probably is not a true antiques expert. Get as much in writing as possible. Even if it means nothing, it is proof that you have been defrauded if later you find out your Ming vase was made in Kowloon, circa 1989. Your invoice should state what you are buying, the estimated age of the item (including dynasty, year), where it was made, and any flaws or repairs done to the piece.

I've noticed that there is a characteristic particular to most quality antiques shops, which is never even imitated in bad shops. In good shops, the dealers want to tell you everything they know about a piece or a style you have expressed interest in; they are dying to talk about the items; they are dying to educate you. They take pleasure in talking about and explaining the ins and outs of entire categories of goods. If you don't find these free lessons readily offered, don't spend a lot of money in that shop.

Blue-and-White

Blue-and-white is the common term given to Chinese export-style porcelain, which reached its heyday in the late 17th century when the black ships were running "china" to Europe as if it were gold. After 1750, Western craftsmen in both England and continental Europe had the secret of creating bone china and were well on their way to creating their own chinoiserie styles and then manufacturing transfer patterns for mass use.

In those years before Westerners were on to the secrets of the Orient (and still believed porcelain was created from baked eggshells), there was such a huge business in export wares that European shapes and styles were sent to Canton for duplication. Thus, a strong knowledge of these forms is required by the shopper who wants to be able to accurately date a piece.

Glenn Vessa tells me that after you've handled a few thousand pieces of blue-and-white you will have complete confidence in what you are doing. I can only tell you that I flunked the test he gave me. And I studied beforehand.

The untrained eye needs to look for the following: pits and holes that indicate firing methods; the non-uniform look of hand drawing versus stencils; the shades of blues of the best dyes; the right shades of gray-white as opposed to the bright white backgrounds of new wares. Marks on the bottom are usually meaningless. Designs may have European inspiration (look at those flowers and arabesques), which will help you determine what you are looking at.

Be careful that you are not looking at English-made blue-and-white passed off as export wares. I saw some in an antiques shop in Macau and while it was nice, it wasn't what I came to China to buy.

Bronzes

Antique Chinese bronzes are featured at several Hong Kong museums and provide a good educational starting place for you to understand the difference between what will cost you thousands of U.S. dollars and what you can buy for a few hundred. The lesser price indicates a fake. As with all Chinese art, you must be able to recognize subtle changes in style and form that indicate time periods and dynasties in order to properly date your fake.

Glenn Vessa says that Japanese bronzes are still a good investment; bronze incense burners begin around $3,000 and go up. Stop by Honeychurch to talk to him about it.

Cameras

Oy! Can we tell you about cameras! You probably don't want to know everything we can tell you about cameras.

First off, we have to deal with fantasy. For some reason, every shopper who comes to Hong Kong thinks he's going to get a great deal; that this is THE place to buy a camera. Wrong. Unless you are a pro, you may not even want to bother with the exercise. But if you insist on playing the game, pay attention:

Start by doing research at home as to what equipment you need. Do NOT allow a Hong Kong camera salesman to tell you what he thinks you should buy, or what is a good deal. Once you feel comfortable that you know what you are looking for, visit several shops (and not all on Nathan Road) and compare prices. We have discovered that prices can vary by as little as $10 and as much as $200 before negotiations begin.

Be sure to ascertain that the price for the camera includes a manufacturer's worldwide guarantee. The store's guarantee (even if printed on fancy paper) is worthless; the manufacturer's guarantee may prove worthless too, but at least get it.

As soon as you start serious negotiations, examine the camera very carefully. It should still be in its original box, complete with Styrofoam that packs it tightly. Remember that camera boxes can be repacked. Check to make sure yours was not. Look at the guarantee to verify that it is a worldwide guarantee and is authentic. There must be a stamp from the importing agent on the registration card. The dealer will add his stamp upon conclusion of the sale. If you are really careful you will call the importing agent and verify the sale. Check the serial numbers on the camera and lens with those on the registration card to make sure that they match. Take out the guarantee before the camera is repacked and ask to have it repacked in front of you. This way the merchandise can't be switched. Ask to have the following information included in the store receipt: name and model of camera; serial numbers of parts;

price of each item; date of purchase; itemized cost of purchase with total sum at the bottom; and form of payment you are using.

Ian, who happens to be a Time-Life photographer, spent a good bit of time on and off Nathan Road doing camera research. His advice: Stay away from Nathan Road completely and know what you are doing if you buy used items. He has done well with used items (see page 254), but notes that many Nathan Road dealers buy from the same sources he does and then sell the goods as new.

Carpets

As the Persian carpet market has dried up, the popularity of Chinese carpets, both new and old, has escalated. China still has a labor pool of young girls who will work for very little money and sit for long periods of time tying knots. Carpets come in traditional designs or can be special-ordered. Price depends on knots per square inch, fiber content, complexity of design, how many colors are used and city or region of origin. Any of the Chinese Arts & Crafts stores is a good place to look at carpets and get familiarized with different styles and prices ranges. You can visit the Tai Ping Carpets showroom in Central and then make an appointment to visit the factory in Kowloon (see page 279) to watch work in progress.

When considering the material of the rug, consider its use. Silk rugs are magnificent and impractical. If you are going to use the carpet in a low-traffic area or as a wall hanging, great. Silk threads are usually woven as the warp (vertical) threads and either silk or cotton as the weft (horizontal). The pile, nonetheless, will be pure silk. Wool rugs are more durable.

Chinese rugs come in every imaginable combination of colors. No one combination is more valuable than the next. Some older carpets have been colored with pure vegetable dyes; more modern ones use sturdier synthetics in combination with vegetable dyes. Avoid carpets that were made with aniline dyes, since these are unstable. These dyes were used on older rugs that were crafted at the beginning of the century. To test for aniline dye, spit on a white handkerchief and then rub the cloth gently over the colors. If only a little color comes off, you are safe. If the carpet has been dyed with aniline dyes, a lot of color will come off on the handkerchief.

Chinoiserie

Exports from the Orient were so fashionable in Europe that they started their own trend. Western designers and craftsmen began to make items in the style of the Orient. Much was created from fantasy and whimsy; there is also a mixture of influence of Indian and other styles with the purely Chinese. Works made in the style of the Orient are considered chinoiserie. Chinoiserie is not actually made in China.

Chops

A chop is a form of signature stamp on which the symbol for a person's name is carved. The chop is then dipped in dry dye and then placed on paper, much like a rubber stamp. The main difference between rubber stamps and chops is that rubber stamps became trendy only in the 1980s, whereas chops were in vogue about 2,200 years ago. Since chops go so far back, you can choose from an antique or a newly-created version. (For more on chops, see page 274.)

Ceramics and Porcelain

Ceramic and porcelain wares available in Hong Kong fall into three categories: British imports, new Chinese and old Chinese. For current British china resources, see pages 270–272. For a short lesson in buying blue-and-white, see page 134.

New Chinese pottery and porcelain is in high demand. Although much of the base material is being imported from Japan and finished in Hong Kong, it is still considered Chinese. Most factories will take orders directly. There are numerous factories in Hong Kong where you can watch porcelain wares being created and place your personal order.

Porcelain is distinguished from pottery in that it uses china clay to form the paste; it is translucent. Modern designs are less elaborate than those used during the height of porcelain design in the Ming Dynasty (A.D. 1368–1644), but the old techniques are slowly being revived. Blue-and-white ware is still the most popular. New wares (made to look old) can be found at the various Chinese government stores, including Chinese Arts & Crafts, in zillions of little shops on and off Hollywood Road, in Stanley Market, in Macau and just about everywhere else. Fakes abound; buy with care.

Chinese New Year

The most important festival of the year, the Chinese New Year, falls on a different day in each year according to the lunar calendar. It is usually in the latter part of January or the first two weeks of February. Each year is identified with an animal that gives character to those born under it. According to legend, when Buddha asked all of the animals to come to him, only twelve showed up. As a result he named the years after them. The animal signs are those of the Rat, Ox, Tiger, Rabbit, Dragon, Snake, Horse, Ram, Monkey, Cockerel, Dog and Pig.

During the Chinese (Lunar) New Year, most stores will close. For a few days preceding the festivities, it is not unusual to find prices artificially raised in many local shops, as shopkeepers take advantage of the fact that the Chinese like to buy new clothing for the new year.

Chinese Scrolls

Part art and part communication, Chinese scrolls are decorative pieces of parchment paper, rolled around pieces of wood at each end. They contain calligraphy and art relating to history, a story, a poem, a lesson or a message. Some scrolls are mostly art, with little calligraphy, but others are just the opposite. Being able to identify the author or artist makes the scroll more valuable, but it is usually not possible. Chinese scrolls make beautiful wall hangings, and are popular collector's pieces.

Cloisonné

The art of cloisonné involves fitting decorative enamel between thin metal strips on a metal surface. The surface is then fired under just the right temperatures and the finish is glazed to a sheen. It sounds simple, but the handwork involved in laying the metal strips to form a complicated design, and then laying in the paint so that it does not run, is time-consuming and delicate, and is an art requiring training and patience.

Antique works by the very finest artists bring in large sums of money. Most of what you'll see for sale in Hong Kong (outside of the finest galleries) is mass-produced cloisonné and is very inexpensive—a small vase sells for about $20; bangle bracelets are $3. You can also find rings, mirrors and earrings for good prices at most of the markets. These make good souvenir gifts to take home. Ian's little girls (then age seven and nine) thought their bracelets were hot stuff. You need to be about that age to really appreciate them.

Computers

All the famous brands, makes and models of computers can be found in Hong Kong, but you had better be computer literate to know if you are getting a better deal than you could get back home. Be sure to check the power capacity, voltage requirements, guarantees and serial numbers of every piece you buy. Clones are also available, and at very good prices. However, "Buyer Beware" applies doubly in this category.

Various software programs are also available; prices are not much less than in the U.S., but can be substantially less than in the U.K. The biggest problem is that you simply must know what you are doing and what you are buying; the more you rely on the sales help, the more likely you are to be taken.

There are several office buildings that specialize in computer showrooms: try the Silvercord Building in Kowloon and Golden Arcade Shopping Center in Sham Shui Po.

Dim Sum

Dim sum are a Hong Kong specialty and are easily ordered in any Western-style restaurant where someone speaks English or the menu is printed in dual languages. If you go for a more adventurous meal, you may need a few basic tips. You may also buy a book on the subject or carry around pictures with you. Some people show photos of the grandchildren. I have in my wallet a picture of my favorite dim sum. The best bet is to learn what you like at home, under Western-style conditions, then learn the names of the items in Chinese or have them written out for you. Of course, that's too easy. It's much more fun to go someplace where they will allow you to stand next to the dim sum cart and point. Don't ask what's inside those little dumplings and you may be a happier person.

We're regulars at Luk Yu Teahouse, where English is not the language of choice. The menu is a tally sheet of red Chinese characters on which you circle items and write numbers according to how many orders of each you require. Good luck. Someone there will speak enough English to help you, but here are two choices that I know will always work:

HAR GAU: My all-time favorite, I can eat six of these babies and be full—I suggest to everyone that this is the winner. H*ar gau* are dumplings filled with steamed shrimp. There are usually three in an order.

SHIU MAI: I'm so-so on these; they are a pork-and-shrimp combo, usually larger than *har gau* and stuffed to overflowing. Orders may have two, three or four pieces in the basket.

Embroidery

The art of stitching decorations onto another fabric by hand or machine is known as embroidery. Stitches can be combined to make abstract or realistic shapes, sometimes of enormous complexity. Embroidered goods sold in Hong Kong include bed linens, chair cushions, tablecloths, napkins, runners, place mats, coasters, blouses, children's clothing and robes—all of these items are new. There is another market in antique embroidered fabrics (and slippers) which is, of course, a whole new category, price-wise.

Traditionally embroidery has been hand-sewn. However, today there are machines that do most of the work. Embroidery threads are made from the finest silk to the heaviest yarn. Judge the value of a piece by whether it is hand-stitched or machine-stitched and what kind of thread or yarn has been used.

One of the most popular forms of embroidered work sold in Hong Kong is whitework, or white-on-white embroidery. Most of it is done by machine, but the workmanship is very good. Hand-embroidered goods are hard to find today, and very expensive. Most of these goods come out of Shanghai and may be competitively priced in your hometown. Don't assume you're getting a bargain.

Furniture

Chinese styles in furniture and the woods the furnishings were made of caused a major sensation in the European market. Teak, ebony and *padouk* were all imported from the Far East and were highly valued in the West. Yet the major furnishing rage was for lacquered goods, usually in the form of small chests of cabinets that were placed on top of stands, which were built to measure in Europe.

True Chinese antique furniture is defined by purity of form, with decorative and interpretive patterns carved into the sides or backs. Antique furniture is a hot collector's item. Dealers and collectors alike are scouring the shops and auction houses. It is better to find an unfinished piece and oversee its restoration, however, than to find one that has already been restored. If it has been restored, find out who did the work and what was done. Some unknowing dealers bleach the fine woods and ruin their value. Others put a polyurethane-like gloss on the pieces and make them unnaturally shiny.

If you do decide to buy, decide beforehand how you will get the piece home. If you are shipping it through the shop, verify the quality of their shipper and insurance. If you are shipping it yourself, call a shipper and get details before you begin to negotiate the price of the piece.

Happy Coats

One of the hottest-selling tourist items is the *happy coat*, a jacket with a stand-up mandarin collar, usually made of embroidered silk with decorative flowers, animals and birds. Happy coats can be extravagant and luxurious or simple and plain. They make great housecoats and are good souvenirs of Hong Kong. Many shops sell them already wrapped and ready to go.

Ivory

One word of warning: No. It's that simple. Articles made from ivory will not be allowed into the U.S. or U.K. It is not smart to try to run them. Antique pieces with proper paperwork will be allowed in.

Carvers in Hong Kong are currently using dentin from walrus, hippopotamus, boar and whale as substitutes for elephant ivory. If you want to make sure you are not buying elephant ivory, look for the network of fine lines that is visible to the naked eye. If the piece you are buying is made of bone, there will not be any visible grain or luster. Bone also weighs less than ivory. Imitation ivory is made of plastic, but can be colored to look quite good. However, it is a softer material than real ivory, and less dense. Many netsuke that you find in the markets are made of bone dust or plastic.

There are very few antique ivory pieces left in Hong Kong. If someone claims to be selling you one, be very wary. Should you snag one, you'll want provenance papers.

Jade

Jade was originally used solely in rituals for the dead. In the late Chou dynasty it became a source of delight acceptable for the living to appreciate; interest in intricately-carved jade ornaments, sword fittings, hairpins, buttons and garment hooks took off.

The term *jade* is used to signify two different stones, jadeite and nephrite. The written character for jade signifies purity, nobility and beauty. Jade has been revered in China for 5,000 years, and is available in many forms. It is considered by some to be a magical stone, protecting the health of one who wears it. The scholar always carried a piece of jade in his pocket for health and wisdom.

Jade is also reported to pull the impurities out of the body.

Jadeite and nephrite have different chemical properties. Jadeite tends to be more translucent and nephrite more opaque. For this reason, jadeite is often considered to be more valuable. If you are shopping for jade, you need a quick lesson in Chinese: *chen yu* is real jade; *fu yu* is false jade. Jadeite comes in many colors, including lavender, yellow, black, orange, red, pink, white and many shades of green. Nephrite comes in varying shades of green only. The value of both is determined by translucence, quality of carving and color. Assume that a carving that is too inexpensive is not jade. "Jade" factories work in soapstone or other less valuable stones. White jade (of little value) can be dyed into valuable-looking shades of green. Buyer beware.

Jade should be ice-cold to the touch and so hard it cannot be scratched by steel. Unfortunately, it's pretty hard to test these properties in a store or marketplace. Yet shoppers make it common practice to quick touch or lick-touch a piece. You may also want to "ring" a piece, since jade, just like fine crystal, has its own tone when struck.

The Jade Market (see page 165) is a fun adventure and a good way to look at lots of "fake" and real jade. Test your eye before you buy. If you are determined to buy a piece of genuine jade, we suggest that you use a trusted jeweler or other reputable source; you'll pay more than you might in a market or a small jewelry shop, but you'll be paying for peace of mind. Please note that jade (real jade) is very, very expensive. Fake jade may be what you really have in mind. Don't be shy.

If you are interested in carved jade figures, bring out your own jeweler's loupe and watch the dealer quake. If the carving is smooth and uniform, it was done with modern tools. Gotcha! A fine piece and an old piece are hand-cut and should be slightly jagged on the edges.

What are those green circles you see in the market and often in the street? They are nephrite and should cost no more than $1 per circle. They make fabulous gifts when tied to a long silken cord and turned into a necklace.

I've been buying brown jade over the last few years—I don't know if it's real or not; dealers claim it is "antique." Willie is something of an expert on jade and my pieces look like his pieces, but getting a handle on true value is difficult. I pay between $10 and $20 per piece and am happy with what I've got. What's it's really worth is anyone's guess. I've been attaching my jade pieces to the zippers or straps of various handbags—very chic. But heavy.

Lacquer

No, I don't mean nail varnish. I'm talking about an ancient art form dating as far back as 85 B.C. when baskets, boxes, cups, bowls and jars were coated with up to 30 layers of lacquer in order to make them waterproof. Each layer must be dried thoroughly and polished before another layer can be applied. After the lacquer is finished, decoration may be applied. Black and red are the most common color combinations. (Black on the outside; red for the inside.)

You may date an item by the colors used; by the Han dynasty metallics were used in the decorative painting.

Modern (post-1650) versions of lacquer may be European-inspired Chinoiserie; beware.

Monochromatic Wares

You may adore blue-and-white porcelains as much as I do, but please remember that most of them were created for the export market because locals thought they were ugly and beneath them. The good stuff was usually monochromatic. Go to a museum and study the best and brightest before you start shopping because, again, fakes abound.

Celadon is perhaps the best known of the Chinese porcelain monochromes. It is a pale gray-green in color and grew to popularity because of the (false) assumption that poisoned food would cause a piece of celadon pottery to change color. The amount of green in the piece is based on how much iron is in the glaze.

Netsuke

A *netsuke* is a Japanese-style carving, usually small, of an ornamental figure. Netsuke were originally designed to enable the kimono wearer, who has no pockets, to carry a small case looped over the belt. The netsuke was fastened to the kimono belt with a short cord. The quality of the carving indicated the importance of the wearer. Most old netsuke are carved out of ivory; you need papers to import them into the U.S.

New netsuke figures are being made in Hong Kong, carved out of bone or plastic. They are stained or colored to look old, but don't quite achieve the patina or grace of aged ivory; the carvings are somewhat coarse.

Please note that a large number of netsuke are erotic; examine what you buy carefully so you are not embarrassed later.

Nintendo

Aaron Gershman reports: When Castlevania III was hot news in the States, in Hong Kong you could already get Castlevania IV. You can find game cartridges with eighty-two games in one cartridge (about $100). Some of the familiar American games have different titles in their Hong Kong versions. For instance, Mega Man is called Rock Man in Hong Kong, and Power Mission is Power Blazer. With prices at a fraction of U.S. prices, who cares? Typical Hong Kong price for Super Mario Brothers 3: $25. This game costs $50 in the U.S. You'll also find a bigger selection of games you haven't heard of than you might imagine. When in doubt, just go by what looks good. You can always try games in the store. If you are planning on buying any Nintendo games in Hong Kong, have an up-to-date *Nintendo Power* issue with you so you can show it to salespeople, who might be able to match up the games in case of different names.

You must buy a converter ($8–$10) in order to use Japanese-style game cartridges on a U.S. Nintendo, because you can't use the Japanese size on your machine. The converter attaches to the cartridge to make it compatible with your machine. This is technology at its best. Take advantage of the opportunity to get a new game, and get something your friends don't have. You can have games before anybody else gets them. Buy the converter in Hong Kong, because they aren't sold in Japan.

Super Nintendo is also available in Hong Kong; you will need a converter, also easily bought in Hong Kong.

Opals

Hong Kong is considered the opal-cutting capital of Asia. Dealers buy opals, which are mined mainly in Australia, in their rough state, and bring them to their factories in Hong Kong. There they are judged for quality and then cut either for wholesale export or for local jewelry. Black opals are the rarest, and therefore the most expensive. White opals are the most available; they are not actually white, but varying shades of sparkling color. The opal has minuscule spheres of cristobalite layered inside; this causes the light to refract and the gem to look iridescent. The more cristobalite, the more "fire." An opal can contain up to 30% water, which makes it very difficult to cut. Dishonest dealers will sell sliced stones, called doublets or triplets, depending upon the number of slices of stone layered together. If the salesman will not show you the back of the stone, suspect that it is layered. There are several opal "factories" in Hong Kong. These shops offer tourists the chance to watch the craftsmen at work cutting opal, and offer opal jewelry for sale at "factory" prices. It's an interesting and informative tour to take, but we couldn't vouch for the quality of any opal you might buy from a factory. Again, it's best to trust a reputable jeweler if you wish to buy a quality stone.

Papercuts

An art form still practiced in China, papercuts are hand-painted and hand-cut drawings of butterflies, animals, birds, flowers and human figures. Often they are mounted on cards; sometimes they are sold in packs of six, delicately wrapped in tissue. We buy them in quantity and use them as decorations on our own cards and stationery.

Pearls

Pearls have been appreciated and all but worshipped in Eastern and Western cultures for centuries. Numerous famous women in history have had enviable pearl collections—from Queen Elizabeth I to Queen Elizabeth II, to say nothing of Queen Elizabeth Taylor, Coco Chanel and Barbara Hutton, whose pearls were once owned by Marie Antoinette.

The first thing to know about shopping for pearls in Hong Kong is that the best ones come from Japan. If you are looking for a serious set of pearls, find a dealer who will show you the Japanese government inspection certification that is necessary for every legally exported pearl. Many pearls cross the border without this, and for a reason.

Pearls are usually sold loosely strung and are weighed by the *momme*. Each *momme* is equal to 3.75 grams. The size of the pearls is measured in millimeters. Size 3s are small, like caviar, and 10s are large, like mothballs. The average buyer is looking for something between 6 and 7 millimeters. The price usually doubles every 1/2mm after 6. Therefore, if a 6mm pearl is $10, a 6-1/2mm pearl would be $20, a 7mm $40, and so on. When the size of the pearl gets very high, prices often triple and quadruple with each 1/2mm.

Most pearls you will encounter are cultured. The pearl grower introduces a small piece of mussel shell into the oyster, and then hopes that Mother Nature will do her stuff. The annoyed oyster coats the "intruder" with nacre, the lustrous substance that creates the pearl. The layers of nacre determine the luster and size. It takes about five years for an oyster to create a pearl. The oysters are protected from predators in wire baskets in carefully controlled oyster beds.

There are five basic varieties of pearls: freshwater, South Sea, *akoya*, black and mabe. Freshwater pearls are also known as Biwa pearls, and are the little Rice Krispies-shaped pearls that come in shades of pink, lavender, cream, tangerine, blue and blue-green. Many of the pearls larger than 10mm are known as South-Sea pearls. They are produced in the South Seas, where the water is warmer and the oysters larger. The silver-lipped oyster produces large, magnificent silver pearls. The large golden-colored pearls are produced by the golden-lipped oyster. The pearls you are probably most familiar with are known as *akoya* pearls: these range from 2mm to 10mm in size. The shapes are more round than not, and the colors range from shades of cream to pink. A few of these pearls have a bluish tone. The rarest pearl is the black pearl, which is actually a deep blue or blue-green. This gem is produced by the black-lipped oyster of the waters surrounding Tahiti and

Okinawa. Sizes range from 8mm to 15mm. Putting together a perfectly-matched set is difficult and costly. Mabe pearls (pronounced maw-bay) have flat backs and are considered "blister" pearls because of the way they are attached to the shell. They are distinguished by their silvery-bluish tone and rainbow luster.

Pearls are judged by their luster, nacre, color, shape and surface quality. The more perfect the pearl in all respects, the more valuable. Test pearls by rolling them—cultured pearls are more likely to be perfectly round and will therefore roll more smoothly.

You needn't be interested in serious pearls, whether natural or fake. In fact, prices being what they are, I'm in favor of fakes. Hong Kong sells fake versions of cultured pearls rather readily; specialty items such as baroque style or gray pearls are hard to come by. Chanel-style pearl items may be found in fashion stores, but not at pearl dealers.

Postcards

I'm a great believer in taking all the free postcards you can from hotels, especially famous ones. I must also confess that the Peninsula sends some of its guests printed stationery that bears your name with the slogan "in residence" underneath—this beats any postcard you can send to friends and relatives.

But if you're forced to buy your postcards, as most mere mortals are, then poke around a good bit before you plunk down $2 H.K. per card. Not that you are overpaying (that's about a quarter), but you can find better deals.

In the Lanes, and about town everywhere, you'll find postcards from the early 1960s sold in red boxes—some 25 cards are in the set, which sells for $25 H.K. Not only is this a better deal than new modern cards, but the cards have a kitschy, wonderful quality to them that add to their charm. Do note that none of the new build-ings in the Hong Kong skyline are included in these cards, because they are so old.

If you're looking for postcards that showcase the current architectural wonders of the city, take the escalator up into the HongKong and Shanghai Bank (the Norman Foster-designed masterpiece that looks sort of like a spaceship), explore the bank and buy four postcards in a souvenir enve-lope for $2 H.K. Each is a different shot of the famous landmark building.

My favorite postcards come from Kwong Sang Hong, which has four or five branches around town—I found my cards in Western Market. They are reproductions of Chinese ephemera in post-card form; they are not cheap but they are stun-ning.

Sega

Consult the section on Nintendo (see page 147). If you are buying for a child and are not per-sonally familiar with all aspects of the game car-tridges, bring a U.S. game with you so you can make sure you buy a compatible game type. You may need to buy a local converter, which is not a problem.

Silk

Anthropologists will tell you that silk is China's single greatest contribution to world cul-ture. The quality of Chinese silk has always been so superior that no substitute has ever been deemed acceptable; thus trade routes to bring silk around the world were established—the same routes that brought cultural secrets from ancient worlds into Europe's own local melting pots.

The art of weaving silk originated some 4,000 years ago in China. Since that time it has spread throughout Asia and the world. China, however, remains the largest exporter of cloth and garments. Hong Kong receives most of its silk fabric directly from China. Fabric shops in the markets sell rolls of silk for reasonable prices, although silk is not dirt cheap and may be priced competitively in your home market.

Be sure, when buying silk, that it is real. Many wonderful copies are on the market today. Real silk thread burns like human hair and leaves a fine ash. Synthetic silk curls or melts as it burns. If you are not sure, remove a thread and light a match.

Snuff Bottles

A favorite collector's item, snuff bottles come in porcelain, glass, stone, metal, bamboo, bronze and jade. They also come in old and new old-style versions. In short, watch out, this is a category that has been flooded with fakes, due to tourist demand.

A top-of-the-line collectible snuff bottle can go for $100,000, and that is American moolah, so if you think you are buying a fine example of the art form for $10, do reconsider your position. The glass bottles with a carved overlay are rare and magnificent; there are specific schools of design and style in snuff bottles that are especially valuable to collect. You can find more ordinary examples in any of the markets. But you want to buy from a fine dealer if you are serious about your collection. If you just want a few ornaments for the house (or tree), the markets or shops on Hollywood Road will have plenty.

Sports Shoes

If you haven't shopped with a preteen, you might not know just how important it is to be wearing the "right" sports shoes to school. Much of our time in Hong Kong was spent discussing the Pump (a type of shoe made by Reebok) and the various copycat styles. Since the Pump costs over $100 in the U.S., there is some hope for a deal in Hong Kong. Indeed, there are tons of name-brand sports shoes sold everywhere, from stores to Stanley Market to street. For the most part, they cost 20% more than they do in the U.S. We know they are made in Korea and should be cheap, but so far our findings have been sorry.

If you must buy the Pump, do so in the U.S., where you know what you are getting. If your child will be satisfied with a high-style substitute, you'll have many choices. Expect to pay over $50, though. You can still do better at Marshall's at home!

Ian did just fine with non-big-name branded sports shoes and found prices to be a small fraction of the price in London. But then, he's not a preteen in need of the latest status shoe.

Tea

The Museum of Tea Ware is a good place to start an exploration into the mysteries of tea. Tea has been grown in China for over 2,000 years, and reflects the climate and soil where it is grown, much as European wines do. There are three categories of tea: unfermented tea, fermented tea and semi-fermented tea.

It is customary to drink Chinese tea black, with no milk, sugar or lemon. Cups do not have a handle, but often do have a fitted lid to keep the contents hot and to strain the leaves as you sip. Since Hong Kong is a British colony, you may also find many hotel lobbies and restaurants that serve an English high tea (a great opportunity to rest your feet and gear up for a few more hours of shopping).

Because tea is relatively inexpensive and often comes in an attractive package or tin, it makes an excellent gift. Your choices are wide—there are many fancy tea shops selling high-priced and well-packaged goods, but there are also many choices in grocery store and local herbal/medicine shops that are equally attractive. All the Chinese department stores have a wide selection of teas and tea containers.

Xiying Pottery Teapots

Tea utensils are a popular item to purchase in Hong Kong, with Xiying pottery teapots being one of the most popular and expensive. They are made from unglazed purple clay and are potted by hand to achieve different forms of balance. They often resemble leaves, trees or animals. Proportion is achieved by changing the balance of the base, top and handle. Xiying teapots are always signed by the artist who made them, and the more famous artists' pots sell for over $1,000.

CHAPTER FIVE

MARKETS AND MALLS

Double Happiness

Double Happiness is a common Chinese wish, often inscribed on beads and pottery, even written across trams. For those who can shop in both malls and markets, you too will achieve Double Happiness. If your time in Hong Kong (especially your shopping time) is limited, you're going to have to make some choices.

Shoppers in Hong Kong have a very serious reality to face up to very quickly—you may even be forced to make this decision BEFORE you get to Hong Kong, as you plan your daily schedule of sightseeing. The question at hand? To mall or not to mall.

Hong Kong is famous for its malls; these lavish pieces of real estate and architecture do indeed represent a very specific slice of the local shopping scene. Perhaps you cannot understand the whole shopping scene without looking at some of these malls.

But the truth is, the malls have the fanciest shops and the fanciest shops have the highest prices. I don't come to Hong Kong to spend money; I want to save. And frankly, I don't want to be indoors in a sterile mall or observing Western-style shopping. At least, not for a great deal of my time.

The more I come to Hong Kong, the less I am attracted to the malls. Don't get me wrong, these malls are fabulous. But there's so much of the real Hong Kong to see out in the streets, that I am drawn to the markets, not the malls.

With luck, you'll be able to see both, to decide for yourself which style of shopping you prefer. With luck, and enough time, you'll find Double Happiness.

Market Heaven

Hong Kong is truly market heaven. There are fruit and vegetable markets, general merchandise markets, jade markets, thieves', ladies' and men's markets. There are market lanes and market areas. There is even a market city (Stanley).

Markets are a way of life in Hong Kong, and we love them. But they are a very real slice of life. Some are not pretty or fancy. If you have a squeamish stomach, avoid the food markets that sell live chickens or ducks and slaughter them on the spot. Steer clear of wriggly snakes and lizards staked out on cardboard. Many visitors who have only seen chicken wrapped in cellophane in their local supermarket can find the realities of a street market to be distasteful.

But it is the way of life in Hong Kong. Open-air food markets like Jardine's Bazaar are a little easier to take than indoor ones, like Central Market, where the sights and smells are intense. You should have no trouble with fruits and veggies; indoor markets are the ones that normally house the livestock.

Merchandise markets are busy and hectic. There are no spacious aisles or racks of organized clothing. Some markets exist only during certain hours of the day or night. At a pre-appointed time, people appear from nowhere, pushing carts laden with merchandise. They set up shop along the street, selling their goods until the crowds start to dissipate, at which time they disappear into the night.

Markets have their own rules, just like stores. If you want to be successful at bargaining and come home with good buys, we offer a few suggestions:

- Dress simply. The richer you look, the higher the starting price. Most goods on carts do not have price tags. If you have an engagement ring that broadcasts RICH AMERICAN, turn it around, or leave it in the hotel safe. We like to wear blue jeans and T-shirts to the market. We still look like visitors, but no one can tell what our budget is.

- Check with your hotel concierge about the neighborhood where the market is located. It may not be considered safe for a woman to go there alone, or after dark. We don't want to sound chauvinistic or paranoid, but crime in market areas can be higher than in tourist areas, especially at the night markets. Arrange your handbag or money carrying situation to be as crime-proof as possible.

- Carry the local currency and have a lot of change with you. Most market shops or stalls do not take credit cards. It's also difficult to bargain and then offer a large bill and ask for change. As a bargaining point, be able to say you only have so much cash on hand.

- Branded merchandise sold on the street can be hot, counterfeit or of inferior quality.

- Sizes may not be true to the tags.

- Go early if you want the best selection. Go late if you want to make the best deals.

- Never trust anyone who does business from the street to mail anything for you.

- Don't give your hotel address to anyone who wants to bring you some other samples the next day.

- Make sure you are buying something you can legally bring back to the States. Don't buy ivory; all varieties are illegal to import. Don't buy tortoise shell; it will be impounded by Customs.

- Don't think less of yourself if you end up paying the asking price. After all, when that steal of the century is only $10, why haggle if you're not in the mood?

Most markets have no specific street address, but are known by the streets that are boundaries or intersect in the middle of the market area. The majority of cab drivers know where the markets are by name. However, it is always a good precaution to have your concierge write the name of the market and location in Chinese before you leave. You probably won't need it, but it can't hurt. Buses, trolleys and the MTR usually service the markets as well. Your concierge can give you exact directions from your hotel. Take a hotel business card with you, so you'll have the address in Chinese in case you need directions back home.

STANLEY MARKET

Stanley Main Street, Stanley Village, Hong Kong

Stanley Market is world-renowned. Any tourist coming to Hong Kong knows about Stanley. Shopping legends abound about fabulous bargains on designer clothing. After all the buildup, we find the reality a bit disappointing. Since honesty is the name of our game, we are going to tell you the truth about Stanley Market: Stanley ain't what it used to be.

But wait! That doesn't mean Stanley is a disaster. Stanley is merely a Tourist Trap. It's still a fabulous place and very much worth doing. Even Ian, who cannot stand touristy places, likes Stanley. It's one of the best markets for husbands and children who normally hate to shop. And yes, it still has enough bargains to satisfy the most intrepid shopper.

Furthermore, Stanley is located in a beautiful part of Hong Kong Island. The drive here is one of the best things about the adventure. When you go around the curve at Repulse Bay and you see the inlet beaches and the sun gleaming off the water, your heart will simply miss a beat. When you get to the actual shopping experience, your heart may miss another beat: There are more tourist goods here than anywhere else.

Here is concentrated shopping for just about anything you might want to buy. It's fun, it's clean and it's festive, but you will pay for the privilege. You will probably overpay for the privilege.

I have received a few angry letters from people who were annoyed that they spent the time and money to go to Stanley; they felt that it was expensive and a waste of time. I mention this outright because I go there frequently, ready to change my mind. And the truth is simple. I still love Stanley.

First of all, if you are traveling with children, Stanley is great entertainment for them. It's safe, it seems exotic (to them), they can wander a little but not get lost, and there is merchandise for sale that interests them—including souvenirs, toys and running shoes. Ditto the husbands—there is enough men's merchandise from $3 ties to $100 leather bomber jackets, to $15 copied Swiss Army watches to engraved chops and lessons in Chinese calligraphy—that even the non-shopping man can be content for an hour or two. Which is all you really need here.

If you have the time, go on the bus and return by taxi (since you will have a lot of packages). You can go with your car and driver and make a stop at Repulse Bay to see the elegant shopping there in the mini-mall (109 Repulse Bay Road); you may also want to go for a swim in the lovely little bay right before you get to Stanley. There is a public beach. If all you care about is the shopping, don't arrive before 9:30 or 10 A.M., as the vendors don't really set up too early.

We often travel to Stanley by the No. 6 or No.

260 bus, which leaves from the Central Bus Terminus or in front of the Star Ferry terminal, and takes about forty-five minutes in moderate traffic. If our schedule is tight, I simply splurge for a taxi—it costs about $10 U.S. to get from Central to Stanley. For the distance involved and the beauty of the ride, this is one of Hong Kong's best bargains. When Ian saw the meter all he could sputter was, "Do you know how much a taxi ride like that would cost in London?"

Start your tour of Stanley Market at Watson's—this is a Western-style chemist shop right at the beginning of the market village—and use it as a landmark in case you get separated from friends or family. (They also have restrooms.) From Watson's, walk straight down Stanley New Street toward the water, and when you reach the main street of the market, choose left or right. We usually go left first, and explore the main market street, then the alleys that lead up the hill. The restaurants are located in this area. If you really are in a hurry, there are fast-food stands in the market as well.

When you retrace your steps along the main street and continue on the other side of Stanley New Street, you will have a beautiful view of the beach and can stop to take pictures. You can take a right on Stanley Market Road and circle around back to Watson's and the taxi stand afterwards. The main street is where you can expect to find your more substantial purchases. These shops are housed in buildings, and have been in the same location for years. Many of them take credit cards and traveler's checks. If not, there are two banks on Main Street.

If you haven't bought too much to carry and are taking the bus home, the stop is across the main road at the top of the market. Ask for directions. You can get off at Admiralty to connect to the MTR. Market hours are seven days a week, 10 A.M. to 7 P.M.

What goes on sale at Stanley is a never-ending parade of designer merchandise, department store (mostly American names) private-label goods, non-branded silk items, T-shirts, ties, linens, ceramics and souvenirs. You rarely see the same stuff twice, even in the same week. Many of the stores are simply regular stores with regular prices, so don't assume that this is a factory-outlet situation or a true bargain area. It's a true tourist area.

There are hand-painted T-shirts by a local folk artist, which I think are real items of art; you can have a chop made in less than an hour ($15); you can order (or choose from the ready-made) a small calligraphy painting, which includes the name of your choice in Chinese with an analysis of the name's meaning on the back. At $3 each, this is a great gift for the kids or the people back home.

The name of the stand that sells this item is YIP'S; they also have a shop at the Convention Centre in Wan Chai. Yes, of course it's a tourist gimmick. But for $3? Give me a break—it's fabulous!

LADIES' MARKET (MONG KOK MARKET)

Argyle Street and Nathan Road, Mong Kok, Kowloon

The market sets up a short distance away from the Mong Kok MTR station; it begins around 4 P.M. and goes into the evening, until about 10 P.M. or so.

The streets have the feeling of a carnival, with lots of people parading by the stands, stopping to examine shirts, socks, sewing sets, buttons and bras. There are some toys and sunglasses, but mostly lots of trinkets, shirts, socks and everyday goods. This market is not a great one; there are no live snakes, however.

Getting there is easy on the MTR. Take the train from Central, Admiralty or Tsim Sha Tsui to

Mong Kok. Exit in the direction of the Sincere department store. Cross Sai Yeung Choi and turn right on Tung Choi. This is where the market begins. Walk on Tung Choi until it dead-ends into Dundas. If you turn right and cross Sai Yeung Choi again you will be on Nathan Road. The Mong Kok station will be to your right, and Yau Ma Tei to your left. There will be more action on the other side of the station as well, toward Mong Kok Street.

TEMPLE STREET MARKET (KOWLOON NIGHT MARKET)

Temple Street and Jordan Road, Yau Ma Tei, Kowloon

If you are only going to one market in Hong Kong, this is the one. It's a night market. You can go out for dinner wherever you like and come here afterwards. There's action until 11 P.M. and sometimes later (on Saturday nights). You can also eat in the street as this is one of the homes of the *dai pai dong*—the street vendor selling dinner from a cart.

And yes, this is where the opera singers are; this is where you can have your fortune told by a bird!

The market can be extremely crowded, with people pushing and shoving to get past, especially on weekends. If you are nervous in crowds, don't go. If you do go, don't carry a lot of cash. Dress down; don't carry a purse. You can't help but get carried away with the sheer joy of the place, the shopping is secondary.

Getting to this market is very simple, but entering the market at exactly the right place in order to start off with the opera singers takes a little know-how. I just heard from a reader who couldn't find the action, so pay attention.

Take the MTR to the Jordan Road station. Exit onto Nathan Road toward Yue Hwa Chinese Products Emporium. You will see Yue Hwa; you can't miss it. Stay on the Yue Hwa side of the street which, if the harbor is to your back, is the left-hand side of the street. You will be walking north on Nathan Road for about two or three blocks.

Keep looking to your left. You are looking for a tiny entranceway, a small alley crammed with people. This is where the opera singers do their thing on little patios. When you spot the alley, turn left into the crowd. Opera singers will be on your right and left, but mostly on your right. This alley is only about 50 yards long. When you emerge from the alley you will be on Temple Street and at the corner of a real temple, hence the name of the market.

Walk straight forward one block, so that you have the sidewalk that borders the grounds of the temple yard on your right side. On this sidewalk you'll see a long row of fortunetellers, each with his own gimmick. One or two may speak English. Ian and I went with Peter and Louisa Chan one time, and Peter was able to translate my fortune for me. I wouldn't have missed it for the world.

Peter explains that this is not a joke and you must take it very seriously. To joke or be a smart-ass would be very rude. I found a fortuneteller with a cage filled with birds. I picked the bird I wanted. Said bird then hopped out of the cage toward a row of cards laid on the pavement. He hopped around a bit, then pecked a card into his beak. He gave the card to the fortuneteller. (The bird was rewarded with a snack.) The fortuneteller then told my future in Chinese, and Peter translated. It was a very good fortune (thanks to Peter or the bird, or both) and the entire experience began the night with just the right note of magic.

We have been back to the Temple Street Market on our own and found it just as much fun, but we had no one to translate the bird words to us. So we just went shopping.

The shopping is the typical street-market fare: first a block of carts and stalls, then many, many blocks of stalls lining Reclamation Street. You can do this same market in another form on Sundays in daylight (see below). When you get to Reclamation Street, note that there are stores along the sidewalk and many of them have bargains too. Like Levi's for $10. Running shoes (no-name brands) for $25. The stalls in the main thrust of the market all seem to be selling the same things after a while: imitation Hermés and Picasso scarves, alarm clocks that beep and peep, belts, socks, T-shirts with characters from video games, chinos and every now and then jade or jade-like things. A few vendors have novelty items—fake Montblanc pens for $3 were a must for Ian's teenagers; the vibrating pillow was essential. I bought fresh fruit for the hotel room and a set of china porcelain mugs with lids for $23 H.K. I mention this only because I found similar ones in Macau for $10 H.K. But at the time we thought $23 H.K. was fair enough. The mugs were great for instant hot chocolate in the hotel and for $3, how could we go wrong?

JADE MARKET

Kansu and Battery streets, Yau Ma Tei, Kowloon

The Jade Market is located very close to the Temple Street Market; while the markets are entirely different affairs, you will find some similarities. You can take a taxi to the Jade Market or get there by walking along Nathan Road until you get to Temple Street. But then you would miss all the fun of the fabulous street market on Reclamation Street that's held on Sundays. In fact, Sunday mornings were made for Jade.

The Jade Market is a day market where you will find your best buys on those little green (or violet or pink) stones that everyone will expect you to bring home. The scene varies according to the day, time and season. One time we went, it was so crowded we could hardly squeeze our way in to look; another time, we were the only ones there.

We can't guarantee what you will find, but we do know that you won't be disappointed if you are looking for variety and a chance to hone your bargaining skills.

The market is located in two free-standing tents under the overfly of the highway at Kansu and Battery streets. I can't say if one tent is better than the other; what happens is that you use up so much energy in the first tent that by the time you get to the second one, you will have lost a lot of your enthusiasm for jade. This is all a matter of what feels good to you and what you are looking for. I don't actually buy much green "jade," so I look for dealers in old jade and in other colored trinkets. Ian likes carved stone animals. We both like big ethnic pieces that make a dramatic fashion statement, rather than the touristy junk that passes for souvenirs. Your eye will take you to the booths that sell what most appeals to you and since there are a total of about 500 vendors in the two tents, you'll have no trouble spending your budget. At the end of our spree, we had pooled our resources and were down to lunch money.

The Jade Market is an official market organized by the Hong Kong and Kowloon Jade Merchants Workers' and Hawkers' Union Association. Each merchant inside the fence is licensed to sell jade, and should display his license above his stall. It is a good idea when buying to note the number next to your purchase, just in case you have a problem later on and the jade turns out to be plastic.

If you are hoping to buy quality jade, there are a few things to check. Make sure that the color is pure and strong. There should be no hint of black (unless the jade is black) or yellow. If the color is translucent, that is a good sign of value. Make sure that the color is as even as possible. A carving will have variations, but a jade circle should not. Also, check for fault lines. A good piece of jade will not have them. If any of the above faults appear in the piece of jade you are buying, bargain accordingly. (See page 144 for more information on jade.)

As you walk into the market, stop and get your bearings. The area is laid out in rows of tables and stalls, back-to-back in the middle and around the perimeter. We like to do one walk-through before we get serious. There is more for sale than just jade, so keep your eyes open for other good buys.

The jade merchants have very similar merchandise; it's just a matter of how much you want to spend and which one will make you the best deal. I find a table I like and then try to bargain hard. You could spend a day here, but you'd be exhausted.

If you are not willing to bargain here, don't buy. The merchants in the Jade Market expect to lower their price by 20% to 40%, depending on your bargaining skill and their need. We have always had our best luck by pulling out a single bill and saying, "This is all we have left." If the shopkeeper says no, we walk away and try again elsewhere. We also do the "you don't need it" routine. I act like the interested party, Ian plays the part of the husband who tells his wife to forget it. I say I have to shop fast before he gets angry at me, and make a low offer; Ian glares at me. Don't knock it; it works.

Please note that we bought a big, heavy necklace of amber-colored beads with the twelve animals of the Chinese zodiac carved into twelve different beads. We paid $100. Two days later I spotted the same necklace at the Chinese Arts & Crafts store in Star House for $500.

Market hours are 10 A.M. to 3 P.M., although many of the vendors close up shop at 2 P.M. Go early rather than late.

To get there from the street market, exit the MTR at Jordan Road and turn right. Walk along Jordan Road for two blocks until you get to Shanghai Street, turn left onto Nanking, and then turn right onto Reclamation Street. Follow it, right through the market, to Kansu Street. You'll see the overfly of the highway and know you are approaching the Jade Market. When you leave the Jade Market, drop down a block and hit Temple Street, so you can visit the temple in the park. Light joss sticks and think of us.

JARDINE'S BAZAAR
Causeway Bay, Hong Kong

If you stay in Causeway Bay, you have a foot up on the rest of the world when it comes to Jardine's Bazaar, Jardine's Lookout (a hillside residential area) and the web of streets between the two. This is what we came to China for. This is the little street market in the back alley that weaves through a hole in the world no one knew was even there.

The first half of the market is full of fruit, vegetables and other foodstuffs. At midpoint Jardine's becomes a dry-goods market and sells the same stuff you'll find everywhere. Jardine's is also in a home-sewing neighborhood, so you may enjoy wandering around looking at fabrics and notions, which are upstairs.

In truth, by the time you get to the dry goods, the market is rather ordinary. It's the fruits and veggies that I love so much—so colorful and exotic and yes, you can find them at other street markets, but there's something about this narrow and tiny bend in the road that makes it all the more appealing.

CENTRAL MARKET
Queen's Road Central, Hong Kong

The major food and produce markets for Hong Kong Island are located in specific areas. Central Market serves the area of Central. As you get even remotely close to Central Market on a sunny summer day, you can sniff your way there.

It's a four-story warehouse, and the ventilation is not terrific. The market sells every variety of fresh produce and meat that you might imagine. There are three levels of gleaming vegetables and fruit, clucking chickens and quacking ducks in cages waiting to be picked for dinner.

This is not a pretty tourist sight for children or the weak of heart or stomach.

WESTERN MARKET

Des Voeux Road, Western, Hong Kong

Once upon a time Western Market was in the same shape as Central Market—possibly worse. Then along came a developer with some sort of Western travel experience who has obviously seen American malls and developments like Faneuil Hall in Boston and Covent Garden in London. While the Hong Kong thing to do would be to tear down the building and build a modern gleaming high-rise, good sense prevailed and this colonial structure was restored and preserved and turned into a festival marketplace.

We have very mixed feelings about it, because the space seems so American and not very Chinese at all. But there are a few wonderful dealers there, many of them handicraft-oriented. There's a branch of FOOK MING TONG, the fancy tea brokers; there are toy soldiers and plenty for kids to see and buy.

Many of the cloth merchants who were disenfranchised when Cloth Alley was destroyed have taken space on the second floor of Western Market. On the third floor there is a nice Chinese restaurant.

Flags fly, banners flap, people shop. There's a lot of energy in the space and a number of unique stalls that sell merchandise I have not seen in other places in town.

KOWLOON CITY MARKET

Lion Rock Road, Kowloon

This one is a bit far out, but is especially entertaining because this is where the young locals like to hang out. Merchandise is a little more with-it;

there's more fun in the air. This is one of the few markets where you'll find china sold. There are lots of blue jeans, factory-outlet rejects and fashions from young Japanese and Chinese designers. This market only operates during the day; do not forget to make a detour to the DD WAREHOUSE nearby (see page 123).

CAT STREET MARKET

Central, Hong Kong

Cat Street Market is Hong Kong's answer to a flea market: Used merchandise of the tag sale variety is sold from blankets and a few stalls on a two-block street of pedestrian pavement just below Hollywood Road.

Some dealers specialize: One guy sells only used typewriters and used sewing machines. Others move around—the man with the Chairman Mao buttons was in one place in May and a different one in November. A few dealers sell the kind of old jade I like; one vendor has old Chinese sunglasses from the 1930s that are truly sensational, but not worth the $100 H.K. asking price. The shops behind and around the market specialize in formal antiques; some of these stores are reputable and even famous.

After you pass the Man Mo Temple on Hollywood Road, turn right onto Ladder Street. Walk down Ladder Street just a few steps and you'll see the blankets almost immediately. Turn left onto Cat Street, which is a pedestrian-only alley. There is an official Cat Street Market Building behind the street vendors, where you can buy furniture and antiques. The market operates during normal business hours.

The Lanes

"The Lanes" is a collective term for a group of small markets set amongst the streets and alleys; usually each market is only one block long. Except for Pottinger Street, which resembles a stairway filled with booths, the Lanes are built between large buildings. They're sort of the Hong Kong version of the Burlington Arcade in London.

The Lanes are all in Central, and are within walking distance of each other. They are also near many other places in Central, so it's likely you will pass them in your daily travels.

LI YUEN STREET EAST

If you're looking for an inexpensive look-alike designer handbag, Li Yuen Street East is just the place. There are not a lot of inexpensive, high-quality leathergoods available in Hong Kong, and while Li Yuen Street East is not Neiman Marcus, it is the location of choice for locals who need handbags or briefcases. Expect to pay between $40 and $50 for a nice leather handbag of the current fashion rage, or of the Hermès flavor. If you look hard, you can even find a nice Chanel-style bag. It won't have the CCs, but the styling and design will be exact. Assorted versions of the Louis Vuitton-colored leather tote bags are also a viable choice. Li Yuen Street East is also famous for its knitting shops, fabric stores, notions and padded brassieres.

LI YUEN STREET WEST

Perhaps you want one of those satin quilted happy coats or vests that you associate with a trip to China. Li Yuen Street West is crammed with them. Be sure to try them on, as the shoulders sometimes run small. Whatever you didn't see on Li Yuen Street East will be on Li Yuen Street West. To get to these two streets, follow the signs as you exit the Central MTR stop.

POTTINGER STREET

After a big lunch, give your leg muscles a work-out and make the steep climb up Pottinger Street. There's nothing unusual for sale here, merely notions. But they are about 20% cheaper here than in a regular Hong Kong department store. If you buy jade circles for gifts, you can buy polyester or silk cord in rainbow colors in Pottinger Street. Hang the cord through the circle and you have a beautiful necklace. One meter of cord per necklace will be perfect.

MAN WA LANE

If you are looking for fun, Chinese atmosphere and maybe some business cards in Chinese, don't miss Man Wa Lane. Man Wa Lane is headquarters of the chop business. But whether you are looking for chops or not, you should see this small, neat street, which spans about three blocks and has a few other stalls that sell general merchandise. If you do buy something from one of the shops and have to return for it, make sure you get a piece of paper with the shop address in both English and Chinese. The stalls do not have numbers but symbols, and they're all in Chinese. We tell you from embarrassed experience: You will never find your way back to a given stall unless you have the address in Chinese. Man Wa Lane is halfway between Central and Western, leaning more toward Western. Catch it as you walk back from Western (and the Western Market) toward Central.

New Territories

SEK KONG MARKET

Sek Kong, N.T.

This is my latest discovery, my new favorite market in Hong Kong, my new thrill to pass on to others. It takes some organizing to get here, so pay close attention:

First off, this is a Friday-morning market. It's over by 1 P.M. There is no market on holidays which fall on Friday, and there probably isn't a market if the weather is awful since this is held outdoors.

Outdoors indeed. The market is held in a field in the New Territories near the community of Sek Kong and near the Ghurka camp. If your taxi driver takes you to the Ghurka camp (mine did), you've gone too far.

Just as the drive to Stanley is part of the fun of that experience, so is the drive out in the New Territories, where you will be just a few kilometers from the border. The rural scenery adds to the adventure. And then the scenic serenity is suddenly shattered when you see the hordes of locals (mostly Westerners) who flock to this market for the bargains. Indeed, the word is out.

I've discovered that the market does have a bit of a pattern to it. Walk around the paths and into the various fields to inspect blankets and tables laden with goods. Linens, school supplies, toys, T-shirts; they're all in abundance. Then there are entire fields filled with pieces of china and pottery strewn around as if they were planted. There are boxes of silk and plastic artificial flowers, ribbons and some crafts supplies. There's tons of children's clothing. You name it, they had it. Even Ralph Lauren/Polo shirts.

This is where I bought the "Gap" bookbags, one of which proceeded to fall apart a little bit more on every day of the trip (see page 48).

Get here via private bus during holiday seasons; city bus (No. 51) from the Tsuen Wan MTR station, or taxi. There are several factory-outlet stores nearby and you might want to make a big morning out of it. I took a taxi here from Kowloon and the fare was $200 H.K. on the meter; I offered the driver a total of $400 H.K. to stay with me, wait, take me to the outlet stores, to Kowloon City and then back to the Regent. It was worth it to me; if you go with several people and split this amount, you're down to peanuts. ($400 H.K. is about $50 U.S.)

LUEN WO MARKET

Luen Wo, N.T.

The market at Luen Wo, also in the New Territories, is a very authentic local food market. It is not enormously different from markets you can see in town, so the trip may not be worth your time. On the other hand, if you plan a day in the New Territories, you can get in a lot of experiences and a few rides on the KCR.

Take a taxi from Kowloon to the KCR station, which is in Hung Hom. It's a huge modern train station. Buy a ticket to Fanling, which will cost a few dollars. Trains are modern commuter-style trains. Exit at Fanling and grab the No. 78 bus (clearly marked at its stand) or take a taxi to Luen Wo. The taxi will cost about $10 H.K., so you can splurge on this one.

The market fills one square city block. There is some overflow into a nearby parking lot. The people who are shopping are far more rural-looking than those you might find in downtown Central, but the goods for sale are not that different. You go here for the total experience, for the fact that it's real. This is a nice Sunday excursion. For a complete tour that includes this market stop, see page 321.

Shopping Centers R Us

Rumor has it that the shopping mall was invented in Hong Kong by a brilliant British tycoon who knew that all tourists want to go shopping and that rain prevents them from doing some of that shopping. Indeed, once you set shoe in any of the plethora of shopping centers and buildings you will not know—or care—if it is day or night, light or dark, winter or summer, rainy or dry outside.

Hong Kong is totally overrun with shopping centers. It's like a contagious disease spreading to all architects, who now feel compelled to equip a hotel or an office building with three floors of retail shops before they get to the actual offices. Somewhere, somehow, they find tenants for all those shops. While stores do come and go in these locations, and there is always some new rumor as to which location is hotter than any other, these shopping centers and buildings do offer all of the riches of the Orient under one roof.

The Cha-Cha Theory of Retailing

In our years of shopping Hong Kong, we have come to the conclusion that every retailer in town is constantly doing the cha-cha. Word spreads that a certain development, an area, a new mall, a building site will become hot (for whatever reasons) and suddenly, one, two, cha-cha-cha: everyone moves, or opens a branch store.

In their wake, a dozen dead dance partners lie gasping in the streets. The Landmark, the greatest Hong Kong upscale mall of them all, is still holding its own. But other locations grow pale or become shadows of their former selves, taken over by local mom-and-pop shops, while the glitzy showbirds amble off.

The hot "new" property in malls/buildings is right now in Pacific Place, the shopping part of which is also known as The Mall at Pacific Place. We believe the Mall at Pacific Place will hold its own, not only because it has two huge and gorgeous hotels to anchor it, but because the Japanese department store SEIBU has put in their first Hong Kong store. Seibu, in case you aren't up on Japanese department stores (see page 201), rhymes with "I love you."

If you go to a lot of the malls and shopping buildings, you'll see a huge amount of overlap. The stores all look alike (they *are* all alike; you are not crazy), and soon the buildings themselves start to look alike (they really don't look alike). Your head swims. Your feet ache. Your brain shouts: "Why?"

We cannot tell you who will be leading the cha-cha next month, or that you will care. At a certain point, you choose your shopping by what buildings are convenient to you. We list the following main malls and shopping buildings in the order that we think is most current, interesting and essential (all at the same time), so you can pick and choose according to your time frame and your location. We don't suggest that you try to do more than three malls unless you have a *lot* of patience and a lot of curiosity.

A corollary to the continuing cha-cha theory: Stores sometimes move around within a mall. Or malls can renumber the shops during a renovation, as they did in Harbour City. If you are seeking a specific store, ask at the information desk or use the directories. We were so lost in the Mall at Pacific Place, a relatively small space compared to something like Harbour City, that we almost cried. If you like to just wander, go: Enjoy. If you want to find something, ask.

The Centres of Central

With the pressure on in Hong Kong, and Pacific Place blooming into a major force in mall history, some of the older buildings have banded together for advertising and promotional purposes. I'm speaking specifically of what is advertised as the "Centres of Central;" this is an organization of the main buildings in Central that house shopping malls. Their ads can be confusing; there is no one big mall called Centres of Central. The individual member buildings are detailed in the section below. Unless otherwise noted, the MTR stop at Central will get you close to any of these shopping centers.

THE LANDMARK

The most famous of the Central malls, the Landmark has the reputation and the big names, but is having to fight to stay ahead of the game.

Many of the big names that started here have remained, but have opened other shops around town, so they are are no longer exclusively in the Landmark. Surely the mall is a must for visitors, who will be awestruck by the glitz and the fountain and the money it takes to make a place like this work.

The multilevel mall is topped by Gloucester and Edinburgh towers. We often suggest this mall as a jumping-off place for Westerners who want to see something but aren't quite ready for Kowloon. After a quick survey you'll probably find that everything is gorgeous but very expensive, and that you are ready to move on. There are a few cafes here for lunch, including FOUNTAINSIDE.

Among the upscale and big-name tenants you'll find GUCCI, BALLANTYNE, CÉLINE, COURRÈGES, ESPRIT, BENETTON, LANVIN, VALENTINO, BURBERRYS, THE BODY SHOP, KENZO JUNGLE JAP, CERRUTTI 1881, MANDARINA DUCK, WEDGWOOD, BULGARI, MEISSEN, SHU UEMURA, TIMBERLAND, LOUIS VUITTON and many, many more.

THE LANDMARK
16 Des Voeux Road Central, Hong Kong

CENTRAL BUILDING

Next door to, and occasionally adjoining the Landmark in some doorways, the Central Building is styled in the same tradition, but without the fountains. In fact, it's hard to tell where one center stops and the other starts. The newness of the stores in the Central Building make it feel as if new life had been breathed into the Landmark. The space is not as large and therefore not as overwhelming; it's sort of the appetizer before the main course. More big names are here, of course, including BASILE, CHARLES JOURDAN, PRADA, S.T. DUPONT, PIERRE BALMAIN, BRUNO MAGLI, JUNKO SHIMADO, MAUD FRIZON CLUB and LACOSTE.

CENTRAL BUILDING
   19-23 Queen's Road Central, Hong Kong

PRINCE'S BUILDING

This office building with five levels of shopping has so many big names now that it competes with the Landmark and the Central Building, both of which are across the street. The Prince's Building is easy to shop because it is perfectly square! It connects by bridge to the Mandarin Oriental Hotel (don't miss shopping there, either), and may be more fun than the Landmark for you. It is not mind-boggling like the Landmark, so you can shop and enjoy yourself. Among the many upscale tenants are DIANE FREIS, CARTIER, FOGAL, ROYAL COPENHAGEN, CHANEL, ASCOT CHANG, and BREE (Italian natural leather handbags). Then there's the useful category, such as the BANYAN TREE (arts, crafts, home and table decor), LAURA ASHLEY and trusty old WATSON'S, the drugstore that sells everything.

PRINCE'S BUILDING
   Chater Road, Hong Kong

THE GALLERIA AT 9 QUEEN'S

Why does the Galleria announce itself with its address? Because it's the new kid on the block. This is a small, luxe, luxe, luxe mall that is rumored to be owned by Joyce. Joyce, a famous character in fashion and retailing in Hong Kong, owns most of the big-name designer stores in Hong Kong anyway, so a mall of her own makes perfect sense.

There are numerous JOYCE BOUTIQUES in the building as well as branches of famous name shops such as HERMÉS, ALEXANDRE DE PARIS (the hairdresser who owns a few accessories shops that sell hairbands for $50 each), etc. There are a few tony restaurants/snack bars here so that it makes for a very upscale pit stop.

THE GALLERIA AT 9 QUEEN'S
9 Queen's Road Central, Hong Kong

SWIRE HOUSE

I don't think Swire House makes much of a mall, but you can't beat the location in Central, between the Mandarin Oriental Hotel and the Landmark. The lobby floor does still have several big-name shops and a few of the winners you may be looking for, like BOTTEGA VENETA, DAKS, ISSEY MIYAKE, MOSCHINO, KENZO PARIS and FILA. The building has entrances on Connaught Road Central, Pedder Street and Chater Road.

SWIRE HOUSE
Connaught Road Central, Hong Kong

Hong Kong Shopping Buildings

PEDDER BUILDING

We are going to be brutally honest about our feelings about the Pedder Building, with the understanding that no matter what we say, you're going to visit here anyway. (As well you should.)

The Pedder Building is not swank. Some people might even say it's creepy.

It's especially bad if you go in summer when the air is heavy and your feet are heavy and your shopping bags are heavy, and the stores here are not too enlightening. But we digress. First, the facts:

The Pedder Building couldn't have a better location in all of Central.

Also, the Pedder Building has several factory-outlet stores in it (see page 115). The Pedder Building could stand to be spruced up a little bit, which they happen to be doing now. There are several shops that are fancy, expensive and not at all outlets—beware.

In the building there are several adorable spaces (if you can stand to find them), including

DAVID SHEEKWAN and CHINA TEE CLUB for lunch or tea. (This is a private club; you need permission to eat here—ask at the door; if they have room, they'll seat you.) There's the utterly swank English-style J.R. PEDDERS with gift items and expensive objects that aren't what you came to Hong Kong to buy, but are popular with locals.

Complain as we may about the building's decor, we do want to make it clear we had no trouble buying a knit dress for $20 and feeling good about it; this is Ian's first stop when he's shopping for his wife. He knows he'll get quality in one stop, without being taken. Businessmen, take note.

PEDDER BUILDING
12 Pedder Street, Hong Kong

Kowloon Shopping Buildings

NEW WORLD CENTRE

Despite my love affair with the Regent Hotel, I am far from wild for the New World Centre, even though the two properties are attached at the hip. They certainly aren't Siamese twins.

New World Centre is pretty much a yawn, except for a few stores that are fine if you are just killing time. I cannot in good conscience send you on a trip out of your way to shop this mall.

The New World Centre is yet another massive, multilevel, spic-and-span, concrete-and-cold-floor shopping center filled with little shops, one-hour photo stands and ice-cream vendors. It has one of the best air-conditioning systems in Hong Kong (important in summer), as well as a cute Japanese department store (TOKYU—open 10 A.M. to 9 P.M.; closed Thursday) on the street level. There's a branch of EPISODE and a few other nice places, but really, don't waste your time.

Now then, not to muddy the waters, but if I get

confused on this perhaps you will too. On the other side of the harbor, on Victoria Island, there is a big business tower called NEW WORLD TOWER. It is not a shopping mall, but on the ground floor is the biggest (and best) branch of AMERICAN EXPRESS. If you look up American Express in the phone book or elsewhere, do not get mixed up—it's not in this shopping mall. The American Express in Kowloon is in the Park Lane Shopper's Boulevard on Nathan Road.

NEW WORLD CENTRE
   18-24 Salisbury Road, Kowloon

SILVERCORD BUILDING

Located at the upper end of Tsim Sha Tsui, across from Harbour City, right there on beautiful downtown Canton Road, the Silvercord Building is best remembered for its sublevel computer shopping.

If you're interested in computers, fax machines or other high-tech electronic goodies, head straight to the basement, where the EAST ASIA COMPUTER PLAZA shops are located. It's a great place to begin your research before buying electronics.

There is also a CHINESE ARTS & CRAFTS store that is big and fun (four floors), although frankly you've already passed the one at Star House, which is even more fun (see below).

Upper-level shops in Silvercord are rather average, but the sensational secret of the building is LACE LANE, where one of the best selections of linens and whitework in Hong Kong is housed in a small shop (see page 263).

If you are not interested in computers or linens, you can easily pass on this one.

SILVERCORD BUILDING
   30 Canton Road, Kowloon

STAR HOUSE

Star House is the first building you come to on your left as you exit the Star Ferry. It's got a

MCDONALD'S, a FOTOMAX for one-hour film processing and a number of stores. You will also see a large branch of CHINESE ARTS & CRAFTS store. There's more shopping upstairs in the office building, where there are some outlets such as HANNAH PANG, who made her rep with LEATHER CONCEPTS (see page 117), and specialty stores with little outlet set-ups.

Don't let the tacky hotel-style arcade turn you off; there's a wonderful Tourist Trap here in between the tacky, boring stores, called STAR-TRAM. Besides the usual tourist wares, they sell a fortune cookie with a condom inside it. Unfortunately, the cookie will crush when you pack them to take home (just ask me) and the condom would fit your Ken doll, but not your best beau. Oh well, it's still a funny gift item. Startram is a chain with branches elsewhere in Hong Kong.

STAR HOUSE
Canton Road, Kowloon

Hotel Arcades

Ever since the 1950s, Holiday Inns of America has hosted little shops in their motel offices where you can buy toothpaste, aspirin and tampons. Hotels in Hong Kong have taken this basic idea and carried it one step further. They have little shops in their lobbies—or in their arcade areas—that sell everything you might want or need. For life.

There are several reasons for the popularity of hotel arcades in Hong Kong. They're dry in rain; they're cool in summer (like shopping malls); they're handy for the tourist who will spend according to convenience; and, most important, they receive the benefits of trust. Shoppers have come to judge the shops in a hotel to be as reliable as the hotel itself. Thus the fanciest, most deluxe hotels have the most trustworthy shops.

Shoppers believe there is a direct correlation between the quality of the store and the quality of the hotel.

Certainly the shops in the Peninsula, the Mandarin Oriental and the Regent are the most expensive and most exclusive. But that doesn't mean there's anything wrong with the shops in the Holiday Inn. And get a look at what's going on underneath the Kowloon Hotel: You'll find some big names for a hotel that no one has ever heard of. (It's part of the Peninsula Group, which explains everything.)

Some hotel arcades offer a handful of shops. Others have three levels of stores and hundreds of choices. Often, a hotel arcade connects to a main shopping center. From the Omni Prince Hotel at the far end of Harbour City, you can walk through a shopping arcade to connect to the Omni Marco Polo Hotel, and then go into another shopping center and keep on connecting for a few miles to several hotels and thousands of stores, end up at Omni The Hong Kong Hotel...and step right onto the Star Ferry.

These are my favorite hotel shopping arcades in both Central and Kowloon:

MANDARIN ORIENTAL HOTEL

The glitziest stores in town fight to get space in the Mandarin Oriental Hotel, not only because the hotel is so fabulous and its clientele so tony, but because the location is prime. Part of your Central shopping spree must include a visit to the stores, which include FERRAGAMO, KAI YIN LO, FENDI, DAVID'S SHIRTS and GEMSLAND, which is the jeweler I happen to use.

MANDARIN ORIENTAL HOTEL
5 Connaught Road, Central

THE HONGKONG HILTON HOTEL

If you aren't staying at the Hilton but have stayed here in the past, you owe it to yourself to come by the hotel, gawk at the new lobby and poke into the stores. This is the soul of Hong Kong: Where else can you be re-created into glitz and marble and come away with a new image as fresh as new money?

The lobby is simply breathtaking; the stores here combine the usual hotel standards with a few chains of big names and some more-upscale players.

THE HONGKONG HILTON HOTEL
2 Queen's Road, Central

THE REGENT HOTEL

As the hotel arcade/shopping center/mall sweepstakes heat up, the Regent enters the fray with perhaps the best of the bunch—to date. But stand by, we are awaiting an announcement that more shopping will pave the mall-way from the Regent to the Pen.

Right now, the Regent's mall is light and bright, with higher ceilings than in the basement levels of the Pen, so you don't get so claustrophobic. The usual combinations of drugstore and needed stores is here with big names like DIANE FREIS, DONNA KARAN, CHANEL, JOYCE, VAN CLEEF & ARPELS, ASCOT CHANG, CARTIER, BASILE, JAEGER, LONGCHAMP, etc.

THE REGENT HOTEL
Salisbury Road, Kowloon

THE PENINSULA HOTEL

Small, cell-like shops fill the eastern and western wings of the hotel, with more on the mezzanine and still more in the basement. We expect it might improve when the new tower is completed. Meanwhile, no one seems to mind the low ceilings—every big name in the world has a shop here. The arcade hosts a number of big-name, high-ticket designers: THE PENINSULA BOUTIQUE, KENZO, LLADRÓ, GIEVES & HAWKES, LONGCHAMP, HERMÈS, POLO/RALPH LAUREN, TIFFANY, PRADA, CÉLINE, BELTRAMI, GENNY,

NAF-NAF, GUCCI, MATSUDA, LÉONARD, GIANNI VERSACE, CARTIER, MCM, CHARLES JOURDAN, etc. I am embarrassed to admit that I adore the Peninsula Boutique with all the Pen logo merchandise. My goal is to own my own tea set, because to me, one of the ultimate souvenirs of a trip to Hong Kong is the experience of having tea in the lobby or having tea service in your room as you arrive. Tea for two anyone?

THE PENINSULA HOTEL
Salisbury Road, Kowloon

KOWLOON HOTEL

A small, underground arcade you reach by escalator directly from the street. There are two levels of basement stores, all small but uncrowded. Because of its association with the Peninsula Hotel, the hotel has a classy retail arcade with big-name designer tenants. If you do pop in, check out: PRADA, HUNTER'S, CLAUDE MONTANA, ISSEY MIYAKE, TRUSSARDI, CRAIG'S for China from England.

KOWLOON HOTEL
19-21 Nathan Road, Kowloon

HYATT REGENCY HONG KONG

A very fancy hotel in a prime shopping area, with stores including: DUNHILL, LANVIN, CARLOS FALCHI, FRATELLI ROSSETTI, ZOE COSTE, ÉTIENNE AIGNER and our fave, SHIRT STOP, one of many branches of this discount house that sells men's shirts and sweaters, some women's and unisex. When we were there last we scored a pile of gorgeous terry-cloth bathrobes (unisex). This is pleasant shopping, right in the middle of the Golden Mile. The street-level back shops are not as nice as the front and basement shops.

HYATT REGENCY HONG KONG
67 Nathan Road, Kowloon

Hong Kong Malls

THE MALL AT PACIFIC PLACE

This is the hottest location in town, the one that made everyone do the cha-cha; the one that houses SEIBU (the best of the Japanese department stores); the one that's trying to push the Landmark to the limit. If you are staying in one of the many hotels built next to the mall, this place is a natural for you. If you are not staying nearby, you will need a high dose of curiosity in order to come explore. I have been lost in this mall; I have cried in this mall. Yet it remains one of the best combinations of high-end shopping and eats in the territory.

Please note that the official name of this place is the Mall at Pacific Place, but everyone calls it Pacific Place. Technically speaking, Pacific Place includes the office tower above the mall and the congregation of fancy hotels grouped around the tower (Marriott, Conrad, Island Shangri-La).

The nicest approach to Pacific Place is from either the Marriott Hotel or the Conrad Hotel, or from your limousine, but of course the MTR will do just fine (Admiralty stop). You may also take a tram to the Queensway stop.

This upscale mall offers a hefty dose of everything you want to see, including a small but good LANE CRAWFORD and the first SEIBU Japanese department store in Hong Kong. Most stores are open 10 A.M. to 8 P.M. daily, although not every store is open on Sunday, and the stores that do open on Sunday usually open at 1 P.M.

There are a few gourmet food stores (OLIVER'S); some antiques shops (C.P. CHING); some eateries, including an American barbecue restaurant (DAN RYAN); and the usual big names like DUNHILL, BOSS, ERMENEGILDO ZEGNA, DAVIDOFF, BALLANTYNE, CARLOS FALCHI, KAI YIN LO, JOSEPH HO STUDIO, ZOE COSTE,

DANIEL HECHTER, DIANE FREIS and MAR-
GUERITE LEE. There are also more casual chains,
such as THE ATHLETE'S FOOT, THE BODY SHOP,
CITY CHAIN (watches), BENETTON, etc.

THE MALL AT PACIFIC PLACE
88 Queensway, Hong Kong (MTR: Admiralty)

ADMIRALTY SHOPPING CENTRE
Yuck. I think Admiralty just plain missed the
ferry. Although this is a major MTR stop and a
great location, the stores here are mostly small-
time local jobs for the population working in the
surrounding buildings. Don't waste your time,
unless you are writing your dissertation on Hong
Kong retail real estate.

ADMIRALTY SHOPPING CENTRE
Harcourt Road, Hong Kong (MTR: Admiralty)

Kowloon Malls

HARBOUR CITY
The shopping complex that occupies most of
Tsim Sha Tsui's western shore is generally known
as Harbour City. It includes Ocean Terminal,
Ocean Centre and Ocean Galleries along with
Omni The Hong Kong Hotel, the Omni Marco
Polo Hotel and the Omni Prince Hotel. There are
four levels of shopping from end to end, and if
you can successfully negotiate your way from one
end to the other, you won't even have to come up
for air.

The idea of a shopping complex on the waterfront originated with OCEAN TERMINAL, which is
the building that juts out into the water alongside
the Star Ferry Pier. Ocean Terminal was so successful that Ocean Centre and then Ocean Galleries were developed. It is hard to tell one from
the other unless you detect the different patterns
in the floor tiles. I find Ocean Terminal to be the
least claustrophobic part of the complex, because

there are windows. Once you get into the bowels of Ocean Centre and Ocean Galleries you need your compass and lots of luck to find your way back out.

Do make a point of finding the area called THE SILK ROAD, which is a small gallery of antiques shops that's kind of fun to visit (see page 284).

Ocean Terminal has chic china shops like ROYAL COPENHAGEN and HUNTER'S; designer boutiques, including DIANE FREIS, ALAIN MANOUKIAN and BENETTON; handicrafts shops and lots of food shops. The entire basement is a children's specialty floor containing a TOYS R US store and also furniture, clothing and other baby-related shopping. There's even an optical shop that just sells children's eyeglass frames. As you walk into Ocean Terminal, stop at the information desk to pick up a complete listing of all the stores in Harbour City, along with the Harbour City map of Hong Kong. This map shows building locations and will help you get around town more easily.

OCEAN CENTRE is the next shopping complex as you walk away from the Star Ferry, followed by OCEAN GALLERIES. Although there are official lobbies and entrances to each, one seems to flow into the next, punctuated with an occasional hotel along the way. The best hotel arcade in Harbour City is at the Omni The Hong Kong Hotel. There is a JOSEPH HO shop on the main level and a mezzanine devoted to antiques shops. We must say that finding your way around Ocean Centre and Ocean Galleries can be confusing. The shops are in blocks and it is easy to get turned around when looking for a number. We avoid coming here if there is a branch of the shop we want anywhere else. However, if it is raining, there is a typhoon or the weather is so hot that you cannot breathe outside, Ocean Galleries and Ocean Centre start to look better.

One stop farther up Canton Road is the CHINA HONG KONG CITY shopping complex. It is a major mall with many fine, and several big-name stores to browse in case you are not exhausted already. Because this mall is so far "uptown" and also contains a ferry terminal, the stores are more geared for locals or those on the go. You certainly wouldn't pick China Hong Kong City to browse as a fun shopping spot.

HARBOUR CITY
　　Canton Road, Kowloon

HONG KONG PLACE

If you think Harbour City is a monstrosity, get a load of Hong Kong Place, which is currently the largest mall in Southeast Asia. The two-story mall has 200,000 square feet of space, which means that it's not as big as a giant U.S. regional mall or even the combined three-mall glory of Harbour City. But to locals it's a big deal.

To me? Well, I'm getting to hate Hong Kong malls. I cannot in good conscience tell you to go out of your way to come here. But if it's a rainy day and you're terribly curious, well, OK.

The various levels are named after local streets with implied (but lacking) charm. I recommend the real live Granville Road for shopping, not the part of this mall named Granville Road. But the space seems to appeal to locals rather than tourists anyway. Promoters are trying to add shoppers' incentives to the mall to make it a hot spot; stay tuned.

There is bus service from the Star Ferry, or you can take a taxi here—this is technically Hung Hom, although it is sometimes written as East Kowloon. There is no direct MTR service.

HONG KONG PLACE
　　Whampoa Gardens, Hung Hom, Kowloon (MTR: None)

PARK LANE SHOPPER'S BOULEVARD

This is a strip mall of unique architectural proportions that will certainly catch your eye (and maybe your credit card) as you stroll the infamous Nathan Road (MTR: Tsim Sha Tsui). The two-level mall has a park growing on its roof. It's made of white tile, but broken up at intervals with quasi-Japanese *torii* in bright colors. About half of the space is occupied by YUE HWA, a Chinese department store making a rather upscale, modern and Western debut in this branch store. There's also an AMERICAN EXPRESS BANK for changing traveler's checks (go upstairs).

PARK LANE SHOPPER'S BOULEVARD
  Nathan Road, Kowloon

Suburban Malls

CITYPLAZA

If you are in town for a very, very short time we don't suggest you visit Cityplaza and its various malls. But if you are game for adventure, if you want to see how Chinese yuppies live, if you want a glance at housing "mansions" and an understanding of an entirely different aspect of Hong Kong living, then this is for you.

Traveling to the MTR stop at Taikoo Shing takes a while (figure a half hour to get to Cityplaza from the island side), but if you go in a hired car you'll get a magnificent view of Hong Kong Harbour and a tour of much of Victoria from your limo. Obviously, you're not going to spend the day here, but we do find it exhilarating. This is the kind of mall that has a multiplex cinema where the movies are in Chinese, not English. And that sums up the neighborhood. Don't forget while you're here that the newer and smaller Kornhill Plaza (see below) is out the back end of Cityplaza III.

Cityplaza is a pair of malls (Cityplaza II and III) that are the underpinnings to several high-rise towers. There is a bridge between the two malls.

Both are very American; this is where the upper-middle-class locals come to shop and get away from downtown and tourists. There are levels and levels of stores, there's a food court and there's a kiddie area called WHIMSEYLAND, with small rides for little ones. Cityplaza II is halfway filled with the many floors of UNY, a Japanese department store. There's also a supermarket, MANNINGS (like Watson's), AMAZING GRACE (crafts) and WING ON (a Chinese department store). Across the way at Cityplaza III is a multilevel MARKS & SPENCER, as well as the usual other shops and branch stores.

To round off the opportunities for non-shopping family fun, there's an ice-skating rink, bowling alley and Rollerworld.

CITYPLAZA
    1111 King's Road, Quarry Bay, Hong Kong

KORNHILL PLAZA

Located directly over the MTR station, Kornhill Plaza is not as big, as exciting or as fancy as neighboring Cityplaza. There are two towers, north and south. North connects to Cityplaza; South has JUSCO. Jusco is a Japanese department store, and it has a fascinating supermarket on the lower level. This store has 250,000 square feet of shopping opportunities—the same size as a branch of Nordstrom's.

The beauty of being here isn't actually that you buy so much, but that you see and absorb so much. This is the future of China. This is their definition of what success buys. If you care, don't miss it.

KORNHILL PLAZA
    2 Kornhill Road, Quarry Bay, Hong Kong

NEW TOWN PLAZA

One of my favorite things to do in Hong Kong is to ride the KCR and get out to the New Territories to see how real people live. We adore the contrasts and send you to Sha Tin only if you are interested in this kind of thing academically: The point is that a yuppie mall is a yuppie mall, so you don't really come here to shop, you come to observe.

The KCR (Kowloon–Canton Railway) station is in Hung Hom; take a taxi from anywhere in Kowloon. It's about three minutes from the Regent. Get off the KCR at the Sha Tin station. Sha Tin is a new city comprising mostly mansion blocks and high-rise towers; my friend Liam, who lives out here, compares it to living in New Jersey when you really want to be in Manhattan. But more things are going on in Sha Tin than in Fort Lee, at least as far as I can tell. This mall has a branch of all the usual suspects, as well as a number of young kicky shops that must appeal to the young kicky shoppers who are on their way up.

Weekends are very crowded. To me, the point of being is Sha Tin is that after visiting the mall, I can continue to other communities, like Luen Wo (see page 173).

NEW TOWN PLAZA
New Town Road, Sha Tin, N.T.

CHAPTER SIX

THE HEART OF HONG KONG

Chinese Department Stores

Welcome to the real Hong Kong and the kind of department store shopping we want you to do. If you aren't in a street market, you should be in the Chinese department stores!

There are several Chinese department stores in Hong Kong, but few of them are glamorous. They are a real experience for the traveler, are a fine source of visual treats and very often have some bargains. They are a great place to shop for souvenirs, silks, arts and crafts items and teas and traditional medicinal products.

CHINESE ARTS & CRAFTS STORES (H.K.) LTD.

This store is shocking to most Americans, because it is elegant. There are several branches, the biggest one (but not necessarily the best) being in Wan Chai, but all are very nice. Stores are open every day of the week, including Sunday. Locals sometimes call this store by its initials: CAC.

Each shop is slightly different, but most of the merchandise is the same. *One warning*: The shops are meant to bring cash into the Communist Chinese government. To make the most, the most is asked. These stores happen to be very expensive for what they are selling. By American standards, the prices are good. By local standards, they are outrageously high.

The silk fabric (yard goods) department is fun, although the prices are cheaper in Jardine's or the Lanes. We love the porcelain, baskets and tablecloths. We've been told by those who know that this is a reputable place to buy jade. There's no imitation passed off as real here. Be warned, however: Real jade is quite pricey. The store will ship for you; sales help have been very pleasant to us. A good place for souvenirs. This is the most Western of the various Chinese department stores. Hours in all stores are basically Monday to Saturday, 10 A.M. to 6:30 P.M.; Sunday hours vary with the location. The Wan Chai branch is convenient to the new convention center.

CHINESE ARTS & CRAFTS STORES (H.K.) LTD.

The Mall at Pacific Place, 88 Queensway, Hong Kong (MTR: Admiralty)

Star House, Canton Road, Kowloon (next to Star Ferry)

Shell House, Queen's Road, Hong Kong

Silvercord Building, 30 Canton Road, Kowloon

China Resources Building, 26 Harbour Road, Hong Kong (MTR: Wan Chai)

WING ON

Wing On is not much of a tourist resource, yet it sometimes has Western-style merchandise at a savings over the U.S. price. Many prices are lower than at Stanley Market. We're not talking Calvin Klein, but you can find some inexpensive work clothes here. Large-size Americans need not apply. Avoid weekend shopping. It's very crowded at all branches.

WING ON

361 Nathan Road, Kowloon (MTR: Yau Ma Tei)

26 Des Voeux Road, Hong Kong

62 Mody Road, Tsim Sha Tsui East (MTR: none)

Riviera Plaza, 28 Wing Shun Street, Tsuen Wan, N.T. (MTR: Tsuen Wan)

YUE HWA CHINESE PRODUCTS EMPORIUM

This is one of my favorite stores; please come by here if only to gawk. The main store at Jordan Road is the one that I love by the way, the one at Park Lane is way too Western for my tastes. Hmmmmm.

If you can't make it all the way to China, stop by here for a taste of the real thing. If you need acupuncture needles, stop by the counter on the first floor. (Promise her anything, but give her acupuncture needles....) The main store is rather jampacked and junky, but the newer Park Lane store is almost as nice as Macy's. Ignore the Western goods and buy Chinese. They mail to the U.S. Hours are daily from 9:30 or 10 A.M. to 8 or 9 P.M.

YUE HWA CHINESE PRODUCTS EMPORIUM

Main store: 301-309 Nathan Road, Kowloon (MTR: Jordan Road)

Park Lane Shopper's Boulevard, Nathan Road, Kowloon

Basement store, 54-64 Nathan Road, Kowloon

SHUI HING CO. LTD.

I mention this Chinese department store because we like it. I find it has a very unique handle on Western-style shopping. Very few Chinese stores understand the Western concept of fashion or style. However, this store is on to it. When you approach the store on a rainy day, there is a basket filled with plastic umbrella shields for you to choose from. We've only seen this done elsewhere in Fendi and at the back door of the Peninsula Hotel.

When you get to the handbag section where the cheap copies of good bags are, you'll find the only plastic copies in the world of Paloma Picasso's handbags. Furthermore, the store is located right in the heart of downtown Kowloon, so you'll automatically pass by as you prowl Nathan Road.

SHUI HING CO. LTD.

23-26 Nathan Road, Kowloon

Wai Fung Plaza, 664 Nathan Road, Mong Kok, Kowloon (MTR: Mong Kok)

CHUNG KIU CHINESE PRODUCTS EMPORIUM

Since you already know we are fond of Chinese department stores, let us now say this is one of our faves. The sales help is usually rude. The visual stimulation in the store is nil. The prices are high when compared to the street. And yet it is packed with things we like to look at, and we consider it a valuable resource for Chinese arts and crafts. We've bought many a souvenir here as well.

The store locations make it a must; two are deep in "real-people" Kowloon, and one is right under a factory-outlet building in downtown Kowloon (the Sands Building). One of my basic gifts to send to children is an embroidered sateen Chinese hat with a long black yarn braid attached (OK, I know it's tacky)—they sell this particular item in many places, but I always get mine at Chung Kiu in the souvenir department. About $4 each.

CHUNG KIU CHINESE PRODUCTS EMPORIUM

Sands Building, 17 Hankow Road, Kowloon

528-532 Nathan Road, Yau Ma Tei, Kowloon (MTR: Yau Ma Tei)

47-51 Shan Tung Road, Mong Kok, Kowloon (MTR: Mong Kok)

SINCERE

A department store with a local reputation, Sincere doesn't appeal to tourists very much because it feels junky and crowded. The big news here is that Sincere is actively going after the new Chinese money and is opening stores in Shanghai (their first since the Communist takeover in 1949) and possibly in economic zones like Guangzhou and Shenzhen. Remember this name.

SINCERE
   83 Argyle Street, Mong Kok (MTR: Mong Kok)
   173 Des Voeux Road, Hong Kong (MTR: Central or Shueng Wan)

Japanese Department Stores

Japanese department stores must be considered the eighth wonder of the world. They are so total, so complete, so very staggering in their stock that they're somewhat overwhelming. Visitors to Japan often go nowhere else but department stores. Visitors to Hong Kong should take some time to take in a few of these stores, just to see what they are like, if not to buy anything.

Basically, Japanese department stores in foreign (foreign to Japan) countries are there to serve Japanese expats. The Japanese department stores in London sell the same things Harrods does. The ones in Hong Kong sell a little of everything; they are particularly known for their inventive gift items and for their food halls.

If you expect just Japanese merchandise, you are very, very wrong. Every big-name French and Italian designer is represented in the bigger Japanese department stores. Japanese cosmetics (fabulous) are sold in quantity; and selection of all types of products is maximal. Causeway Bay has several Japanese department stores right near each other, so you may want to check a few of them out while you are there. The biggest and best in Tokyo and Hong Kong is SEIBU (Pacific Place); YAOHAN is worth the trip to Sha Tin.

Prices in Japanese department stores tend to be high, and we don't buy a lot here. We do drool.

One final word to claustrophobics: Don't go during rush hours. Stores are open until 9 or 10 P.M., so relax and enjoy yourself away from the madding crowd.

YAOHAN

While I am loathe to send you to out-of-the-way locations, it just may be that Yaohan is worth the effort. This Japanese department store has recently expanded to Hong Kong with stores in both Whampoa Gardens and Sha Tin. They are best known for their food departments and, trust me, this place is a sight to see.

I'm not sure what you'll do with all the items you'll be tempted to buy here, but any serious foodie should consider this a must. A stop at Yaohan is also important for those who want to study the Chinese yuppie scene and see what's going on in the New Territories. The mall in Sha Tin is just a mall, true, but it's a study in hot new local trends and manners.

YAOHAN

Whampoa Gardens (ground floor), Hung Hom (take a bus from Star Ferry; no MTR)

New Town Plaza, 18 Sha Tin Centre Road, Sha Tin, N.T. (KCR to Sha Tin)

DAIMARU

Closed on Wednesday in the traditional Japanese habit of closing one day a week, Daimaru is OK, but pales when compared to the competition. Asian pop music blares; major designer goods are abundant. Prices are not bargain-basement, but are no higher than at other Japanese department stores. This just simply isn't one of the best examples of Japanese retailing, so I think you can take a pass.

Daimaru is divided into two large department stores, one for fashions and one for housewares and furniture. The stores feel much more Japanese than the other department stores. This is a good "real-people" resource if you live in Hong Kong.

Inexpensive Japanese (a fashion style you will grow to appreciate when you see it) is cute and fun—great for teens. There are watches and pearls here, but the selection and quality are not as snazzy as at Mitsukoshi. Daimaru is more middle-class than some of the other stores. Hours are 10:30 A.M. to 9:30 P.M.

DAIMARU
Fashion Square, Paterson Street, Hong Kong (MTR: Causeway Bay)

ISETAN

Isetan is more young-at-heart than the other Japanese department stores. It's also a bit hard to shop, due to the crowding of merchandise and the weird shape of the store itself. It's a smallish store, across the street from the Regent; it only offers a small hint of Japanese taste. This store also has several basement levels. Fun for teens; convenient enough to your basic Kowloon shopping spree that you can pop in for a few minutes. Hours: Daily, 10 A.M. to 9 P.M.

ISETAN
Sheraton Hotel, Salisbury Road, Kowloon

MATSUZAKAYA

This department store feels a lot like Sears, but has pockets of designer clothes here and there. If you crave Godiva chocolates, you can buy them here. The ground floor has cosmetics, perfumes, handbags and accessories; the first floor is ladies' and children's ready-to-wear; the second floor is men's and sports; and the third floor is housewares, stationery and toys.

The overall quality is everyday Hong Kong, which probably is not your look back in the U.S. Display of fashion is not good, and we aren't wild for the store, except for its good cosmetics department and those marvelous Godiva chocolates.

Hours are daily from 10:30 A.M. to 9:30 P.M.; closed on Thursday.

MATSUZAKAYA
Paterson Street, Hong Kong (MTR: Causeway Bay)

MITSUKOSHI

There are now two branch stores of Mitsukoshi in Hong Kong, one on each side of the harbor. Mitsukoshi can be appreciated even before you set foot in the actual store. But then, Mitsukoshi is a legend in its own time.

In Causeway Bay: The store takes up most of the ground floor of the Hennessy Centre; it is one of the largest and fanciest of the Japanese department stores in Causeway Bay. Just looking at it is exciting. Fine watches, pearls, leather handbags and some designer labels dot the ground-floor display cases. Compared to other Japanese department stores, Mitsukoshi is one of the most lovely and elegant, especially on the main floor. Prices here are Japanese standard, which means there are no bargains.

As you descend into the guts of the store, each floor gets less and less American. The lower-level fashions downstairs are geared more for Hong Kong taste and budget. As you go down, the lights get brighter and the music seems louder. Don't go if you have a headache.

Mitsukoshi has designer clothes and accessories—Gucci, Lanvin, Christian Dior, Guy Laroche, Chloé, Mila Schön, etc. The housewares department is great fun; there is also a grocery store on B3.

In Tsim Sha Tsui, Mitsukoshi is across from Harbour City at the high end of Canton Road, closer to the Silvercord Building than the Star Ferry. It takes up much of a block and leads into a mall that is part of the Ramada Renaissance Hotel. Speaking of renaissances, this whole block and the surrounding area has been building and building and growing to house a number of big stores, so Mitsukoshi actually brought a boom with it.

The store is big and modern, with a nice kids' department downstairs where your children can play and test Nintendo games to their hearts' delight. This is where you can buy the transformer that will allow you to play a Japanese-style Nintendo game on your child's American Nintendo. The plastic transformer costs about $8–10.

The goods sold in this store are very yuppie-oriented; name-brand everything is available. You'll recognize many American names; European names are the big draw. Even if the designer has his own boutique in town, he still seems to get floor space at Mitsukoshi.

The store is large, deluxe, expensive and overwhelming. Go early when you feel strong.

Hours are Sunday through Friday, 10 A.M. to 9 P.M., and Saturday until 9:30 P.M. (closed Tuesday).

MITSUKOSHI
> Sun Plaza Arcade, 28 Canton Road, Kowloon
> Hennessy Centre, 500 Hennessy Road, Hong Kong (MTR: Causeway Bay)

SEIBU

Remember the old days when Bloomingdale's really was something special? Seibu reminds me of those days. I honestly believe they took everything Bloomie's had to offer and then made it better. Locals complain that the store is as expensive as Lane Crawford. Surely Seibu considers Lane Crawford the competition, instead of the other Japanese department stores. Frankly, I think it's MORE expensive than Lane Crawford and certainly more with-it.

Seibu has fabulous stores in Tokyo (and all of Japan), and now offers Hong Kong its upscale lifestyle and fashion. The store here is no larger than Lane Crawford (far smaller than the one on the Ginza), but it gives you a fine taste of what retailing refinement can be.

If you are at all interested in the creative aspects of retail, wander this store just to stare and maybe take notes. There are no bargains, but there is power in the beauty of the choices.

SEIBU

the Mall at Pacific Place, 88 Queensway, Hong Kong (MTR: Admiralty)

SOGO

Sogo is right over the Causeway Bay MTR station, which makes it very convenient. (Or, if you are driving, there is free parking for two hours at Windsor House.) It's open late, so you can get in some nighttime shopping with pleasure. All the big designers are represented here. Prices are good on Japanese designers, such as Hiroko Koshino, whom we have been buying in Milan or at Alma in New York.

Sogo plays recognizable Muzak as you zip up and down escalators —designers on the ground floor; ladies' fashions, cosmetics and shoes on B1; food on B2. There are more ladies' fashions on floors 1 and 2; don't miss the cosmetics bar on the first floor; men's fashions are on 3; 4 is sports and hi-fi equipment; 5 is household goods and furniture; 6 has babies' and maternity items; and 7 offers stationery. On the first floor there's an adorable "Café City" decorated in pink-and-black Art Deco and ready to convince you that you aren't in Hong Kong. Sogo claims to be the world's largest department store; their branches in Japan are to die for.

Hours are daily from 10:30 A.M. to 10 P.M.

SOGO

Lockhart Road, Hong Kong (MTR: Causeway Bay)

British Department Stores

It seems perfectly normal for there to be British department stores in a British Crown Colony— especially one that was set up for the sole purpose of trade—but there's still no Harrods or Liberty. Oh well, Marks & Sparks isn't so bad.

LANE CRAWFORD

Lane Crawford is the most prestigious Western-style department store in Hong Kong, and a jewel to those who work and live here, but who crave the elegance of Old World charm in a retail setting. Lane Crawford is not huge by American standards, but it's comfortable and you'll find all the familiar brands of quality merchandise. It is not really there for tourists, but it does offer the guarantee that you are not getting fakes, seconds or inferior merchandise. Snobs often like to buy their jewelry here.

Lane Crawford was created as a full-service English department store for the people who live here. It doesn't have the food halls of Harrods or the selection of suitable work clothes for younger women of Selfridge's, but it does offer cradle-to-grave services along with the merchandise. The name has snob appeal in Hong Kong, similar to that of Neiman Marcus in the U.S.

We have never seen anything in Lane Crawford we didn't see anywhere else, and find the store worthwhile only if you seek to escape the realities of Hong Kong (and many do, if only for an hour), or want to see a lot of merchandise in a manner you can deal with, as opposed to the wretched excesses elsewhere in Hong Kong.

LANE CRAWFORD

Lane Crawford House, 70 Queen's Road, Hong Kong

74 Nathan Road, Kowloon

The Mall at Pacific Place, 88 Queensway, Hong Kong (MTR: Admiralty)

MARKS & SPENCER

Marks & Sparks, as it is fondly called in Britain, has come to Hong Kong, and in a big way. Every place you turn (especially in the malls), you spot a new one. Willie and his architectural firm are now finishing one in the Landmark. Hooray!—a chance to buy more St. Michael's underwear.

Now then. As much as we love M&S, we admit that there are no great Hong Kong bargains here. Being in the store, especially the grocery department, is just like being in England. Right down to the prices. What you are paying for is the M&S reputation for quality and value, but we are not talking factory-outlet prices.

If you shop the Hong Kong outlets or street markets, you'll do better than M&S prices on regular ready-to-wear. Locals depend on M&S; tourists shouldn't really have to.

Please note that in some malls the various M&S departments appear to be in different boutiques or on different levels of the mall so you don't get a sense of shopping the whole store or of being in a department store.

Expats, please note that M&S will pay the freight home (to any address in the U.K.) on your Christmas hamper as long as you spend 40£ or more per hamper. This could be the deal of the century. Of course, the goods come from a warehouse in the U.K. in the first place, but still, it's the thought that counts.

MARKS & SPENCER

Harbour City Ocean Galleries, 25-27 Canton Road, Kowloon

The Landmark, 16 Des Voeux Road, Central, Hong Kong

Cityplaza III, 1111King's Road, Quarry Bay, Hong Kong (MTR: Taikoo Shing)

Designer Goods

Hong Kong gets more and more designer shops every day; I cannot come to town without being annoyed that so many new shops have opened. Truly annoyed. First of all, how can I possibly keep count or keep it straight? Second of all, who in the world is shopping at these places? And finally, did any of us come to Hong Kong to buy big-name designer clothes at regular retail prices? I mean, really.

Every now and then you can get a break on designer goods. Hermès is cheaper than in the U.S. and U.K. Escada can be cheaper. Some Chanel items (like makeup) are cheaper. Most items are not cheaper than at home. Therefore, if you have interests in a certain designer line, I suggest you shop the line at home and come to Hong Kong with notes in hand.

It is possible that you will find designer lines in Hong Kong that have not yet come to the U.S. or U.K., so you can be the first on your block to wear a certain style. For the most part, however, I'd much rather you were out on the streets, in the markets, eating dim sum with your fingers or going to Macau than shopping the high-end, fancy, drop-dead-chic stores in hermetically-sealed malls and stalls. Of course, I know some of you will ignore my advice and head for the high-end fashion. You know what to expect from each of your favorite designers, so you don't need me to describe the ware in their shops. Following is a directory of where to find the biggies. End of speech.

British and Continental Big Names

GIORGIO ARMANI

The Landmark, Gloucester Tower, 16 Des Voeux Road Central, Hong Kong

Mandarin Oriental Hotel, 5 Connaught Road Central, Hong Kong

EMPORIO ARMANI

Harbour City/Ocean Centre, 5 Canton Road, Kowloon

16 Queen's Road Central, Hong Kong

ÉTIENNE AIGNER

The Mall at Pacific Place (Shop 338), 88 Queensway, Hong Kong (MTR: Admiralty)

Alexandra House, Des Voeux Road, Hong Kong

The Landmark, 16 Des Voeux Road Central, Hong Kong

The Regent Hotel, Salisbury Road, Kowloon

Hyatt Regency Hong Kong, 67 Nathan Road, Kowloon

BALLANTYNE

The Landmark, Gloucester Tower, 16 Des Voeux Road Central, Hong Kong

The Mall at Pacific Place, 88 Queensway, Hong Kong (MTR: Admiralty)

BALLY

The Peninsula Hotel, Salisbury Road, Kowloon

The Landmark, Gloucester Tower, 16 Des Voeux Road Central, Hong Kong

BELTRAMI

The Landmark (Shop 109), 16 Des Voeux Road Central, Hong Kong

The Peninsula Hotel (basement), Salisbury Road, Kowloon

BENETTON

The Mall at Pacific Place (level 1), 88 Queensway, Hong Kong (MTR: Admiralty)

Cityplaza II, 1111 King's Road, Quarry Bay (MTR: Taikoo Shing)

Harbour City/Ocean Centre (Shop 003), 5 Canton Road, Kowloon

Harbour City/Ocean Terminal (Shop 217-20), Canton Road, Kowloon

BOTTEGA VENETA

Swire House (ground floor), Connaught Road Central, Hong Kong

BURBERRYS

The Landmark, 16 Des Voeux Road Central, Hong Kong

BULGARI

The Landmark, 16 Des Voeux Road Central, Hong Kong

The Peninsula Hotel, Salisbury Road, Kowloon

BYBLOS
Harbour City/Ocean Terminal (Shop 201), Canton Road, Kowloon

CACHAREL
The Landmark, 16 Des Voeux Road Central, Hong Kong

Harbour City/Ocean Centre, 5 Canton Road, Kowloon

CARTIER
Prince's Building (ground floor), Chater Road, Hong Kong

The Peninsula Hotel, Salisbury Road, Kowloon

The Mall at Pacific Place (Shop 3/F), 88 Queensway, Hong Kong (MTR: Admiralty)

The Regent Hotel, Salisbury Road, Kowloon

CÉLINE
Repulse Bay Shopping Arcade, 109 Repulse Bay Road, Hong Kong (MTR: None)

The Landmark, 16 Des Voeux Road Central, Hong Kong

The Peninsula Hotel, Salisbury Road, Kowloon

CERRUTTI 1881
Harbour City/Ocean Centre, 5 Canton Road, Kowloon

The Peninsula Hotel (basement), Salisbury Road, Kowloon

The Mall at Pacific Place (Shop 367), 88 Queensway, Hong Kong

The Landmark, 16 Des Voeux Road Central, Hong Kong

Repulse Bay Shopping Arcade, 109 Repulse Bay Road, Hong Kong (MTR: None)

CHANEL
Prince's Building, Chater Road, Hong Kong
The Peninsula Hotel, Salisbury Road, Kowloon
The Regent Hotel, Salisbury Road, Kowloon

COURRÈGES
The Landmark, Gloucester Tower, 16 Des Voeux Road Central, Hong Kong

Harbour City/Ocean Centre (Shop 207), 5 Canton Road, Kowloon

CHRISTIAN DIOR
The Landmark, Edinburgh Tower, 16 Des Voeux Road Central, Hong Kong

The Peninsula Hotel, Salisbury Road, Kowloon

CHRISTIAN DIOR MONSIEUR
Prince's Building, Chater Road, Hong Kong

DAKS
Prince's Building, Chater Road, Hong Kong

The Peninsula Hotel, Salisbury Road, Kowloon

DOLCE & GABBANA
Harbour City/Ocean Centre (ground floor), 5 Canton Road, Kowloon

The World of Joyce at The Galleria at 9 Queen's, 9 Queen's Road Central, Hong Kong

ALFRED DUNHILL
The Peninsula Hotel, Salisbury Road, Kowloon

Hyatt Regency Hong Kong, 67 Nathan Road, Kowloon

Prince's Building, Chater Road, Hong Kong

The Mall at Pacific Place (level 3), 88 Queensway, Hong Kong (MTR: Admiralty)

ESCADA
Central Building, Pedder Street, Hong Kong

The Peninsula Hotel, Salisbury Road, Kowloon

Kowloon Hotel, 19-21 Nathan Road, Kowloon

China Hong Kong City, Canton Road, Kowloon

ETRO
The Peninsula Hotel (basement), Salisbury Road, Kowloon

FENDI
Harbour City/Ocean Centre, 5 Canton Road, Kowloon

Mandarin Oriental Hotel, 5 Connaught Road Central, Hong Kong

FERRAGAMO

Harbour City/Ocean Terminal, Canton Road, Kowloon

The Regent Hotel, Salisbury Road, Kowloon

Mandarin Oriental Hotel, 5 Connaught Road Central, Hong Kong

The Peninsula Hotel, Salisbury Road, Kowloon

JEAN-PAUL GAULTIER

Prince's Building, Chater Road, Hong Kong

Harbour City/Ocean Centre, 5 Canton Road, Kowloon

GENNY

The Peninsula Hotel, Salisbury Road, Kowloon

The Landmark (Shop 232), 16 Des Voeux Road Central, Hong Kong

GIEVES & HAWKES

The Peninsula Hotel, Salisbury Road, Kowloon

Prince's Building, Chater Road, Hong Kong

Repulse Bay Shopping Arcade, 109 Repulse Bay Road, Hong Kong

Harbour City/Ocean Terminal, Canton Road, Kowloon

GIVENCHY

The Landmark, Gloucester Tower, 16 Des Voeux Road Central, Hong Kong

GOLDPFEIL

Swire House (Shop 19), Connaught Road Central, Hong Kong

The Peninsula Hotel, Salisbury Road, Kowloon

China Hong Kong City, Canton Road, Kowloon

GUCCI

The Landmark, Gloucester Tower, 16 Des Voeux Road Central, Hong Kong

The Peninsula Hotel, Salisbury Road, Kowloon

Repulse Bay Shopping Arcade, 109 Repulse Bay Road, Hong Kong (MTR: None)

HERMÈS

The Galleria at 9 Queen's (ground floor), 9 Queen's Road Central, Hong Kong

The Mall at Pacific Place (level 3), 88 Queensway, Hong Kong (MTR: Admiralty)

The Peninsula Hotel, Salisbury Road, Kowloon

ICEBERG

The Landmark (Shop 236), 16 Des Voeux Road Central, Hong Kong

IKEA

Sun Plaza Arcade, 28 Canton Road, Kowloon

JAEGER

The Regent Hotel, Salisbury Road, Kowloon

KENZO

The Landmark, 16 Des Voeux Road Central, Hong Kong

The Peninsula Hotel, Salisbury Road, Kowloon

GUY LAROCHE

The Landmark (Shop 102B), 16 Des Voeux Road Central, Hong Kong

KARL LAGERFELD

The Landmark, Edinburgh Tower, 16 Des Voeux Road Central, Hong Kong

LANVIN

The Landmark, Gloucester Tower, 16 Des Voeux Road Central, Hong Kong

The Regent Hotel, Salisbury Road, Kowloon

Hyatt Regency Hong Kong, 67 Nathan Road, Kowloon

LÉONARD

The Peninsula Hotel, Salisbury Road, Kowloon

The Landmark (ground floor), 16 Des Voeux Road Central, Hong Kong

LONGCHAMP

The Peninsula Hotel, Salisbury Road, Kowloon

The Regent Hotel, Salisbury Road, Kowloon

LOEWE

The Landmark, 16 Des Voeux Road, Central, Hong Kong

Repulse Bay Shopping Arcade, 109 Repulse Bay Road, Hong Kong (MTR: None)

The Peninsula Hotel, Salisbury Road, Kowloon

BRUNO MAGLI

Central Building (ground floor), Pedder Street, Hong Kong

The Regent Hotel, Salisbury Road, Kowloon

Harbour City/Ocean Terminal (Shop 233), Canton Road, Kowloon

China Hong Kong City, Canton Road, Kowloon

MISSONI

The Peninsula Hotel, Salisbury Road, Kowloon

CLAUDE MONTANA

The Landmark, Edinburgh Tower, 16 Des Voeux Road Central, Hong Kong

Kowloon Hotel, 19-21 Nathan Road, Kowloon

MOSCHINO

Swire House, Connaught Road Central, Hong Kong

The Regent Hotel, Salisbury Road, Kowloon

THIERRY MUGLER

The Landmark (Shop 242), 16 Des Voeux Road Central, Hong Kong

HARVEY NICHOLS

The Landmark (Shop 218), 16 Des Voeux Road Central, Hong Kong

NINA RICCI

China Hong Kong City, Canton Road, Kowloon

The Peninsula Hotel, Salisbury Road, Kowloon

The Regent Hotel, Salisbury Road, Kowloon

Mandarin Oriental Hotel, 5 Connaught Road Central, Hong Kong

JIL SANDER

The Regent Hotel, Salisbury Road, Kowloon

PAUL SMITH

Harbour City/Ocean Centre (Shop 005), 5 Canton Road, Kowloon

TRUSSARDI

The Galleria at 9 Queen's, 9 Queen's Road Central, Hong Kong

Harbour City/Ocean Centre (Shop 209), 5 Canton Road, Kowloon

VALENTINO

The Regent Hotel, Salisbury Road, Kowloon

VAN CLEEF & ARPELS

The Landmark (atrium), 16 Des Voeux Road Central, Hong Kong

The Peninsula Hotel, Salisbury Road, Kowloon

GIANNI VERSACE

Kowloon Hotel, 19-21 Nathan Road, Kowloon

The Landmark (For Men, Shop G19; For Ladies, Shop 14A), 16 Des Voeux Road Central, Hong Kong

The Peninsula Hotel, Salisbury Road, Kowloon

VERSACE VERSUS

Harbour City/Ocean Terminal, Canton Road, Kowloon

LOUIS VUITTON

The Landmark, Gloucester Tower, 16 Des Voeux Road Central, Hong Kong

The Peninsula Hotel, Salisbury Road, Kowloon

Repulse Bay Shopping Arcade, 109 Repulse Bay Road, Hong Kong (MTR: None)

The Regent Hotel, Salisbury Road, Kowloon

ERMENEGILDO ZEGNA

The Mall at Pacific Place (Shop 250), 88 Queensway, Hong Kong (MTR: Admiralty)

American Big Names

Rarely are American goods less expensive in Hong Kong, except maybe at Esprit. Or if you find them in an outlet or on the street. If you want to feel faint with disbelief, check out the prices at Donna Karan.

ESPRIT

88 Hing Fat Street, Hong Kong (MTR: Causeway Bay)

Auto Plaza, 65 Mody Road, Tsim Sha Tsui East, Kowloon

Park Lane Shopper's Boulevard, Nathan Road, Kowloon

Cityplaza II, 1111 King's Road, Quarry Bay, Hong Kong (MTR: Taikoo Shing)

DIANE FREIS

Prince's Building, Chater Road, Hong Kong

Harbour City/Ocean Terminal, Canton Road, Kowloon

The Regent Hotel, Salisbury Road, Kowloon

The Mall at Pacific Place, 88 Queensway, Hong Kong (MTR: Admiralty)

DONNA KARAN

The Regent Hotel, Salisbury Road, Kowloon

RALPH LAUREN/POLO

Central Building, 19-23 Queen's Road Central, Hong Kong

The Peninsula Hotel, Salisbury Road, Kowloon

TIFFANY & CO.

The Peninsula Hotel, Salisbury Road, Kowloon

The Landmark, 16 Des Voeux Road Central, Hong Kong

PALOMA PICASSO

The Landmark (Shop G44), 16 Des Voeux Road Central, Hong Kong

TOYS R US

Harbour City/Ocean Terminal, Canton Road, Kowloon

Asian Big Names

MATSUDA

Swire House, Connaught Road Central, Hong Kong

ISSEY MIYAKE

Swire House, Connaught Road Central, Hong Kong

ISSEY MIYAKE PERMANENTE

The Landmark, 16 Des Voeux Road Central, Hong Kong

KAI YIN LO

The Peninsula Hotel, Salisbury Road, Kowloon

Mandarin Oriental Hotel (mezzanine), 5 Connaught Road Central, Hong Kong

The Mall at Pacific Place, 88 Queensway, Hong Kong (MTR: Admiralty)

DAVID SHEEKWAN

Pedder Building, Pedder Street, Hong Kong

Up-and-Coming Talent

More and more young designers are finding that Hong Kong is a fine place to be discovered. Although many of the young designers in town are not yet represented in boutiques, they are busy designing private-label goods for large stores. You may never have heard their names, but you may dig their designs.

Find the latest and wildest designs by these hot young talents in the shops that line Kimberley Road and Austin Avenue. These two streets, in the northern end of Tsim Sha Tsui, have become the SoHo of Hong Kong. The decor of the shops is avant-garde; the prices are affordable. Start at the corner of Austin and Nathan roads, walking east. Austin Road turns a corner and becomes Austin Avenue, which will turn again and become Kimberley Road, heading back toward Nathan Road.

Another great place to search out talented new designers is a store called HONG KONG DESIGNER'S GALLERY. The main shop is in the New Territories, at the Hotel Riverside Plaza Arcade, Tai Chung Kiu Road, Sha Tin, N.T. This is quite a bit out of the way for most tourists. A smaller but much more convenient shop is located at Paliburg Plaza, 66 Yee Wo Street (MTR: Causeway Bay). Here you will find bits and pieces from many up-and-coming designer lines.

Made-to-Measure for Him

Another of the famous Hong Kong fantasies is that made-to-measure suits grow on trees, or that they are easily and inexpensively obtained with a snap of the fingers and a few hundred dollars. Not!

Yes, there are still tourist joints and rip-off tailors who will make you a suit, with two pairs of trousers, for $250. Maybe even less. But I have to lay it on the line, guys: The suit you get for $250 does not look like the suit you get for $650, and you don't really want the suit for $250. At least, I can't take responsibility for what you will look like in a $250 Hong Kong-made suit. However, I guarantee you'll look like a million bucks if you go to one of Hong Kong's better tailors and spend what it takes for Savile Row quality.

True, you can go to any American discounter or outlet mall and buy an off-the-rack suit for $250, maybe less. Ian bought two suits for $99 each at a blowout sale at Filene's Basement. They're great cheap suits. (Made in Mexico, by the way.) But they are cheap suits and cannot be compared in fit, fabric, life span or appearance to a more expensive suit. Ian happens to be a 40R and easy-to-fit, and he looks good in everything. If a bespoke suit looks so enormously different on him, imagine how much better the man with the less-than-perfect figure will look.

Remember the first law of Hong Kong custom-made suits: A bargain is not a bargain if it doesn't fit. Furthermore, the whole point of a bespoke suit is psychological—you must feel (and look) like a king in it. Its impact derives from the fact that it was made for your body, that it moves with your body as no off-the-rack garment can.

I've gotten a few angry letters from readers who were not happy with the famous (or infamous) cheapie Hong Kong tailors suggested in past editions. So I've modified my plan. It's simple: If you want a truly fine bespoke suit, Hong Kong can give you British quality at a Hong Kong price. If you cannot afford to trade up to a quality suit, please do not waste your money on an inferior product.

• Start your search for a tailor the minute you arrive. Leave yourself time for three fittings while in Hong Kong. The first will be for measurements and choice of fabrics; the second fitting will be a partially-finished suit with only one sleeve in place; the third will be to detail the finished garment, if it is not perfect. Good tailors usually have everything wrapped up by the third fitting.

If at all possible, choose your tailor before you leave home and fax ahead for an appointment so you can meet shortly after arrival in Hong Kong. After you check in to your hotel, the tailor should be your first stop. While it is not difficult to get across the harbor in Hong Kong, you may want to choose your hotel based on the convenience to your tailor. We make more trips to W.W. Chan than any other address in Hong Kong or Kowloon; it helps to be staying nearby.

• Most tailors carry a full line of imported fabrics from Italy, England and France. If your tailor is not one of the Big Three, ask whether the thread they use is imported also. If it is not, ask to see the quality, and test it for durability. Remember all those horror stories you have heard about suits falling apart? It wasn't the fabric; it was the thread. You do not need to worry about quality at the Big Three tailors.

- Again, if you aren't certain of your tailor's quality, check the lining fabrics. The better tailors have beautiful choices, some imported and some not, but all in good taste. Be sure to specify a fully-lined jacket. No fine tailor would consider giving you anything but the best lining.

- If you still have questions about the quality of your tailor, check the inner-facing material to make sure it is stiff enough to hold the shape of the suit.

- Check the quality of the shoulder pads, the buttons and the buttonholes. A tailor could save a lot of money by using inferior goods. A bad tailor cannot make a good buttonhole. The mark of an excellent tailor is the fact that the handmade buttonholes actually work.

- Well-made suits from a Hong Kong tailor are no longer as inexpensive as they used to be. Gentlemen who came to Hong Kong in the 1960s paid $99 for a suit; that is no longer the going price—even from a cheapie tailor. Imported fabrics run about $20 to $80 per yard, and an average-sized suit will take 3-1/2 yards. The silk/wool blends and cashmeres cost more. The finished price for a top quality, killer suit will run in the area of $500–$800. You could do better in some cases with an off-the-rack suit in the U.S., but the quality would not be the same. Ask for tailoring prices with and without the material. In some cases you might wish to supply your own.

- The shop will want a 50% deposit to start the work. You may be able to pay with a check in

U.S. dollars or pounds sterling. Ask ahead of time.

- If you are having the tailor ship the suits to you, remember to figure in the Customs charges and shipping. On average, it costs $20 per suit to air-freight them to you. Shirts can be shipped for $30 per dozen. U.S. Customs charges about $75 in duty on a single new suit. Once you have established an account with a tailor or a shirtmaker and he has your measurements on file, you can simply get the fabric swatches sent to you for the new season and do your shopping through the mail—or in a local hotel.

- Check to see if the tailor you have chosen makes trips to the U.S. to visit customers. Chances are, if you live in a major city (New York, Washington, San Francisco, Los Angeles or Chicago), he will. Most of the tailors we recommend either come in person once a year or send a representative with fabric books and order forms. At that time, new measurements can be taken in case you have lost or gained weight.

- The tailors we recommend have been tried and tested by one of us (Ian Cook; my husband Mike; our son Aaron; or relatives or friends). There are many other tailors in Hong Kong. There is at least one in every hotel shopping arcade. There are even tailors who set up booths at the various night markets. Unless you have a personal recommendation, let the buyer beware.

The Big Three

H. BAROMON LTD.

Tycoon alert: This is a No. 8 warning! If you wonder where the real financial heavyweights have their clothing made, wonder no more. H.

Baromon has been in the business for forty years, serving the elite. His reputation is so above the rest of the world, we are surprised his shop hasn't been moved to Savile Row. When you go to choose suit fabric from H. Baromon, you receive a little booklet containing a photo of the shop, a brief description of the H. Baromon philosophy, a page where you can paste your sample cutting, a memo page for notes, a dollar conversion chart and a very nice map to help you find your way back.

A made-to-order suit takes at least seven days. The average suit price is well over $750. Shirts average $100. H. Baromon does not send representatives to the U.S.

H. BAROMON LTD.

Swire House, Connaught Road Central, Hong Kong, 011-852-523-6845

A-MAN HING CHEONG CO. LTD.

Fondly referred to as "Ah-men," this tailor shop in the Mandarin Oriental Hotel turns out quite a few garments for the rich-tourist-and-businessman trade, and therefore has become very adept at relating to the European-cut suit. They don't even blink twice when you ask for an extra pair of trousers. They just smile and ask for more money. The prices here are on the higher side, with a suit costing about $650. However, the quality is excellent, and that is what you are paying for. Anyone can buy off-the-rack. This is a Savile Row-quality suit.

A-Man will also do custom shirts for approximately $50–$150. If you wish to cable them, their cable name is "Luckylucky." You will feel lucky lucky when you get home and enjoy your new bespoke clothing. Fax 011-852-523-4707; phone 011-852-522-3336.

A-MAN HING CHEONG CO. LTD.

Mandarin Oriental Hotel, 5 Connaught Road Central, Hong Kong

W.W. CHAN & SONS TAILOR LTD.

My personal choice for myself, my husband, my son and for Ian is W.W. Chan. Note that this is the only tailor in the Big Three which has a division that makes women's clothing (see page 226).

Peter Chan carries on a family business, which he has built and expanded over the years. He is the only Big Three tailor with offices in Kowloon. The average price for a suit is $500–$650; the mink/cashmere blends do run up the price.

The W.W. Chan showroom is decidedly more relaxed than the other two big-time contenders. The showroom itself is neat, clean, modern and even spacious, which is hard to find in Hong Kong. But the location in Kowloon and the approach to the actual showroom are not so swank; businessmen who are used to wall-to-wall carpet may need a moment to adjust, until they are inside the showroom (which has wall-to-wall carpet). Peter had a showroom in the Peninsula Hotel (George Chen), but now uses the single showroom in the Burlington Arcade to accommodate W.W. Chan clients as well as those who frequent George Chen (which Peter owns) and Irene's Fashions, the women's division of W.W. Chan.

The showroom is wood-paneled and divided into two parts; one half is primarily for men, although there are more men's fabrics on the side that appears to be for women. The walls are divided into bins, which house zillions of bolts of fabric, most of which come from Europe. More booklets and fabric swatches lie around. When we are picking fabric for suits, we always try to give Peter a hint at what we want (gray flannel, for instance), because the task of just looking at all the possibilities can be daunting.

Peter's eye and good taste will guide you to the right stuff. Peter also knows the cut—he'll explain the differences between American and European cuts, a Brooks Brothers-type cut and more. Alterations to garments made at W.W. Chan are free for the lifetime of the garment, and a fine men's suit lasts twenty years, or more.

The quality of the Chan product is equal to its first-rate reputation; customers here tend to be those who demand the best and like to find it for themselves. The Bijan crowd may prefer H. Baromon; the British tycoons may be happier in Central. The people who come to W.W. Chan feel like they are members of a club. I've actually made friends with other customers who were having fittings; there is a constant flow of airline pilots and businessmen coming through the door. Single women may want to hang out just to meet men.

The company sends out tailors twice a year; you may request their U.S. schedule and make an appointment to be fitted stateside. There is no schedule for London. Fax: 011-852-368-2194.

W.W. CHAN & SONS TAILOR LTD.

Burlington House (2nd floor), 92-94 Nathan Road, Kowloon

Made-to-Measure: Shirts

Having a shirt made is not quite the science that having a suit made is, but there is a big difference between a well-made shirt and a poorly-made one. Furthermore, men with hard-to-fit figures will always look better in custom-made shirts. A made-to-measure shirt allows you to combine fit, fabric and quality. And you get a monogram at no extra cost.

There are a lot of choices to be made: the fit of the body, the type of collar and cuffs, the fabric and the possible use of contrast fabric. Prices usually depend on the fabrications; 100% cotton fabric costs more than a poly blend; Sea Island cotton costs more than regular cotton. Expect to pay about $75 for a Sea Island custom-made cotton shirt, although such a shirt can cost more, depending on the maker.

Many shirt houses have a minimum order on shirts; most tailors make shirts as well as suits. If you are buying the shirt and the suit from the same tailor, there is usually no minimum order on shirts. Most shirt houses make pajamas and boxer shorts as well as shirts.

All the men in my family (including Ian) have their custom shirts made at W.W. Chan, as it is tremendously easier to order shirts and suits at the same time and from the same quality maker. There are other choices, obviously.

W.W. CHAN & SONS TAILOR LTD.

Mike, Aaron and Ian all have their shirts made from our regular tailor. Try the white monogram on the sleeve of a white shirt: very sophisticated.

W.W. CHAN & SONS TAILOR LTD.
92-94 Nathan Road, Burlington Arcade (second floor), Kowloon

ASCOT CHANG CO. LTD.

Perhaps the best known of the internationally famous shirt dealers, Ascot Chang advertises heavily in the U.S. and stresses their quality and devotion to fit. This shirtmaker has many branches in Hong Kong and Kowloon. The shops are filled with wonderful fabrics imported from Switzerland and France. Prices are competitive with David's (see below); they offer mail-order once your measurements have been taken. Shirts run between $40 and $125, depending upon the fabric and style. Top of the line. They have a shop in Manhattan.

ASCOT CHANG CO. LTD.
The Peninsula Hotel, Salisbury Road, Kowloon
The Regent Hotel, Salisbury Road, Kowloon
Prince's Building, Chater Road, Hong Kong
7 West 57th Street, New York, NY 10019
9551 Wilshire Boulevard, Beverly Hills, CA 90210

DAVID'S SHIRTS

David's is the other most popular and famous of the custom shirt shops in Hong Kong. (They also have a branch in New York City.) The main shop in Hong Kong is in Kowloon, on Kimberley Road. But there are more conveniently placed branch shops, mostly in hotels like the Regent or the Mandarin Oriental. David's is less glitzy than Ascot Chang, but just as famous to those in the know.

For custom shirts, two fittings are necessary— one for the measurements and then one with the garment. David's will copy any favorite shirt you may have. Just bring it with you and plan to leave it. They also have a framed illustration of collar and cuff styles you can choose from. Mail-order is not only possible but common with repeat customers. If you cannot get to Hong Kong, ask for a current swatch and price list. Return a shirt that fits you perfectly and a check, along with fabric and collar/cuff choices. Approximately four to six weeks later a box of new shirts will arrive. If you want to contact their New York store, call (212) 757-1803.

DAVID'S SHIRTS

Victoria Hotel (unit 201), Shun Tak Centre, Hong Kong (MTR: Shueng Wan)

Mandarin Oriental Hotel, 5 Connaught Road Central, Hong Kong

Wing Lee Building (ground floor), 33 Kimberley Road, Kowloon

10 Rockefeller Plaza, New York, NY 10020

Other Tailors

JIMMY CHEN

Jimmy Chen has a good reputation and nice shops in the city's best tourist locations. His shop is especially known for making a little of everything: suits, shirts, men's clothes and women's clothes. He also makes cotton summer suits for men, which many other tailors refuse to do. Prices are equal to those charged by the Big Three.

JIMMY CHEN

The Landmark, Edinburgh Tower, 16 Des Voeux Road Central, Hong Kong

The Peninsula Hotel, Salisbury Road, Kowloon

Harbour City/Omni The Hong Kong Hotel, Canton Road, Kowloon

GIEVES & HAWKES

Talk about bringing coals to Newcastle—this always gives me a kick: Here you have one of the most famous Savile Row tailors opening shop in Hong Kong, the city where tailors commit their lives to bettering Savile Row. Gieves & Hawkes does a very good business with those who do not trust a Chinese tailor (silly chaps) and who want the status associated with one of London's veddy, veddy best. They also appeal to status-conscious travelers from other countries who want a London label.

GIEVES & HAWKES

Prince's Building, Chater Road, Hong Kong

The Peninsula Hotel, Salisbury Road, Kowloon

Less-Expensive Tailors

I'm seriously down on inexpensive tailors, because I've seen work that makes me wince, especially compared to the Big Three. Since not everyone has $500 or more for a suit, there should be alternatives, right? These come from reader suggestions; I have not used them personally.

WILLIAM CHENG

Reader Muriel Mitzman from New York wrote to recommend this tailor, whom she found refreshing after visiting the infamous Sam (who is no longer in these pages). She and her husband bought suits and shirts and were happy with make, fit and price.

WILLIAM CHENG
Han Hing Mansion, 38 Hankow Road, Kowloon

DE LUXE TAILOR

This is from Barbara Basler, writing for the *New York Times*, claiming well-made suits at a good, although not low, price ($350–$400).

DE LUXE TAILOR
Yip Fung Building (Room 708), 2-18 D'Aguilar Street, Hong Kong

Men's Alterations

It was Ian who brought up the subject of alterations in Hong Kong, an especially good point given the fantasy that most people have about tailoring being so cheap in Hong Kong. Ian happened to have a favorite sports jacket: years old, it was sagging in the pockets, a little stretched across the shoulders (don't ask what a photographer can do to a jacket), and it possessed a tattered lining.

We took the jacket to Peter Chan at W.W. Chan, since he is our regular tailor. His advice: DON'T bring regular old alterations to a fine Hong Kong tailor, because the time and labor needed to do the job properly can bring you to a costly solution. DO bring your favorite jacket (or whatever), a family heirloom or garments that have emotional meaning to you.

The new lining for Ian's sports jacket cost $100, which he was happy to pay because he loves that jacket. Some men would rather buy a new jacket for the same $100. The new lining was silk; hand-stitched with pleats to allow for maximum movement; gapping pockets were brought together; the weave of the jacket seemed tighter because of the strength of the new lining.

Also note that with a fine tailor, alterations to clothes they have made are usually free. Ian's new navy jacket, made by Peter, would have a life expectancy as great as Ian's. In twenty years (or sooner), if it needs a new lining, Peter will make one...for free.

If you want a new lining to a sport jacket that your tailor has not made, request this service and ask the fee. Peter Chan will only take alterations from regular customers; the flat fee for a new lining in a sports jacket is $100.

But wait, there's more to it. I bought an absolutely perfect Brooks Brothers navy blazer at a tag sale in Connecticut for $10. It was a large size, way too big for Ian. But I knew he needed a navy blazer and that we were going to Hong Kong. Could Peter fix the jacket at a worthwhile price?

Well, yes, Peter could fix the jacket and have it come out perfect, but no, it didn't make sense: He suggested a brand-new jacket.

According to Peter, the rule for major alterations is simple: bigger or smaller can be easily achieved (especially smaller); longer or shorter are very serious alterations and require that a garment be completely taken apart and remade—not usually worth the cost of the labor involved.

Also consider the quality of your original garment. Fine tailors do handwork, which is time consuming and therefore expensive. If the jacket (or whatever) you wish to save is machine-made, it's even harder to put it together properly. A new item will cost the same and look better.

W.W. CHAN & SONS TAILOR LTD.
Burlington Arcade (second floor), 92-94 Nathan Road, Kowloon

Made-to-Measure for Her

Men have been having suits made in Hong Kong for years, but women are still learning the ropes. Finding a tailor who can properly drape fabric on a womanly Western figure takes a lot of doing.

I started going to W.W. CHAN for the simple reason that Peter Chan makes my husband's clothes. But there is method to my madness; I didn't just pick an agreeable face from our circle of friends. The three best men's tailors in Hong Kong (see page 218) are so defined because they have their own workshops; only Chan makes women's clothing. After my first suit, I was addicted; now I have most of my good clothes made by Danny Chen at W.W. Chan.

There are scads of tailors in town who will take on curvy clients; possibly some of them can tailor a suit to your liking. You can find tailors less expensive than the Big Three. But for women who want the best, only W.W. Chan will make you a suit that fits like couture.

When you pick a tailor in Hong Kong, know the rules of the game: Absolutely every handmade garment in Hong Kong with the exception of those from the Big Three is contracted out as piecework. In piecework, seamstresses and tailors are paid by the piece, not by the hour. It behooves them to finish quickly. They do not have time to press individual seams, to move slowly, to do painstaking work.

The Big Three pay their tailors by the hour, and will accept only the best, because their clients insist on it. Work is not farmed out; each item is made on the premises. A French atelier or Savile Row shop would not be any more professional. The quality of the garments from these work-rooms is superior on every piece cut.

Prices on men's and women's clothing differ at W.W. Chan. You are charged a flat rate for the making of the garment (no matter what size or how complicated); you pay for the fabric by the yard (or provide your own). A woman's suit totals $350–$500, depending on the fabric. French wools (the same ones used at Chanel) bring the cost up. A dress costs about $170 for labor alone; a jacket, $175.

While three fittings are recommended, especially for a first-timer, the truth is that these guys can get it more or less perfect after the first measurements are taken.

I would have had some women's clothing made at other tailors, but the truth is, I was frightened off in the research stage, and I'm so happy with W.W. Chan that I can't stand the thought of possibly wasting my money. The two other tailors I tried to use did not pass muster after I inspected recently-finished garments on their new owners. I was impressed by MODE ELEGANTE (see page 232), which is a firm used by several women I know. I have not had anything made there.

- If you know you want to use Danny Chen, it's best to write, call or fax ahead for an appointment. If you aren't headed for Hong Kong, ask about being fitted in the U.S., since Mr. Chen travels to major cities once a year. Men can book with Peter Chan. Contact W.W. Chan & Sons Tailor Ltd., Burlington Arcade (second floor), 92-94 Nathan Road, Kowloon, Hong Kong. From the U.S., phone 011-852-366-9738 or fax 011-852-368-2194; cable WWCHAN. You can always drop in, of course, but if your time is limited or you need to work at odd hours, an appointment is smart.

- If your mind is not made up as to which tailor you want to use, spend your first day in Hong Kong visiting shops, looking at the samples, asking questions and feeling goods. Because you should schedule three fittings, you'll need at least three days to have a garment made; five days is preferable. Try to see clothes being fitted on other people, which isn't as hard as it sounds. You don't have to climb into the dressing room, but watch the public waiting area and observe the fit between garment and owner. A well-made garment is worthless if it doesn't flatter the wearer.

- Tailors make tailored clothing best. Don't ask them to make a knit bodysuit or a Diane Freis-style dress with flounces and crystal pleating. Danny Chen will make a bodysuit with finished facing (you must provide the knit; there is none in Hong Kong) at the same charge as a blouse ($75 for labor), but he prefers not to.

- All tailors sell fabric by the yard; the better the tailor, the better the quality and selection of his goods. Be advised that tailors are geared for men's suits and not women's clothing, so fabric choices for ladies can be limited.

- If you bring fabric with you, make sure you have enough. (See our chart on page 230.) If you bring a fabric with nap, a large pattern or a plaid, or if you are larger than size 14, bring more yardage. If you are buying fabric in Hong Kong, it is easiest if you buy from your tailor, but by no means essential. Allow more time so you don't feel pressured. If you bring a pattern with you, look at the fabric chart on the back and figure accordingly. You may want to buy an extra yard, just in case. I looked at the wrong line on a pattern once and had to have a completely different outfit made since I'd goofed and had few choices left.

- Bring your own buttons and trim if you want top-of-the-line polish to your suit. Every tailor in town can make a Chanel-style suit, but none look as classy as the real thing, for lack of proper buttons and trims.

- Have all measurements taken so that you may reorder or have additional items made at a later date without a return trip to Hong Kong. My first suit was a jacket and skirt; I didn't want trousers so we didn't even do those measurements. A year later, when I wanted trousers, it was not so easy. If the measurements existed, I would have been able to fax in an order and have it shipped to me without much ado. Mail delivery from Hong Kong happens to be safe and efficient. Most tailors use air freight, which costs about $50.

- If you care enough to use a master like Danny Chen, have enough sense to listen to what he has to say. He'll make whatever you insist that he make, but if you're smart you'll listen to him before you make a costly mistake. "Suits that look bad have only two problems," he says. "Wrong fabric or wrong style for body." Also listen carefully to what Danny doesn't say. Recently he said to me, "What do you think of your buttons?" What he was really saying is that he thought the buttons I brought with me were wrong for the suit and he wanted me to reconsider. He's a real diplomat, so consider every word.

Fabrications

Fabric Width	Garment	Yardage
44"	long-sleeved dress	4-1/2 yards
44"	blouse	2-1/2 to 3 yards
54"–60"	trousers/woolen	1-1/2 yards
54"–60"	blazer	2 yards
54"–60"	pleated skirt w/jacket	3 to 4-1/2 yards
60" knit	long-sleeved bodysuit	2 yards

Women's Tailors

IRENE'S FASHIONS

In Hong Kong, a city where locals often think Americans are inscrutable, you'll find some unusual marketing practices. Thus it is that W.W. Chan, known as a men's tailor, has a women's division in the same shop, but this tailor has a secondary name (Irene's Fashions), so that customers will know there is a women's tailor on hand. Clothes made at Irene's are made on the premises, which means this is the only one of the Big Three to make women's clothing. Don't mind if some of the women's samples hanging around are a bit dowdy; for the lowdown on having something made here, see page 226.

Since I've now been having my clothes made here for several years, I've a few practices that have worked well: I keep a standard Vogue pattern in Hong Kong. This is a pattern for a dress which covers all my figure flaws and works for all occasions, even sitting on airplanes for twenty hours. I can ask Danny to modify the sleeve or the cut of the skirt or whatever in order to change the dress around a bit (I have six versions of this one dress), but he and I are always speaking the same language since he keeps the pattern.

I've also had coats made: Danny fit me for several different lengths and keeps them on file. That way you can order a coat depending on style plus need. Once you are fitted for a coat, take the time to see where other lengths will hit on your body frame so that you are prepared a few years down the road.

If your weight fluctuates, as mine does, have the tailor keep fat and thin measurements. You can fax information—I'm up or down five pounds, etc. Also have standard styles that will fit under all conditions. My perfect dress has an elastic waist, so I needn't worry about my weight changes too much.

Most important: Give a project plenty of time. The more you put in, the more you communicate, the better your finished garment. You can't go wrong with Danny.

IRENE'S FASHIONS

Burlington Arcade (2nd floor), 92-94 Nathan Road, Kowloon

MODE ELEGANTE

Of all of the zillions of tailors I went to in search of women's clothing, this was the only one that had samples that were not only stunning, but were true fashion and not pale imitations. While I did not have anything made, I was impressed. Furthermore, several of my Hong Kong lady friends—all businesswomen—use this source.

MODE ELEGANTE

The Peninsula Hotel, Salisbury Road, Kowloon

PRINCE'S TAILOR

My friend Isabelle decided on Prince's because her friend living in Hong Kong brought her here. (Do not confuse this resource with Princeton Tailor!) Isabelle was pleased with the work, although one of the skirts she ordered was not in the length she asked for, and she refused to pay for it. (No problem.) The suit she had made was copied from a suit she brought with her, in the tailor's fabric, and consisted of a large blazer with a tiny miniskirt. Since Isabelle is a size 2, she hardly tied up a lot of money in yard goods, and her entire bill for the one finished suit was about $250. This is about half what I pay at IRENE'S FASHIONS, although I require three times the amount of fabric that Isabelle needs.

Of course I needed to inspect her suit immediately and thoroughly to see if there was a bargain to be had. Well, it was nice, but not thrilling. It was better than fine, but it in no way compared with the quality of the W.W. Chan suits I have had made. Furthermore, I think $250 is an awful lot of money for an average suit. I'd rather pay more and have something stunning. But that's just my philosophy.

PRINCE'S TAILOR
Sheraton Hotel, Salisbury Road, Kowloon

Made-to-Measure: Shoes and Leathergoods

If you are a shoe fanatic, read carefully, because there's no business like shoe business in Hong Kong.

First things first: In Hong Kong, shoes are usually sized in the European manner. There are few, if any, women's shoes above a size 40 (U.S. 9-1/2). American and European women with large feet spend a lot of their time in Hong Kong complaining about the difficulties in finding shoes. If you wear a large size, and are in an emergency situation, the good news is that the Marks & Spencer department stores carry large-sized shoes (up to size 10 or 10-1/2). These are private-label, not designer, styles but they are good, "sensible" English shoes, and are reasonably priced at around $50 a pair.

I remain disappointed in the shoes available on Leighton Road in Happy Valley. The shoes are manufactured in Hong Kong and then printed with Italian labels. Expect that they will not last that long. However, at these prices you might not care how long they last. For the most part, these are inexpensive copies of fashion styles. They sell for about $40–$60 a pair.

There are many European shoe boutiques in Hong Kong, and many of them have quality goods at prices about 20% lower than in the U.S. Charles Jourdan has an extensive stock at savings against

U.S. prices. Gucci is more expensive; Bally is about the same. Ferragamo is much more expensive. Go figure.

Finely-crafted leathergoods are available at all the designer boutiques. Shop with a price list from home, lest you overpay.

You may find inexpensive fashion shoes and handbags in Stanley Market; many more inexpensive and imitation designer handbags are sold in the Lanes, but Hong Kong is not headquarters for great, high-quality handbags. There are running shoes galore in Stanley and in most street markets.

I've investigated having shoes made and found it's cheaper to buy a ready-made shoe and not gamble. There are customers who are thrilled with made-to-measure shoes from Hong Kong. I take my big feet to Ferragamo and pay retail. But nothing goes wrong. The latest rumors are that the made-to-measure shoe business is dying in Hong Kong because the last makers have all gone to Japan, where they make more money. It is possible that having shoes made here is no longer as smart as it once was.

Custom-shoe shops usually look like holes in the wall, junked up with dusty shoes. Even the fanciest ones in the fanciest hotels don't look like John Lobb in London. If you really want shoes made, ignore the surroundings and walk in. The shoes you see displayed are samples of what can be made. Some people come to Hong Kong with shoes and ask to have them copied. Others decide once they are there, and have no idea what they want. All of the custom shops have similar policies:

- Once you have decided on a style, a canvas will be made of your foot. This will then be turned into a mold from which the shoe will be made. If the shoemaker you have chosen simply takes measurements, leave. This is not what you are paying for. You won't be happy with the results.

- Unless you specifically ask to pick out your skins, the shoemaker will do it for you. I suggest you pick your own and mark the backs so that no one else will use them. In the case of leather, ask to see the hides and examine the quality. Be able to verify that your skins were indeed used.

- Many kinds of leather or skin are used in making exotic shoes and boots. The following cannot legally be shipped into the U.S.: kangaroo, elephant, shark, antelope, gnu, sea lion, lizard, sea turtle or alligator. Crocodile shoes must enter the U.S. with proper certification.

- The shoemaker usually has a base price list from which he works. A basic pair of men's Cordovans cost $150, say. Then you add the extras. This is especially true of boots, where you might decide to have fur lining ($20), zipper sides ($5), or double leather soles ($4). If a man's foot is bigger than 12-1/2, a special price will be quoted.

- If you are having shoes shipped to you, allow for shipping charges. Surface mail postage for shoes or a handbag should cost $15. Airmail for the same will be $20–$30.

- The shoemaker will want a deposit (at least one-third, possibly one-half) or full payment before he starts to make the shoes. This is often negotiable, depending upon the store.

- If at all possible, pick up your shoes yourself. If they are uncomfortable, it is easier to remedy the problem while you are there.

- Prices vary from $20 to $100 on the same shoe style from shop to shop. Some shops will bargain; others will not.

- Made-to-measure shoes are usually more expensive than U.S. designer or top-of-the-line brand shoes.

I once tried to have shoes and a handbag made in Hong Kong, but after visiting several shops and working with several reputable makers, I gave up. With size 10-1/2B feet—maybe even size 11 (OK, they are a size 11, want to make something of it?)— I found that the risk and expense were just too great. Who needs the extra aggravation on a short trip?

The case of the handbag was even more interesting, because I have a real Chanel bag, and wanted it copied, line for line. My model did not come with Cs embroidered on it in the first place, so I was not talking copyright violation or anything shady. I just wanted the same size and style. Not one of the five places I went to could come up with quality hardware that would make the bag look as expensive as the real thing. They had the leather; they could quilt. They didn't have hardware (without Cs) that could pass muster; the chains were cheap-looking and far too yellow.

For the record, if you are willing to buy fake from the street, there are several dealers in the Lanes with Hermès-style Kelley bags that look great. And word on the street is that fabulous Chanel imitations are yours for a song when you travel to Seoul or Bangkok.

So if you're out doing the town, you may want to try some of these sources:

SAM WO

This is my friend Rose Kettle's source; I've used him enough to know that he's the best in town. Rose has been buying here for years. The deal is strange because Sam's merchandise appears to be the same as everyone else's and his prices are much higher. Then you examine two pieces and see the difference—Sam's quality is much more like the real item.

Furthermore, if you have the time and the inclination, you can tell Sam what you are looking

for and see if he can get it for you. . . .
please.

SAM WO
Li Yuen Street West, Hong Kong

KWONG WING CO.

This is a store behind the stalls in the lower beginning part of the Lanes. It sells pretty much the going thing. Quality is not so high as at Sam's, but prices can be 50% lower. Inspect carefully; note that some of the chains on Chanel bags can be rather yellow and cheap-looking. The Epi-style Vuitton (in colors) comes in a zillion styles and a wide enough price range to allow you to stock up on gifts. However, discriminating shoppers can tell this is not real Vuitton. Still, this is one of the few places in town for this kind of Vuitton look.

KWONG WING CO.
21 Li Yuen Street East, Hong Kong

LEE'S

This stall at the top of Li Yuen Street East sells a great Chanel-style bag for about $15. Honest.

LEE'S
Stall Nos. 58 and 59, Li Yuen Street East, Hong Kong

MAYER SHOE COMPANY

European-styled shoes and handbags sold in such a pleasant atmosphere, without hype, that it is a delight to shop here. They understand the Ralph Lauren school of elegance perfectly. They have shoes in stock or will make a pair for you. Our choice.

MAYER SHOE COMPANY
Mandarin Oriental Hotel, 5 Connaught Road Central, Hong Kong

LILY SHOES

Lily has a huge reputation among Westerners, probably because one of their shops is in the ever-convenient Peninsula Hotel. Prices are high for Hong Kong, but moderate when compared to the rest of the world. (A Chanel-style handbag: $175 from Lily, $795 from Chanel.) They will make women's shoes for about $200 a pair (100£). The store in the Kowloon Hotel Shopping Arcade is always empty and will bargain with you; the one in the Peninsula is mobbed and not too big on customer service. Frankly, they leave me cold. Others have been thrilled.

LILY SHOES
    The Peninsula Hotel, Salisbury Road, Kowloon
    Kowloon Hotel, 19-21 Nathan Road, Kowloon

LEE KEE SHOES AND BOOTS
    Another big name, especially for men's shoes. I've seen nice shoes from this source, but my last visit didn't impress me.

LEE KEE SHOES AND BOOTS
    65 Peking Road, Kowloon

SHOEMAN LAU
    The best bet for men's made-to-measure shoes, with an international reputation to match.

SHOEMAN LAU
    Hyatt Regency Hotel, 67 Nathan Road, Kowloon

VIP SHOES
    Uncle Lennie adores his shoes from here and can't wait to go back for more.

VIP SHOES
    The Regent Hotel Shopping Arcade, Salisbury Road, Kowloon

Big-Name Leathergoods (Not Easily Found in the U.S.)

COMTESSE
    Leathergoods handmade in Germany and considered a major status symbol by both Europeans

and Japanese. If you believe in a very expensive bag that makes a statement, and your goal is to have something different from everyone else's, this store is a must. The line is also sold at Duty-Free Shoppers.

COMTESSE

The Landmark, 16 Des Voeux Road Central, Hong Kong

The Peninsula Hotel, Salisbury Road, Kowloon

PITTI

Pity me, but I've never heard of this Italian-sounding handbag resource where many of the bags aren't even leather—they're linen, raffia, nylon, etc. All are chic, unusual, sort of expensive, but definitely the kind of thing that reminds you why you need to look in a few designer shops in Hong Kong. Several branches around town.

PITTI

Kowloon Hotel, 19-21 Nathan Road, Kowloon

LANCEL

A big name in France, known for well-made handbags and leathergoods that often have the heavy stitching of the chic Country look. Their collection of bags with white stitching on dark leather is timeless. Sold in several Japanese department stores because of the appeal to that market, but also in their own shops, which are either in hotel arcades or in the giant Harbour City malls.

LANCEL

Harbour City/Ocean Terminal, Canton Road, Kowloon

LONGCHAMP

French leathergoods that aren't overdone in the U.S., but are a huge status symbol in parts of the Orient. Their refined sporty elegance gets a lot of attention. The rich man's Dooney & Bourke.

LONGCHAMP
   The Regent Hotel, Salisbury Road, Kowloon
   The Peninsula Hotel, Salisbury Road, Kowloon

LOEWE
   They are standing three deep at the counters, and they are not American.

LOEWE
   The Landmark, 16 Des Voeux Road Central, Hong Kong
   The Peninsula Hotel, Salisbury Road, Kowloon
   The Regent Hotel, Salisbury Road, Kowloon

Dress-Up Handbags

ASHNEIL
   The neighborhood is convenient enough, but slightly offbeat; the building is actually frightening. Never mind. When you get inside Ashneil and see the Judith Leiber look-alike merchandise, you will be happy you came here.
   If the address isn't familiar, this street is right off Nathan Road a half block from the Regent and right behind The Sheraton. Easy as pie.

ASHNEIL
   Far East Mansion (first floor), 5-6 Middle Road, Kowloon

FINE 'N RHINE
   You won't believe this, but in the space of one week I got two different unsolicited letters from readers, both recommending this source. This happens to be around the corner from Far East Mansion and the other "Judith Leiber" source; it is not in Tsim Sha Tsui East, which is what I thought at first. Mody Road is the main drag in Tsim Sha Tsui East, but it begins right at Nathan Road. This address is in the first block.
   Besides handbags, they also have a selection of belts.

FINE 'N RHINE
15 Mody Road (first floor), Kowloon

Jewelry and Gemstones

Hong Kong trades every variety and quality of gemstone. It is the fifth-largest diamond-cutting center in the world. The money changing hands in this industry totals billions of dollars per year.

The good news about buying gemstones in Hong Kong is that you can bring them (unset) back to the U.S. for a negligible duty (or for no duty at all). The bad news is that finding good stones requires a Ph.D. in gemology.

The jewelry and gemstone businesses are separate, and converge only at the wholesale level, where you will never be admitted without a bona fide dealer. If you are serious about buying stones, you should be introduced to the wholesale dealers. This requires personal contact from a dealer here, or from a friend who is Chinese and living in Hong Kong. It is a very tight business. Don't expect to just walk into a shop off the street and see the best stones or get the best prices.

There is risk in every purchase, but if you are dealing with a reputable jeweler that risk is minimized. Reputation is everything. If you are looking for good pearls, diamonds, opals, jade or ivory, educate yourself first. Take the time to learn before you leap.

Jewelry

Jewelry is the word I use to describe decorative baubles made of gold and either precious or semiprecious stones. There are almost as many jewelry shops in Hong Kong as there are tailors. As you walk down almost any street in Hong Kong, your eyes are constantly drawn to windows full of magnificent pins, rings and earrings. Much of the Hong Kong jewelry is made with 18K gold, which is popular in Asia. This is a yellower gold than the 14K gold Americans usually prefer. Jewelers used to dealing with overseas clients keep pieces on hand for both markets. Decide which you prefer before you begin serious negotiations on a piece. I usually use 14K because it is less expensive than 18K. Gold will be marked with either a K label or, alternately, "375" (9K), "585" (14K), or "750" (18K).

One of the best buys in the jewelry field is in custom-made pieces. If you have a favorite Tiffany, Harry Winston or Van Cleef & Arpels catalog, take it with you. A good jeweler can translate any basic design into something just for you—at half the cost.

Jewelry can obviously be bought in branch stores of internationally famous jewelers such as CARTIER, VAN CLEEF & ARPELS, etc. These businesses have set prices, which may be geared for the businessman or Japanese customer who is willing to pay top dollar: Price at home first. If you've come to Hong Kong with plans to save money on jewelry, you probably are not looking to do business with the branch stores.

Also remember LANE CRAWFORD: It's expensive, but it has a fine reputation and a guarantee on whatever you buy.

- Look at many things in the shop, both expensive and inexpensive. This allows you to assess the range, the workmanship and possibly how fair the pricing system is, and if there's any give from the jeweler. You never know what the jeweler will use as a promotion piece in order to get you going as a client.
- Ask questions. If the jeweler is not willing to spend time with you, leave.
- Negotiate prices on a few items before you get down to business on the one that you really want. If the jeweler knows that you are

looking for a good price at the beginning, the process will happen faster.

- Ask if you can get an outside appraisal of the piece of jewelry that you are considering. If the jeweler hesitates, question why.
- Remember that you will pay duty on set versus unset stones coming into the U.S. Use this as a negotiating tool.
- Always get a written certification of the gold content of your piece of jewelry. This is important for insurance and Customs.
- Also get a receipt from the store, quoting the exact price that you paid. Don't leave it up to U.S. Customs to evaluate your goods.
- If you choose to have the jewelry sent to you, confirm that it will be insured, and for how much.
- If you are buying a piece of jewelry with large stones, have a separate appraisal done on them. It should include a photograph and a detailed description of each stone.

Expensive Jewelry

GEMSLAND

A great source for custom work, pearls and set pieces at fair prices. Ask for Richard Chen or his mother, Mrs. Helen Chen. Judith got this source from a friend of hers years ago; Richard Chen has been our regular jeweler in Hong Kong for many years. He carries many classic ready-made pieces suitable for international clientele, or he will custom-make your order in five to seven days.

GEMSLAND
Mandarin Oriental Hotel, 5 Connaught Road Central, Hong Kong

KEVIN

This shop on the Golden Mile has some very unusual and creative pieces of jewelry. Not the usual stuff you see in the hotel arcade shops. For the person who wears the jewelry and doesn't let the jewelry wear her.

KEVIN
Holiday Inn Golden Mile, 50 Nathan Road, Kowloon

LARRY JEWELRY
This jeweler specializes in glitzy and large pieces for the Texas-Palm Beach-L.A. new-money crowd. Not for the British at all. Several branch stores.

LARRY JEWELRY
The Landmark (Shop G49-50), 16 Des Voeux Road Central, Hong Kong
The Mall at Pacific Place (Shop 232), 88 Queensway, Hong Kong
Harbour City/Ocean Terminal (Shop 239), Canton Road, Kowloon

RICCO RICCO
Very Italianate styling in gold or gold with diamonds, much more suited for European taste and big spenders who like fancy, glitzy shops.

RICCO RICCO
The Mall at Pacific Place (Shop 341), 88 Queensway, Hong Kong

RONALD ABRAM
Rare jewels for the connoisseur; prices to match.

RONALD ABRAM
Prince's Building (Shop 128), Chater Road, Hong Kong

KAI YIN LO
Hong Kong's best with an ethnic flavor that's both serious and fun. Her designs using gold and semiprecious gemstones are unique in Hong Kong and sold worldwide. You will save money by buying in Hong Kong. Several branch stores.

KAI YIN LO
 The Peninsula Hotel, Salisbury Road, Kowloon
 Mandarin Oriental Hotel (mezzanine), 5 Connaught Road Central, Hong Kong
 The Mall at Pacific Place, 88 Queensway, Hong Kong

Not-So-Expensive Jewelry

PAN AM PEARLS

Another of Rose's finds and a serious winner in my book, although I did get one letter from a reader who had confusion with pricing and her bill. So pay attention in your dealings; you can come away as happy as I have been.

I have been here numerous times and had a variety of experiences: One or two times the help was not very friendly and would not give me very good service. (Don't go on a Sunday for that reason.) Other times, they couldn't be nicer—and I could bargain and buy and get a gift with purchase (an enamel ring worth exactly $10 H.K.).

I have seen fluctuations in quality according to stock. Never since have I been able to match my double strand, 8 mm job which cost me $40 three years ago. However, all the faux pearls we bought from here are about the best I've seen at these prices, and I still think this is one of my single best sources in Hong Kong.

A strand of pearls runs about $20 per; they will string together several strands into a single necklace with a new clasp as you wait. Baroque pearls are also available. Susan Granger bought lovely matinee-length pearl and "malachite" necklaces at $15 per strand; when I went to look at them, I was not as pleased with the quality as Susan was—or she got to a better batch than I did.

This is right near the Hyatt Regency Hong Kong, so don't let the address throw you. It is upstairs; take the stairs if the elevator looks too rickety for your taste. They also sell some souvenir-type gifts. Be sure to ask for a silk pouch for each item you buy.

PAN AM PEARLS
   9 Lock Road, Kowloon

AXESSORIUM

With several shops around town, this tiny chain can give you the Chanel-type look in affordable variations. A few years ago, I found a necklace of pearls as big as golf balls—the kind that I had only seen in French *Vogue*—for $60: not cheap, but a fair price. Earrings begin around $25, but go to $50 rather rapidly. There are also belts and hair accessories.

AXESSORIUM
   Harbour City/Ocean Terminal, Canton Road, Kowloon
   Prince's Building, Chater Road, Hong Kong
   Houston Centre, 63 Mody Road, Kowloon

Made-to-Measure Jewelry

With a treasure trove of unset gems just growing old in the underwear drawer, I decided to take some gemstones (bought in Brazil) to Hong Kong and have them made into jewelry. The results were incredible.

I chose GEMSLAND partly because of the recommendation of a friend (Judith), but also because I liked the fact that they weren't so top-of-the line, so fancy you would be intimidated, or so low and funky that you were frightened.

For my first piece, I walked into the shop in the Mandarin Oriental Hotel without an appointment and with my then-ten-year-old. Out came the gemstones and the opinions as to what should be done. My suite of three green tourmalines, two matched ovals and one larger stone, emerald-cut was laid out—I wanted them in one ring, although there was much discussion as to whether or not that was wise. Some were for making them into earrings plus a ring; earrings plus a choker; a ring on prongs; a ring with diamonds; etc.

Finally we were given some clay and started playing with the stones in the clay, molding a ring. A price was quoted ($350), we nervously nodded a go-ahead, and we left.

The next three days were not easy. What if it was ugly? What if I didn't like it? Finally, the big moment. We arrive. We sit. A small silk pouch is brought out. Then the ring is revealed: It is far more gorgeous than ever anticipated!

It also looks far different from what I think we designed. But who cares?

For $350, this is the best bargain in Hong Kong. I pay with American Express plastic so as to gain ninety days' free insurance on the Purchase Protection Plan. Simple enough.

Next trip: I fax for an appointment; I call from the hotel to say I am on my way; they are waiting. I bring Ian (photographer's eye) and another stash of gemstones from Brazil.

Richard Chen takes a good hard look at my best stone, a large citrine, and announces that it is probably a fake. We discuss whether or not to use it. We decide to go ahead, who really cares?

Ian, Richard and I arrange the stones in various positions and decide on a bar pin, estimated price to be "no more than $200." I go for 14K gold.

I get the piece five days later; it's very nice. I get the bill: $230. I do not say anything, but pay it. This time I get air miles on American Express.

Pearls

If you are searching for pearls and pearls alone, you will have many options. Every jewelry store has them in the window. The question is, Whom do you trust? When we were doing our research for Born to Shop: Tokyo, we were told that all the pearls that make it to Hong Kong are the rejects from Tokyo. It is true that pearl prices in Tokyo are higher than in Hong Kong, but we don't believe that all the pearls are inferior. The story does, however, point out that some jewelers might be selling inferior quality. Also, whiter pearls are more prized in Hong Kong than pinker or yellower pearls, and are therefore the most expensive.

The bigger jewelry shops are a safe bet for buying quality pearls. The price tag will be higher than on the street, but you have some assurance that, should you have a problem with your second appraisal back home, they will make amends. The following are all considered reputable shops for pearls:

TRIO PEARL

One of the best places to go to in Hong Kong is Trio, whose reputation for high prices and higher quality is well-known.

TRIO PEARL
The Peninsula Hotel, Salisbury Road, Kowloon

GEMSLAND

Richard Chen or his mother, Helen, are happy to spend hours rolling pearls to find the best ones. We even know people who mail-ordered pearls and were happy with the quality.

GEMSLAND
Mandarin Oriental Hotel, 5 Connaught Road Central, Hong Kong

K.S. SZE & SONS

This showroom is so swank it might make you nervous to enter, although it looks fancier from the windows than it does inside. It is a few doors from Gemsland. While they also sell diamonds and gemstones, they are also well-known for the quality of their pearls and the fairness of their prices.

K.S. SZE & SONS

Mandarin Oriental Hotel, 5 Connaught Road Central, Hong Kong

Opals

I have only one suggestion when it comes to buying opals: Buyer beware. Opals are mined in Australia, among other places, and brought to Hong Kong to be cut, polished and shipped out again. Considering this, it is surprising that there are not more opal stores. You will see opals in fine jewelry stores, but you will not see many. One company in particular, OPAL CREATIONS, has cornered the tourist opal trade. They have set up one shop in Burlington Arcade, 92-94 Nathan Road, Kowloon, that is a re-creation of an opal mine, with illustrations and samples of what to look for and what not to look for. It is informative and fun, especially if you are with children. The mine opens up into the (surprise!) retail store with opal choices galore. There are big stones and little stones, set stones and unset stones. All the opals are guaranteed to be authentic and not tampered with in any way. Prices are high, and the sales pitch is strong, but for small pieces, there are many choices. Comparison-shop elsewhere before coming, and then bargain once you are there. Remember, it is easy to be duped when it comes to opals.

Diamonds

Diamonds come into Hong Kong duty-free from around the world. It is one of the world's largest diamond-trading areas. If you wish to buy diamonds, check with the Hong Kong Tourist

Association, which publishes a list of some 200 jewelers they recommend. Also contact the DIAMOND IMPORTERS ASSOCIATION OF HONG KONG LTD., Diamond Exchange Building (Room 401), 8-10 Duddell Street, Hong Kong, for their list of authorized agents. The Diamond Importers Association also publishes a variety of educational leaflets that you can send for ahead of your trip. Or call 523-5497 when you are in Hong Kong.

When looking for diamonds, judge their value by the four Cs—Cut, Clarity, Color and Carat. The cut of the diamond is determined by your personal choice. No one cut is more valuable than others, although the round cut is the most classic and salable because it allows for the most brilliance and fire. Clarity in a diamond is judged by absence of inclusions, then number, size and position of existing inclusions. A "flawless" diamond is unusual.

Color is an important factor in the value of the stone. A perfect blue-white stone is the most valuable. The more intense the color, the higher the price. Colorless diamonds are rare.

Carat is the weight of the stone. One carat equals 1/5 gram. Price goes up as carat weight increases. There are 100 points per carat. A 4.02 carat stone would weigh 4 carats 2 points. A flawless stone larger than 1 carat is considered of investment quality, because of its rarity.

Before you buy any stone, get an independent appraisal done by the GEMOLOGICAL LAB OF HONG KONG, Luk Hoi Tong Building, 31 Queen's Road Central, Hong Kong. It usually takes five working days to certify a diamond. It's worth the time to make sure that you don't get caught buying a cubic zirconia at a diamond price.

Should you prefer cubic zirconia to diamonds, BLUNCO is a well-known source in Hong Kong—see them at Hanley House, Flat B (13th floor), 68-80 Canton Road, Kowloon.

Watches

I went to Hong Kong wearing my broken (but genuine) Gucci watch with the thought of having it fixed or buying a new one. Since it was either stolen from my wrist or I accidentally knocked the clasp (sure) and it fell off, I did not have a chance to get it fixed, and I quickly soured on the idea of buying a new one. After my adventure trying to buy a fax (see page 56), I was terrified of any experience in which I might be taken.

Certainly there are plenty of watches for sale in Hong Kong, real and fake. Or as they say on the street, "Copy watch, lady?" The trick is finding the right watch at the right price. You can pay anything from $50 to $10,000. If you are in the market for an international brand of watch, you are wisest to go to one of the authorized dealers for that brand. They are all listed in the phone book as well as through the Hong Kong Tourist Association. All of the companies expect to lower their prices by 10%. You might expect to get an even better discount if you pay in cash.

If you are looking to buy a fun or interesting watch, but don't care if it's a name brand, there are some things to be aware of before you buy:

- Check to see that the whole watch and not just the movement was made by the manufacturer. A common practice in Hong Kong is to sell a Swiss watch face and movement with a Hong Kong-made bracelet. The bracelet is probably silver with a gold plating. This can work to your advantage if you do not want to spend $5,000 for a solid-gold watch but want the look. A reputable dealer will tell you that this is what you are buying, and price the watch accordingly. These watches can cost anywhere from $150 to $400. We have found that you have the greatest bargaining power in this area, because the profit for the watchmaker is so high. On the other hand, dealers of name-brand watches have a limited play in their prices.

- Check the serial number on the inside movement with the serial number of your guarantee. If you do not receive a worldwide guarantee, don't buy the watch.

- If you are buying from a name-brand dealer, do the same careful checking as if you were buying from a small no-name shop on the street. We know of someone who bought a name-brand watch from a reputable dealer, got the watch home, and had problems. When she went to the U.S. dealer for that name, they told her that yes, indeed, she had bought one of their name watches, but the movement was five years old. She had bought a current body with a used movement!

- If it's not necessary that you find a name-brand watch, and you are simply looking for something unusual and fun, try the following:

CITY CHAIN: This is a popular chain that carries Seiko, Bulova and Zenith among their name brands. They also carry fashion watches like Smash (a takeoff of Swatch). There's a branch of this huge chain in every mall and shopping district.

SWATCH SHOP: 502 Hennessy Road (ground floor), Hong Kong (MTR: Causeway Bay). Swatch is a big seller in Hong Kong. Prices are no cheaper than in the U.S., but you might see some different styles.

For a list of authorized sole agents of big-time watchmakers and their phone numbers, see the back pages of the free HKTA booklet on shopping.

Cameras

Buying a camera in Hong Kong is confusing unless you are quite knowledgeable about the equipment and comparable prices. Every year there are new top-of-the-line models available in every brand, and they're all for sale in Hong Kong. Most shopkeepers will tout what they have in stock, and not necessarily what you need.

Since Ian is a Time-Life photographer, I sent him out to hunt down both used and new cameras. His report:

- Avoid the dealers on Nathan Road. Period. They're more expensive than need be and they will cheat you whenever possible. Price cameras from shops in Western, Central (there's a few on Stanley Street) and from Kimberley Road in Kowloon—this is right off Nathan Road, it's no trouble at all in finding it—they are much more professional.

- Bring prices and style numbers from home; a newspaper clipping with advertised prices is also a good idea.

- Ask if you can test cameras before you purchase them. There is a Canon showroom in the Silvercord Building where you can test various models. You must supply your own film.

- Once you are quite sure of what you want, price-shop. Try several different stores and bargain as if you were going to buy. Don't buy until you have spent several days getting used to Hong Kong and to the way the camera stores do business. Be prepared to spend a lot of time at this; it's not enough to just "dash in"; work several districts of town and keep a chart or pages in your notebook or Filofax on each possibility.

After you have decided where you are going to buy, insist on the following:

- Each piece of equipment needs its own (worldwide) warranty. The serial number of the piece must be clearly marked on the card, along with the agent's stamp and a complete address of where you purchased the item.

- Make sure you are not being charged for extras that should have been included in the original purchase. For example, camera cases usually come with the camera. You should not pay extra for the case.

- Watch your purchase being packed, and check each item as it goes into its box. Don't trust the store owner to pack and deliver your purchase to the hotel. When you get back you might discover that a few small items somehow got lost.

- Keep your receipts separate. Customs most likely will not want to open and go through all of your equipment if your receipts are clear and in order.

- For the name of an authorized importing agent for a name-brand camera, call the Consumer Council at 736-3322.

Used Cameras

There's an entire arcade of camera dealers who specialize in used equipment (Champagne Court in Kowloon); some items are so new that dealers from Nathan Road come here and buy them and then pass them off as new at manufacturer's prices. Ian has made several trips here on each visit to Hong Kong and has had varied results: When he priced camera bodies, he found them outrageously high. Yet certain lenses were a steal, especially compared to London prices, which on camera equipment are higher than New York's.

DAVID CHAN COMPANY

The HKTA found this resource for Ian and he has done a fair amount of business with them. Luck is a major factor here, as they must have in stock what you are looking for and you must be pleased with the condition. They sell used modern and antique models as well as film and camera supplies. Film prices are 20% less than on Nathan Road.

DAVID CHAN COMPANY
Champagne Court (Shop 15), 16 Kimberley Road, Kowloon

KIMBERLEY CAMERA CO. LTD.
Resource for new and used models; locations on both sides of the harbor. Bigger and more touristy than David Chan.

KIMBERLEY CAMERA CO. LTD.
Champagne Court (Shop 2), 16 Kimberley Road, Kowloon
48 Stanley Street, Hong Kong

LI BROTHERS
This resource has most things put away and sells supplies in bulk. They are happy to deal with pros.

LI BROTHERS
Champagne Court (Shop 13), 16 Kimberley Road, Kowloon

Film and Processing

Ian uses a professional lab in Hong Kong; I've used various one-hour facilities for my snapshots, and the professional lab. The professional lab charges twice as much as everyone else for snapshots, so buyer beware.

Most hotels have film processing services available; the Peninsula offers one-hour service; the price for developing 36-print exposures is about $12. The Hilton uses a service which charges more or less the same amount, but slightly less in H.K. dollars, so it's a few cents cheaper in American dollars. The hotel prices are competitive with outside services and far less expensive than the professional lab!

You may pay for developing only (usually about $1.50) and then pay per print—about 25 cents. Or select a flat rate for processing and printing. There are no deals by which you get a second set of prints for free or for a reduced price. Film may be sold at a reduced rate or promotional rate if you buy two rolls or more. Color print film is about half the price of slide film. Prices on film are no better in Macau, by the way.

Ian shoots almost exclusively Fuji film; he has had trouble buying RDP (professional film) in Hong Kong. Regular Fuji film can be bought at 20% less than tourist prices at any of the many dealers in Champagne Court, the photo supply arcade at 16 Kimberley Road in Kowloon.

Ian finds prices for professional processing and printing to be half those in London and less expensive than New York as well, but warns readers that throughout the world, professional processing is almost always going to be more expensive than regular processing.

ROBERT LAM

This is a professional lab with a few branches in Hong Kong, as well as one in Singapore. They handle the bulk of the professional work in Hong Kong; i.e., "everyone" uses them. Including Ian Cook. They processed the film for the cover of this book. They will also process snapshots, but be advised that prices are less expensive elsewhere and the quality does not appear to be that much greater—on my snapshots, anyway. We paid $114 H.K. for one roll of snapshots; The Pen charges $87 H.K. for the same job and delivers to your room! Lam does take credit cards. There is a small selection of Kodak film only.

Now then, let's say you have your film processed via a less-expensive firm and you see that you have a sensational shot or two that you want blown up to perhaps 8"×10". Take the negative to Robert Lam, and you will get better prices on a print (which can be backed on foam core) than you would get at a professional lab in the U.S. However, the price may be more expensive than some of the cut-rate print deals you can get in the U.S. at non-professional labs. It's all a matter of what kind of quality you want.

The main office is listed below; it is in the boonies.

ROBERT LAM

116-120 Canton Road (ground floor), Kowloon

80 Jaffe Road (ground floor), Wan Chai, Hong Kong (MTR: Wan Chai)

Main office: Robert Lam Building, 22 Lee Chung Street (fourth floor), Chai Wan, Hong Kong (MTR: Chai Wan)

FOTOMAX

There are scads of these one-hour developing booths all over town; I use the one at Star House near the Star Ferry, because it's incredibly convenient. They do give you discount coupons with your first order, so you can better regular prices thereafter. They also sell film at uptown tourist prices.

FOTOMAX

Star House (Shop 6), Canton Road, Kowloon

Computers and Small Electronic Devices

There's one important thing to say about buying computers: EAST ASIA COMPUTER PLAZA, in the basement of the Silvercord Building, 30 Canton Road, Kowloon. Period, the end (well, sort of the end). This is the place to go to, to be safe. Silvercord is a rather boring office building with some fairly decent shopping at street level (Chinese Arts & Crafts has a store here) and some good shops on the mall levels. Downstairs is computer city. There are authorized dealers here for most of the big names in the computer world.

There are bookstores (try LEED & WOOD CO. LTD., Silvercord Building, Kowloon) that sell software programs and have information galore. We admit that the software we priced offered no savings over U.S. discount prices (unless you get lucky); there were some savings over British prices. You can get fax machines, laptops and typewriters with memories. The question is whether you want to or not. (After getting burned on my fax experience I remained shy, but had I come here in the first place, things probably would have gone a whole lot better.)

The big names like Apple, IBM and NEC are sold at authorized stores in the East Asia Computer Plaza. You can haggle and bargain...possibly even make a good deal. Make sure, however, that the machine you buy is wired to work on the voltage where you will be using it. The Hong Kong voltage is 220, while standard voltage in the U.S. is 110. Don't let a salesperson convince you that a converter will do. Computers are much too sensitive, and you don't want to risk losing your program because of a power failure. Also make sure that the equipment you buy will work with the monitor you have at home.

If you are a little more adventurous, take the MTR to Sham Shui Po to visit the GOLDEN ARCADE SHOPPING CENTRE, 44B Fuk Wah Street. My friend Roger, age 14, says this place is "wild." He's right!

This area is not known for its tourist appeal; it's filled with street stalls selling blue jeans for $5, T-shirts, bed linens, ducks and roosters. The street odor is strong. People are jammed into every nook and cranny of the area. In the midst of this craziness is the Golden Arcade Shopping Centre, a supermarket filled with computer hardware, software and educational material.

As you get out of the MTR you will be right there...Just look up to see the arcade marquee.

There is a directory listing all 120 shops, but it really doesn't matter. The only way to shop here is to wander and compare. Each shop has a different type of computer, and many if not most of them are clones.

You have to know your stuff. If you speak Cantonese, it will help as well. But don't be intimidated; even if you don't buy anything, this is the place to go. If you are with men or boys who disdain your desire to shop, send them here for a half day while you take off for outlets unknown. This is such a scene that anyone will enjoy observing it or getting wrapped up in the motion.

Important note: If you buy, please take the time to open the package and run the program right there in the store. One of our readers found that half the program would not boot. They ran a new copy for him on the spot. This is definitely a bargain-hard shopping environment for smart shoppers only.

Video Games

If you are related in any way to a child under the age of 14, you are probably shopping for video games. Please see our expert's assessment of the Hong Kong Nintendo situation, on page 147.

Technologically speaking, the things a not-too-plugged-in parent needs to know are: Game Boy game cassettes are international in form, and they fit the U.S. and Asian machines interchangeably. Nintendo, on the other hand, has a Japanese system and an American system, as well as a laser disc system (a whole other story, but a hot item to think about). Most of the Nintendo game cartridges sold in Hong Kong are for the Japanese system. However, you can buy a plastic converter for about $8–$10. You only need one converter, although we have heard of some cases when the converter simply didn't work. So to be safe, we bought three; they all worked. Sega fits with a converter as well. (Different converter.)

While local talent has not figured out how to bootleg American-style games, there are plenty of inexpensive Japanese versions on sale. The average price of an American game system is $45; a Japanese game is $30, and a bootleg copy can cost as little as $15. Game Boy cassettes sell for about $25 in the U.S. and $15–$20 in Hong Kong. Prices should be negotiable according to how many you buy. They do sell some Nintendo products at the Hong Kong airport.

Most camera and/or small electronics stores sell video games. Japanese department stores have huge selections of games (your kids do not care if the instructions are written in Japanese), but prices tend to be slightly higher than at camera shops. Japanese department stores do sell all versions of the games, including the newer laser disc system.

If you are looking to buy game programs for a PC, shop very carefully. I priced "Where in the World Is Carmen San Diego?" and found Hong Kong to be more expensive than home. Prices may be competitive to London.

Peter Chan's best source for video games is: MASSKEY DEVELOPMENT LTD., Golden Arcade Shopping Centre, 152 Fuk Wah Street, Sham Shui Po, Kowloon. (MTR: Sham Shui Po)

On a much smaller scale, in the realm of touristy shops that also sell video games, I've done well at RICKY LAU, Haiphong Alley, Kowloon. For Nintendo games (Japanese-style) I pay $25, tops.

Optical Goods

In the olden days, Hong Kong was a bonanza of inexpensive eyeglass frames, optical care and contact lenses. No more. While you can still find

inexpensive frames in the $30–$50 [...]
plete pair of glasses is likely to co[...]
thing as what you pay at home at your [...]
chain or discount service center. And if anything
goes wrong at home, you can return to the shop
and have it fixed.

Prices for contact lenses are identical to what I
pay in the U.S.

The clever item to buy is a pair (maybe many
pairs) of fold-up reading glasses. Susan Granger
sent me in search of a pair; she says she pays
about $55 in Hong Kong. I went to my regular eye-
wear source, THE OPTICAL SHOP, where the slim-
line fold-ups were $125—and that's without a pre-
scription!

I just about gave up on the project, until I was
walking along Shanghai Street in Yau Ma Tei on
my way to the Jade Market, when lo and behold,
there was a man seated on the pavement with his
stash of fold-up reading glasses. His price? $10 a
pair! Glasses were available in various strengths;
the vendor provided a fresh chamois wipe with
each pair we bought. I gave a pair to Mike and to
Ian—both were thrilled. This is a great gift for
someone at home, as long as you know what
strength to buy.

Fabrics and Notions

As one of the ready-to-wear manufacturing
capitals of the world, Hong Kong has more fabrics
and notions than just about any other city we've
seen. Prices for even the most luscious Chinese or
Japanese silks are reasonable, although Chinese
silk is much less expensive than Japanese. (Japanese silks are much more intricately printed; the
Chinese rarely run multiple screens on their silks.)

There are two basic fabrics-and-notions neighborhoods: Jardine's Bazaar and the Lanes. When
you go to Jardine's Bazaar, weave in and around

all the little streets behind the market itself; you'll find numerous fabrics, notions and yarn shops with incredibly low prices. The cloth dealers of Wing On Street have moved to Western Market; I don't really think you want to make the trip here just for fabric. But if you're in the area anyway, by all means, stop by.

Wool and synthetic wool yarns are very inexpensive in Hong Kong. You'll find some excellent knitting shops in the Lanes, and there are several in Causeway Bay.

You can buy fabrics from most tailors; there's a large selection of Chinese silks in all Chinese Arts & Crafts stores. A nice silk runs about $25 per yard. This happens to be the same price we pay in New York. Bespoke tailors always have a large selection of fabrics for men's suits and shirts, but you cannot buy these goods off the bolt. For the truly fashion-conscious woman, it might be easier to bring fabrics from home.

Raw silk is available at most Chinese department stores and costs about $15 a yard. This is comparable to the U.S. price, but the color selection may be better in Hong Kong. Brides, note: White-and-cream raw silk gowns are "in" (in the U.S.). You can indeed have a wedding gown made in Hong Kong.

Please note that some U.S. cities have discount fabric dealers who sell designer cuts. I buy fabrics in New York and bring them with me to Hong Kong. This takes up room in the suitcase, but saves money. Besides, I seem to have no trouble filling that space on my return trip.

Embroidery and Whitework

For centuries, the Chinese have been famous for their embroidery. There are several styles to choose from: with colored silk threads and with white cotton thread; white thread used on white linen or cotton is called whitework.

Antique embroidered goods are quite valuable and are more likely to be found on Hollywood Road, at Charlotte Horstmann (see page 283) or in antiques stores where slippers, collars and possibly even robes are sold. New versions of tablecloths, napkins, place mats, sweaters, jackets and fabric purses are all sold with embroidery. In terms of quality, you'll do better with antique handwork or newly-made whiteworks.

Whiteworks with cutouts are called drawnwork. The best drawn embroidery is supposed to come from Swatow in China. There is also a huge business coming out of Shanghai and may cost the same in Hong Kong as it does in your hometown.

Be careful to learn the look of hand embroidery versus machine embroidery. The goods coming out of Shanghai are new and machine-made. In fact, most of the shop goods are machinemade. Hand embroidery is very expensive. If you want finely crafted pieces, try:

HANDART EMBROIDERIES

This shop offers a particularly good selection of bed linens, place mats and doilies.

HANDART EMBROIDERIES
Hing Wai Building, 36 Queen's Road Central, Hong Kong

THE CHINESE BAZAAR

This store offers a good selection in table linens, napkins, coasters and children's clothing. They have been in business since 1905.

THE CHINESE BAZAAR
Prince's Building, Chater Road, Hong Kong

LACE LANE

My pick for selection and service. The handsmocked dresses for little girls are especially wonderful. They will special-order for you; they will ship to the U.S. I found linen of a quality here that I couldn't find anywhere else in town.

LACE LANE

Silvercord Building, 30 Canton Road, Kowloon

Wing On Plaza, 62 Mody Road, Tsim Sha Tsui East, Kowloon

WAH SING LACE COMPANY

On Lan Street is a short block full of wholesalers and manufacturers. Not all may offer retail, but this is a good lane for finding bargains. Wah Sing manufactures and does export, in case you want to buy lots.

WAH SING LACE COMPANY

7 On Lan Street, Hong Kong

KAI WAH HANDICRAFT

Don't pass this resource by, although it may seem like a typical little shop, no different from a zillion others. I find the help lacking in manners and unwilling to bargain or deal in any way. Yet I keep returning to buy because of the selection and styles; if you want whitework that is not duded up with flowers and too much embroidery, if you like simple and plain but very nice, this is one of the few sources where you can find it. Also note the Christmas ornaments: For $10 U.S. you get a box of four needlepoint old-fashiony Father Christmas figures (each different) made in the British tradition. Because of the convenient location at the corner of Nathan Road, you can easily dart in.

KAI WAH HANDICRAFT

Sheraton Hotel, Salisbury Road, Kowloon

Please note that good drawnwork is getting harder and harder to find. Young people don't want to do it (wrecks the eyes) and shipment and business procedures from China are dicey, so orders don't come in when anticipated. If you find the real thing, expect to pay dearly for it. Once you have seen finely-made, hand-bound cutwork or drawnwork, you will laugh at what is generally sold in markets, Chinese department stores and crafts stores. Also please see our Bed N Bath Rule of Shopping (page 9), because you may find mass-produced whitework in the U.S. for less than it costs in Hong Kong.

It's very hard to quote prices and remain accurate as the world turns, but we admit that in almost all cases we thought prices for whitework and embroidery in Hong Kong were expensive, especially when compared to the quality we were offered. Expect to pay about $25–$35 for a set of four place mats with napkins. The higher price is for more details, cuts or embroidery.

Needlepoint

One of my great disappointments is that so far we cannot find a source for those fabulous Country and quasi-French needlepoint pillows that we all know are coming out of China. Since these cost about $80 as finished pillows in the U.S., we would expect them to be quite affordable in Hong Kong, and would happily buy them even if they were not made up into throw pillows. Alas, the Chinese department stores all have a counter devoted to finished needlepoint canvas scenes, but we are talking styles and designs that are only slightly classier than a portrait of Elvis painted on black velvet. You might luck into the Last Supper, but you will not find florals or anything pretty.

I am also still looking for someone who will finish all the needlepoints I have started and left half-done. If someone can make a suit in three days, someone else should be able to finish a pillow. Stay tuned.

Cosmetics and Fragrances

Cosmetics and fragrances are not as inexpensive in Hong Kong as in Paris, but may be less than in the U.S. and/or U.K. They can also be more. Please note that these are one of the few categories of goods on which local vendors must pay duty, so that cost is passed on to shoppers.

Best buys are scents that have been introduced in Europe, but not in the U.S. So if you want to sniff out the latest, Hong Kong offers you that opportunity. Whether you save or not becomes meaningless because you'll be the first on your block to have the new scent. If you care.

We have comparison-shopped all the big department stores—British, Japanese, Chinese, you name it—and we find that they all have pretty much the same prices. The variation in prices at the duty-free in the airport is mind-boggling. At a certain point I just buy what I want when it seems like a best guess.

Many of the big names have their own outlets or boutiques—you'll buy Chanel makeup in a Chanel boutique; Elizabeth Arden is sold in a special area of Lane Crawford, etc. Department stores have everything, including high prices. Shop carefully.

Take note: Many big-name cosmetics companies manufacture for the Far East in and around Hong Kong; often they will have a product with the same name as the product you use at home, but it will be slightly different. They may also have a product or shade that you will have never heard of and will never find again anywhere else in the world. I bought two Chanel eyeliner pencils at Chanel. They cost $20 each; a slight savings from the U.S. price and a cost equal to that of the duty-free store at the airport. But they were French colors that did not match U.S. colors. I went in looking for "khaki" and came out with "brun magenta"—a completely different shade, of course. I'm nothing if not flexible.

Another note: The large duty-free shop at the airport is well-stocked and easy to shop; pricing is erratic; don't count on the airport being any better than intown.

FANDA PERFUME COMPANY

Longtime basic for those who live here; prices are discounted on many items, including Baededas. The most convenient store in the path of any (and all) shoppers doing Central up right is the one on Pedder Street—it's sort of across the street from the Landmark and down a sneeze from the outlets in the Pedder Building. You can't go wrong.

FANDA PERFUME COMPANY
21 Lock Road, Kowloon
World Wide Plaza, Pedder Street, Hong Kong
Houston Centre, 63 Mody Road, Tsim Sha Tsui East, Kowloon

THE BODY SHOP

I do love this English natural cosmetics line, but British Correspondent Cook says the prices are so outrageously high in Hong Kong that he is offended. Certainly items cost less in the U.K., but if you're American, you'll find it's sort of a toss-up. No bargains, but a standard to live by if you are in need. All the products come in biodegradable containers and are made from natural ingredients. There is a complete line of cosmetics as well as soaps with scents like sandalwood and jasmine. Treat yourself to a bottle of Peppermint Foot Massage Creme after a hard day of bargain hunting. There are branch stores absolutely everywhere.

THE BODY SHOP
The Landmark, Gloucester Tower, 16 Des Voeux Road Central, Hong Kong
The Mall at Pacific Place, 88 Queensway, Hong Kong

SHU UEMURA

Nobody does better colors in eye shadow. Makeup junkies shouldn't miss the opportunity to buy from the Japanese maven of cosmetics and color. Most good Japanese department stores also carry the line. It is available in the U.S., but is hard to find since the New York store closed. There's a store in Paris, but none in London. Load up now. Get a load of the testing center and try on everything to find the colors that suit you best.

SHU UEMURA

The Landmark, 16 Des Voeux Road Central, Hong Kong

DFS

The initials stand for Duty-Free Shoppers (International). These guys own the airport and a lot of Hong Kong as well. Yep, you've even spotted their store in the international part of the San Francisco airport. The stores are enormous and give you the same thrill as shopping at an airport, without the anxiety. Enormous selection of everything including (but not limited to) perfumes, makeup, beauty treatments and more. The main store is in Tsim Sha Tsui East at the ChinaChem Golden Plaza, but there are at least a half dozen other locations around town, including one at the Convention Centre if that's where you hang out.

DFS

Harbour City/Ocean Terminal, Canton Road, Kowloon

WATSON'S, THE CHEMIST

There's a Watson's on almost every big busy block and mall in Hong Kong; I happen to end up at the one around the corner from the Pedder Building, because it's convenient. There's one in Prince's Building and one on Main Street in Stanley. You will have no trouble finding a Watson where the perfumes and makeup departments are rather complete, and frequent promotional deals are similar to ones in the U.S.: if you buy something, you get a gift or extra item.

WATSON'S, THE CHEMIST

24-28 Queen's Road, Hong Kong

SASA COSMETIC COMPANY

This is my favorite new source for makeup and cosmetics, mostly because I am always on Granville Road at least twice a visit to Hong Kong—maybe twice a day. This is a medium-sized, drugstore-type of place that is mobbed with locals who have never seen such a huge selection of American and European brands of cosmetics and health/beauty aids. There are many items you won't see in America and many that could have been relocated right from your hometown drugstore—at higher prices, of course. Revlon nail polish costs $21 H.K., which sounds like a bargain until you convert and discover it's exactly the same price as at home ($3.75). I found my Dune perfume spray for $34 here; it's $38 at Watson's and at most duty-free sources. It's 20£ onboard British Airways. They don't carry Chanel makeup, but they've got tons of everything else. Have a ball.

SASA COSMETIC COMPANY
25 Granville Road, Kowloon

Beauty Salons

Now that I am middle-aged (and Ian is taking my picture), I have come to rely on the services of a local beauty salon. Before I settled on a regular, I polled my girlfriends and the HKTA for the best in town. I continue to use Hair Image (Kenneth or Dibby), but the word is all of these sources are trustworthy.

HAIR IMAGE

Located in the Regent Hotel shopping arcade (but not owned by the Regent), this Western-style, upscale salon has a mixture of local and visiting clientele. If there's a big ball or local do, it may be hard to get an appointment. A wash and blow-dry cost $31. I tip $80 H.K. when I am thrilled, $50 H.K. for an average job. They are open seven days a week! Call for an appointment: 011-852-721-4431.

HAIR IMAGE
The Regent Hotel (ground floor), Salisbury Road, Kowloon

REVER
Many well-known local ladies use this resource, although I haven't tried them. There are a few locations spread out around town, with a concentration closer to Wan Chai and Causeway Bay; there is a Kowloon salon. Call 011-852-730-3139 for the salon closest to your hotel or your day's activities.

REVER
call for closest branch

COMMAND PERFORMANCE
I stumbled on this salon while exploring the Pedder Building; it's funkier than the other two (fer sure), and not tremendously less expensive. Still, convenience is a lot when you travel. Book either a senior stylist, a top stylist or a stylist; get your shampoo and finishing from another ranking of stylists. A manicure is $85 H.K. They are closed Sunday and holidays; Thursday is their late night. They say that they guarantee their services; if you are unhappy they will correct services as needed. For an appointment, call 011-852-526-5471.

COMMAND PERFORMANCE
Pedder Building (Store 105), Pedder Street, Hong Kong

China and Crystal

The largest china and crystal stores are in or near the major hotels and shopping centers. They all ship and take orders from overseas. The only problem arises when the store is out of stock. You can have many dinner parties before your missing pieces arrive. Check on availability before you place your order.

While you may save on pieces you can carry yourself, once you ship, you wipe out any big savings.

BACCARAT
The Landmark (Shop G3-4), 16 Des Voeux Road Central, Hong Kong

CRAIG'S
St. George's Building, 2 Ice House Street, Hong Kong (next to the Mandarin Oriental Hotel)
Harbour City/Ocean Centre (Shop 341), 5 Canton Road, Kowloon
Harbour City/Ocean Terminal (Shop 122A), Canton Road, Kowloon

RICHARD GINORI
The Mall at Pacific Place (Shop 358), 88 Queensway, Hong Kong (MTR: Admiralty)

HUNTER'S
The Peninsula Hotel, Salisbury Road, Kowloon
Harbour City/Ocean Terminal, Canton Road, Kowloon
Kowloon Hotel, 19-21 Nathan Road, Kowloon
Repulse Bay Shopping Arcade, 109 Repulse Bay Road, Hong Kong (MTR: None)
The Mall at Pacific Place (Shops 308 and 309), 88 Queensway, Hong Kong (MTR: Admiralty)

EILEEN KERSHAW
The Peninsula Hotel, Salisbury Road, Kowloon
The Landmark, 16 Des Voeux Road Central, Hong Kong

LALIQUE
The Landmark, 16 Des Voeux Road Central, Hong Kong

LLADRÓ
The Peninsula Hotel, Salisbury Road, Kowloon

272 BORN TO SHOP • HONG KONG

Alexandra House, Des Voeux Road Central, Hong Kong

MEISSEN
The Landmark (Shop G22), 16 Des Voeux Road Central, Hong Kong

RAYNAUD (LIMOGES)
Harbour City/Ocean Terminal (Shop 124), Canton Road, Kowloon
Prince's Building, Chater Road, Hong Kong

ROSENTHAL
Prince's Building, Chater Road, Hong Kong

ROYAL COPENHAGEN
Prince's Building, Chater Road, Hong Kong
Harbour City/Ocean Terminal, Canton Road, Kowloon

ROYAL DOULTON
The Mall at Pacific Place (Shop 366), 88 Queensway, Hong Kong (MTR: Admiralty)

WEDGWOOD
The Landmark (Shop G7A), Gloucester Tower, 16 Des Voeux Road Central, Hong Kong
The Peninsula Hotel, Salisbury Road, Kowloon

Chinese china also is available, and there are many outlets. One of the easiest sources for vases and tea sets is the Chinese department stores. We like CHINESE ARTS & CRAFTS, in either of their stores, at Star House or the Silvercord Building, Kowloon. Also in Kowloon, try CHUNG KIU CHINESE PRODUCTS EMPORIUM, Sands Building, 17 Hankow Road, or YUE HWA, Park Lane Shopper's Boulevard, Nathan Road.

Chinese China

Chinese porcelain factories are a popular shopper's attraction; you can see some of the goods in production if you are interested, or you can just shop until you fill a container.

The factories are not overly easy or convenient to get to, so we suggest that you plan your day around the visit, leave plenty of time and remember that most factories close for lunch, usually between 1 P.M. and 2 P.M.

All Chinese crafts stores have a selection of china; assume that blue-and-white is fake unless guaranteed otherwise. Do check out the numerous porcelain dives as you parade along Hollywood Road (see page 88). Some shops here do specialize in authentic blue-and-white as well as other wares. Talk to Glenn and Lucille at Honeychurch (see page 89) if you need a lesson in buying porcelain.

AH CHOW PORCELAIN

If you are doing an outlet spree in Lai Chi Kok, this is a must; otherwise I'd rather you go to Wah Tung (see below), which is much larger. Ah Chow is a small outlet that has been servicing a lot of U.S. and British department stores for years. They have excellent prices; they ship (it takes years to get your order—or it seems like years); they will do a custom order for you. I have bought from this factory and been thrilled with my purchases.

AH CHOW PORCELAIN

Hong Kong Industrial Centre (Block B, 7th floor), 489-491 Castle Peak Road, Kowloon (MTR: Lai Chi Kok)

WAH TUNG CHINA COMPANY

You have to take a taxi here, or a car, but you can have lunch in Aberdeen (at Jumbo!). This is the single largest source for Chinese porcelain in Hong Kong. They will send a van to pick you up. We rate this as a four-star shopping dream. There are floors of showroom; prices seem to be rather negotiable, depending on how much you buy and how aggressive you feel. I've bought tons from here and loved every minute of it. They ship. They take special orders.

WAH TUNG CHINA COMPANY

Grand Marine Industrial Building, 3 Yue Fung Street, Tin Wan, Aberdeen, Hong Kong

OVERJOY

Located in the heart of Hong Kong's shipping and container district, where there are a few other porcelian showrooms, Overjoy is the single most famous source to those who have been living here for years. Grab a taxi to this industrial area, walk up one flight of stairs; the selection includes both Western and Chinese patterns. Shipping rates are posted; delivery to your hotel in Hong Kong is free.

OVERJOY

Kwai Hing Industrial Building (Block B, first floor), 10-18 Chun Pin Street, Kwai Chung, N.T.

Chops (And We Don't Mean Lamb)

Of course I know what a chop is. It's served for dinner and comes in the pork, veal or lamb category. Right.

It turns out that in China, a *chop* is a form of signature stamp (not made of rubber) on which a symbol for a person's name is carved. The chop is dipped in dry dye (instead of an ink pad) and then placed on paper to create a signature stamp, much like a rubber stamp.

Antiques are quite pricey, depending on age, importance of the carving, materials used and maybe even the autograph that is engraved. New chops have little historic importance, but make great gifts. Some come ready-made in a standard set of Western names; you can have your own carved.

Although chops vary in size, they are traditionally the size of a chessman, with a square or round base. Up to four Chinese characters or three Western initials can be inscribed on the base.

The quality of a chop varies greatly, based on the ability of the person who does the carving. We have done enough chop shopping to know that the very best place to get a chop, if you crave atmosphere, is in Man Wa Lane. It's also the worst place because it is so confusing—you may never find your way back to the proper vendor when you need to pick up your finished chop.

Every hotel has at least one gift shop that will have your chop engraved. (You must allow at least twenty-four hours.) Many shops will provide one-hour service. At Stanley Market you can sometimes get while-you-wait service.

You can buy little pots of the proper dye in any gift shop ($1) or use a regular old ink pad. I bought a pot of sticky dye, which the dealer told me was inferior to the $7 pot of sticky dye, but I refused to believe him. I am sorry now. I ended up at an office-supply store buying a regular old ink pad.

Folk Arts

Hunting down bargains in arts, crafts and antiques is one of our favorite shopping adventures in Hong Kong. Our definition of arts and crafts is broad enough to include handwork of any kind, from hand-carved teaware to cloisonné that has been done within the last 100 years. We include pottery that is original or copies of originals, ivory carvings, jade carvings, handmade dolls and papercuts.

The Hong Kong Tourist Association publishes a list of factories that produce brassware, carpets, carved furniture, Chinese lanterns, pewter and china, and are open to the public.

EILEEN KERSHAW

This shop, in the Peninsula Hotel, is on the upper end of fine arts and crafts stores. In fact, the store is so fancy (they sell Lalique here), that you can't put it in the same category as many other artsy-craftsy stores. Their business card is a three-way foldout with the Chinese dynasties listed along the entire back half. The front has a list of birthstones, in case you want to buy a present for a friend, as well as a place for notes on what you have seen.

The shop is extremely large, but seems less so because there are pieces of stonework, display cases, packing crates and porcelain jars everywhere you look. The sales help is very understanding and pleasant. Prices are average to high. The antique vases are displayed on the highest shelves, so that curious travelers cannot touch. Antique paintings, china, carpets and wall hangings are a large part of the store's business, but do not involve the usual walk-in tourist. If you are interested in a special type of item, ask. The store will do mail-order as well. For the high roller.

EILEEN KERSHAW

The Landmark, 16 Des Voeux Road Central, Hong Kong

The Peninsula Hotel, Salisbury Road, Kowloon

AMAZING GRACE ELEPHANT COMPANY

Amazing Grace carries handcrafted items from all over Asia. You can also buy silk pillow covers, brass carts, bowls, candlesticks, incense burners, jewelry, Korean chests, paper carvings, fans, dolls, bird cages, mirror frames, tea sets and more. This shop has a broad appeal and can be a good source for small, inexpensive gifts items. Branch stores are as far away as Sha Tin or as near as the Excelsior Hotel in Causeway Bay. This is sort of the local version of Pier 1 or even OXFAM.

The warehouse/outlet, in the New Territories, is open to the public. If you are doing serious shopping, it might be worth the drive. You cannot get there any other way but by car, so take that into consideration. We suggest you stop in the Harbour City/Ocean Terminal shop and get directions.

You can also take the KCR to Sha Tin—there's an Amazing Grace at the big mall there—and make a day out of it. Locals use Amazing Grace for inexpensive goods to do up their homes; I think you can buy a lot of this stuff at home, and it's not worth a lot of your attention. But that's just my opinion.

AMAZING GRACE ELEPHANT COMPANY

Harbour City/Ocean Terminal (Shop 348), Canton Road, Kowloon

New Town Plaza (Shop 526), Sha Tin, N.T.

Excelsior Hotel, 281 Gloucester Road, Causeway Bay

YUE KEE CURIO COMPANY

Yue Kee has many options in fine art curios, including carvings, wall pieces, floor pieces, screens and statues. There are also Chinese vases in every size. The shop is very crowded, and we don't suggest that you bring children or large shopping bags. It will take some time to make your mind up here. Yue Kee also has antiques.

YUE KEE CURIO COMPANY

Harbour City/Omni The Hong Kong Hotel Arcade, 2 Canton Road, Kowloon

MOUNTAIN FOLKCRAFT

One of our favorite shops for handcrafted items, Mountain Folkcraft carries a little bit of everything in a small amount of space. It's also got a rather folksy location in an alley with a tiny temple at the corner. This is a much more authentic environment than Amazing Grace, or just about anybody else, although the crafts come from all over Asia and include: batik fabric, boxes, chests, puppets, baskets, toys and pottery. The location is right behind Wellington Street and actually is easy to find.

MOUNTAIN FOLKCRAFT
   12-15 Wo On Lane, Hong Kong

BANYAN TREE LTD.

Banyan Tree is a mass-market kind of handicrafts shop that sells rattan furniture, fabrics, figurines, lamps, porcelains, rugs, screens and hundreds of other items for the home on both a retail and wholesale basis. They have a large exporting business, and can deliver anything you buy to your hometown. We would trust Banyan Tree to pack and ship anything. This is another version, with a slight Martha Stewart bent, in the Pier 1 mold.

BANYAN TREE LTD.
   Harbour City/Ocean Galleries, 25-27 Canton Road, Kowloon
   Prince's Building, Chater Road, Hong Kong

CHUNG KIU CHINESE PRODUCTS EMPORIUM

This smallish department store inside the Sands Building in Tsim Sha Tsui has four floors, three of which are devoted to handicrafts products. On the main floor look for jade, cloisonné, ivory and semiprecious stone carvings. Upstairs there is jewelry, embroidery, silk and tailoring. For Chinese carpets, go to the fourth floor. This place is a dump, but great fun.

CHUNG KIU CHINESE PRODUCTS EMPORIUM
   Sands Building, 17 Hankow Road, Kowloon

ORIENTAL ARTS & JEWELERY COMPANY

Oriental Arts & Jewellery is an importing company located on the third floor of a Nathan Road office building near the Park Lane Shopper's Boulevard.

Go around the corner to find the entrance, take a rickety elevator, step over straw in the hall, and look for the red door that says "A." Come prepared to stay, because this is arts and crafts nirvana. As you walk into the room you see warehouse-type display racks in front of you. On them are a variety of vases, cloisonné items, porcelain and stone carvings in jade and lapis lazuli. Behind and to the side are crates and more crates. Some have their tops opened; some have not yet been touched. The shipments are, for the most part, from mainland Chinese factories. On our tour through mainland China a few years before, we visited factories where cloisonné work was done. The factories all had shops. The prices here were cheaper for the same-size vase, two years later. (A 6" vase was $20.) The imports are mostly new copies of old pieces. However, there are also some old pieces that are offered for sale. One Chinese couple who were there when we came in sat for the entire hour we were there negotiating the price of a 3' lavender jade carving.

ORIENTAL ARTS & JEWELERY COMPANY
    80 Nathan Road, Kowloon

TAI PING CARPETS

One of the major crafts industries in China is carpet-making. Carpets are still made by hand, and many take years to complete. Tai Ping is one of the leading manufacturers and importers. You can visit their retail shop and order a custom carpet (takes 6 to 12 weeks), or check out the factory shop on Monday and Thursday from 2 P.M. to 4 P.M. In Hong Kong, call 656-5161, ext. 211, to arrange the visit.

TAI PING CARPETS
    Hutchison House, 10 Harcourt Road, Hong Kong
    Wing On Plaza, Mody Road, Kowloon
    Factory Shop: Tai Ping Industrial Park, Ting Kok Road, Lot No. 1687, Tai Po Market, N.T.

Art and Antiques

We have a minimal section on art and antiques, for several reasons:

- The bulk of the internationally famous dealers in Asian art are in London, New York, Tokyo, Brussels and places other than Hong Kong.
- The amount of fakes and frauds in the art business is infamous. The situation is even more intense in Hong Kong, and in no way can we confirm the authenticity of your purchase.
- The antiques scene in Hong Kong is shifting. Some dealers are moving away from Hollywood Road; others have now set up in Ocean Terminal in a space politely called The Silk Road (third floor). Exchange Square is getting more and more high-end tenants, while still others are looking for rents they can afford. There's also a big antiques scene in Macau (see page 302).

We remind you to buy what you know; if you don't know much, buy what you love, regardless of its real value. Bring your own expert with you if you are truly serious, or hire one in Hong Kong. A magazine called *Orientations* is available in Hong Kong—it may help you with news and prices. There are also a number of big-time auctions in Hong Kong; both Sotheby's and Christie's have offices here. Auctions are held in either spring or fall.

If you think you are serious about something, but can't sleep at night because you're not certain if it's real, get a second opinion. Many dealers on Hollywood Road will appraise an item (from another source) for you on a flat-fee basis.

It also pays to get an education before you go shopping. There are excellent museum collections in Hong Kong; the world's leading collection of Oriental art is in the British Museum in London.

LUEN CHAI CURIOS STORE

These are curios like we're Minnie Mouse—this Cat Street dealer has scrolls, antique porcelain and exhibition space to show contemporary Chinese painting. Located near the Man Mo end of the antiques shopping street, this store is in an area concentrated with shops that are borderline Tourist Traps, so it becomes impossible to tell the real from the fake and the good from the too-good-to-be-true.

LUEN CHAI CURIOS STORE
    22 Upper Lascar Row, Hong Kong
    142 Hollywood Road, Hong Kong (MTR: Central or Sheung Wan)

HANART GALLERY

One of the most famous galleries in the world for scrolls. Their exhibition space often represents modern Chinese art. This is the place to go, to know, to be known, to be in. Their reputation is outstanding. They also have galleries in New York and Taipei. See listing below for Harold Wong; you may need an appointment.

HANART GALLERY
    Central Building, Pedder Street, Hong Kong

SCHOENI

You have officially begun to "do" Hollywood Road when you stop in here, at one of Hong Kong's toniest dealers. Art and objets d'art from all over the Orient, so that only a portion of the selection is Chinese, but all of it is serious and expensive.

SCHOENI
    27 Hollywood Road, Hong Kong

TAI SING CO.

A leading dealer in important Han, T'ang and

Sung porcelains, as well as Imperial porcelain (which is outrageously expensive), since 1957. They also sell Chinese export porcelain. (This, too, is expensive.)

TAI SING CO.

122 Hollywood Road, Hong Kong

PLUM BLOSSOM INTERNATIONAL LTD.

While we are not much on contemporary Chinese painting, we have actually seen work at Plum Blossom that we like. Furthermore, it's pretty easy to know that contemporary Chinese work is an area that is getting to be hot and worth investing in. But I digress.

You see, Plum Blossom is one of the best sources in town for antique textile arts, one of my most passionate loves. You can find everything from uncut robes to ready-made carpets to embroidered fragments to Tibetan carpets. This is the kind of place you can look to for guidance in the area of expensive items that will accrue in value. Exchange Square is downtown, near the Mandarin Oriental Hotel.

PLUM BLOSSOM INTERNATIONAL LTD.

Exchange Square One (Shop 305-307), Hong Kong

PETER LAI ANTIQUES

You'll find this dealer in serious Chinese works of art more toward the Man Mo end of Hollywood Road .

PETER LAI ANTIQUES

138 Hollywood Road, Hong Kong (MTR: Central or Sheung Wan)

P.C. LU & SONS LTD.

A fine antiques dealer with showrooms in the major hotels, P.C. Lu's family has been in the business for four generations and runs one of the finest resources for antique ivory and jade, porcelain and decorative work. The three sons, who now run the business, work closely together. Stop in at any of the galleries and browse or get a look when you're prowling The Silk Road (see page 284).

P.C. LU & SONS LTD.

Harbour City/Ocean Terminal, The Silk Road, Canton Road, Kowloon

CHARLOTTE HORSTMANN & GERALD GODFREY LTD.

One of the most popular and well-respected antiques shops in Hong Kong, Charlotte Horstmann & Gerald Godfrey offer a wide range in museum-class Asian antiques. There are pieces from Korea, Burma, China, Japan, Indonesia and India. Choices include Noh masks, Chinese scrolls, Ming tapestries, Tang horses and period furniture made of sandalwood, rosewood and blackwood. I've also spied some fancy junk here. It's worth a look, but may not be your cup of *cha*.

CHARLOTTE HORSTMANN & GERALD GODFREY LTD.

Harbour City/Ocean Terminal, Canton Road, Kowloon

HONEYCHURCH ANTIQUES

Honeychurch Antiques has been our home base on Hollywood Road since the beginning of the *Born to Shop* series, so forgive us if we guide you here, where we know you will be well taken care of by American expats. Located in the beginning part of the antiques run on Hollywood Road, Honeychurch has been run by Glenn and Lucille Vessa for over 25 years. They know everything and everyone; stop by and ask whatever pops into your mind. And yes, there is a Mrs. Honeychurch, but she's retired and she lives in England.

Their store carries a wide variety of merchandise; eclectic is the best summary. The look is sort of Oriental Country; there are goods from Japan and other exotic locations besides your basic Chinese antiques. Try both floors in the main shop and then a warehouse floor next door (ask to be taken over), with larger pieces of furniture and a few other goodies. I found my collapsible bird cage in the warehouse. You never know what's waiting for you.

HONEYCHURCH ANTIQUES
   29 Hollywood Road, Hong Kong

Private Dealers

   GRACE WU BRUCE, phone 011-852-523-0840; fax 521-2641

   HAROLD WONG (Hanart Gallery Ltd.), phone 011-852-868-1811; fax 868-1896

The Silk Road

The Silk Road is an extremely clever marketing ploy to lead tourists to a portion of the mall in Ocean Terminal that is more or less devoted to antiques shops, but there are a few ringers in there, so it's hard to take this theme completely seriously. Nonetheless, there are shops you will enjoy poking into, and the mall is easy enough to get to. The Silk Road portion is marked clearly; you can enter from the Omni Hong Kong Hotel and not have to wander the endless corridors of shopping mall. Pass the coffee shop, then take the escalators straight up to the third floor. If you expect little, you will be pleased. (Confucius says.) Expect too much, and you will cry. Note that Charlotte Horstmann's gallery is right here, although it isn't part of the Silk Road promotional set-up.

CHAPTER SEVEN

MACAU

Welcome to Macau

I welcome you to Macau with an enthusiasm reserved for the newly converted. Truth is, I have been to Macau several times, over a period of many years. On most of my previous trips, I looked around, shopped around and shrugged my shoulders while singing a chorus of "Is that All There Is?"

I mention this, because it took me a number of years to get to this point, to be able to suggest Macau is really worth your time, to be able to genuinely welcome you to this former Portuguese colony, which goes to the Chinese in 1999.

I've changed my tune because I finally found the wonderful antiques neighborhood that I had been missing and because the Hotel Bela Vista has opened. Come to think of it, that's only the beginning. There's plenty more to the story.

So come to Macau. Come for a day, a day and a night; come for a weekend if you insist (not the best time to come) or better yet, come for several days. I know that once you've had a day like my last day in Macau, you'll put this tiny territory on your hit parade and on the list of places you have to come back to. I welcome you to an aspect of Hong Kong life that is too special to ignore.

Macau Traditions

Macau has existed in the Hong Kong reality for a series of specific local traditions:

- You go to Macau to have an affair with someone else's spouse;
- You go to Macau to gamble;
- You go to Macau to save money on antiques.

I'm up for at least one of those options (the antiques), and am beginning to understand the other possibilities. I'd rather spend my money on antiques than gambling, but after inspecting the Hotel Bela Vista, I certainly know the first place I'd go for a fling.

The local tradition is that gambling and affairs are conducted on weekends, so it's better for tourists to avoid Macau at these times whenever possible. Hong Kong crowds consider a trip to Macau in the same vein that Westerners consider a weekend in the country. They go to Macau to slow down, to take it easy, to relax. The notion is surely that Macau operates on a different pace than Hong Kong. But if you think you're headed to a sleepy little island, think twice. Macau is beginning to boom; the skyline may soon look like Hong Kong's. Besides, Macau is not an island. It's a peninsula.

A Short History of Macau

Macau is actually making more history now with the new vision of the territory than it has made in years past. Yet it's here that trade with the Far East was originally, well, uh, anchored. The Portuguese got permission to use Macau as their window on the East in 1556. The black ships departed from the harbor here, laden with the exotic trade which made continental Europe stand up and take note of all things Chinese. And Japanese. And Oriental.

In 1974 there was a coup in Portugal; the new government decided to dump colonies and territories. They tried to give Macau to the Chinese. The Chinese balked. In 1985 they all finally got it together and agreed that Macau would become a special territory (called a Special Administrative Region) for 50 years. The 50 years begin on December 31, 1999. (About two and a half years after the Chinese begin their special relationship with Hong Kong.)

Meanwhile, Macau has always generated its cash flow through gambling. And the antiques and forbidden treasures of China have slipped quietly across the border when no one was looking. And the husbands and wives slipped between the sheets while everyone *was* looking, but pretended not to be.

So international tourism was not a big to-do. Until a few years ago when someone realized that the Chinese were indeed moving into Hong Kong in '97 and Macau in '99, and it was a good time to woo and win them to the ways of capitalism; wouldn't it be fun to transform Macau? The transformation has been just plain dumbfounding.

In fact, I suggest you get to Macau before they ruin it.

Changing Times

I'm about to say something very two-faced and hypocritical: I adore everything they've done to Hong Kong. I love the architecture and the growth and the fast-paced race with money and destiny. But I am sorry to see Macau headed in the same direction. Yet, and here's the catch, I was never in love with the sleepy old colonial Macau (I thought it was a dump), and it's not like Macau is destroying a wonderful past in order to make room for the future.

It's just that I fear for the banyan trees. And I love some of those dumpy buildings. I adore the Apollo Theatre, and I'm not talking about Harlem, my dears. The Apollo is in downtown Macau. What I didn't like about the old Macau was that it wasn't seedy enough to be charming. It just was, and there was no real method to it.

But now I'm afraid that's going to go away.

Growth in Macau is staggering; in the two-year period between my last visits, the place was totally transformed. More changes are planned constantly. Landfill continues to close in the harbor; more hotels are opening, and of course, the water churns red from silt due to construction on the airport in Taipa.

In no time at all (1995), Macau will have its own international airport. (Yes, British Airways has gates there, and you will be able to fly from London to Hong Kong and depart Macau to London.)

Admire the view from the terrace of the Bela Vista while you can because it's going to go, too—landfill and more buildings are planned. Everything's coming up roses in Macau, high roses. Or is that high-rises?

A Short Lesson in Geography

Macau is connected to Hong Kong via a 40-mile sealane; it's actually 64 kilometers and a million miles away. Macau itself is not an island, but the tip of a peninsula that is directly attached to mainland China, also known as PRC. You can walk to the gate. You cannot walk through the gate without a visa.

Aside from modern downtown Macau, there are two islands: Taipa (where the new airport is located) and Coloane, which has the beaches and

Macau

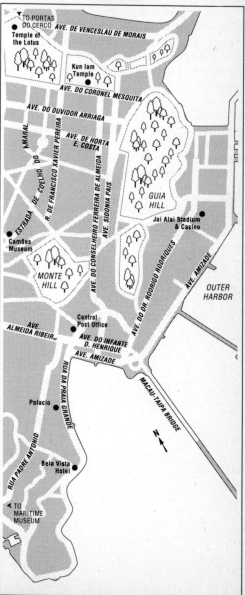

TO PORTAS DO CERCO

AVE. DE VENCESLAU DE MORAIS

Temple of the Lotus

Kun Iam Temple

AVE. DO CORONEL MESQUITA

AVE. DO OUVIDOR ARRIAGA

ESTRADA DO COELHO DO AMARAL

R. DE FRANCISCO XAVIER PEREIRA

AVE. DE HORTA E. COSTA

AVE. DO CONSELHEIRO FERREIRA DE ALMEIDA

AVE. SIDONIA PAIS

GUIA HILL

Jai Alai Stadium & Casino

Camões Museum

MONTE HILL

AVE. DO DR. RODRIGO RODRIGUES

AVE. AMIZADE

OUTER HARBOR

Central Post Office

AVE. ALMEIDA RIBEIRO

AVE. DO INFANTE D. HENRIQUE

AVE. AMIZADE

MACAU-TAIPA BRIDGE

RUA DA PRAIA GRANDE

Palacio

N

RUA PADRE ANTONIO

Bela Vista Hotel

TO MARITIME MUSEUM

several new hotels that are going for the resort business.

There are bridges to the islands and bridges which loop back toward the main gate and China.

The ferry terminal is not near much of anything, except the Mandarin Oriental. And a lot of landfill. It may be closer to something else by tomorrow, at the rate they're building. You will need a bus or taxi to get into town (you can also take a pedicab, if you are game); you will need a taxi to get to various destinations. You can easily explore the core downtown area by foot, but you'll need to get to downtown from the ferry pier if you arrive from Hong Kong via Shun Tak.

A Short Lesson in Getting to Shun Tak Centre

Shun Tak Centre is the name of the rather new and quite modern, two-tower ferry terminal located in the Western district of Hong Kong. The MTR stop is Sheung Wan, which is the end of the line. The building and terminals are located several floors up in the never-ending lobby space; ride several escalators and read a lot of signs. Do not be in a hurry the first time you do this.

Getting There

Assuming you are not flying to Macau via the new airport, or crossing the hills from China, you are most likely coming from Hong Kong and most likely from Shun Tak Centre. Your choices are simple, one if by air and two if by sea.

Lots of high rollers think it's terribly neat to come to Macau via helicopter. Since I am terrified of the things in the first place, and since I have survived number 8 seas between Hong Kong and Macau and wouldn't like to have been in a chopper at such a time, I can only say *bonne chance*, and have fun. The fare for the chopper is just slightly over $100 on weekdays; it runs more frequently on weekends and holidays, as these are peak travel times. The journey takes twenty minutes. Ian's dying to try it. There are several flights a day; eight people fit into the craft. You get tickets at the ferry terminal in Shun Tak Centre (MTR: Sheung Wan); you may also book the ride via any tour organization.

I've always come and gone to Macau via jetfoil. Although there are numerous seafaring vehicles and locals know the difference between a catamaran, a hydrofoil and a jetfoil, I can only tell you that speed is my choice here, and so I go via jetfoil. I've tried to sample the other methods, but fate was not with me. And I don't plan to be caught dead in a helicopter. So there.

HYDROFOILS take 75 minutes, but have an open deck. (Nice in a Number 8.)

HOVER-FERRIES take slightly more than an hour and depart via China Hong Kong City.

HIGH-SPEED FERRIES take almost two hours, so they are misnamed.

JETCATS take 70 minutes and are similar to JUMBOCATS; they too depart China Hong Kong City.

JETFOILS are made by Boeing, which will bring you great comfort when you begin to panic. The crossing takes an hour.

The fares do change with the times, but the variables include the day of the week (weekends cost more), the time of day (night costs more) and the class of service (first costs more). First-class service on a weekday is basically about $12 each way for an adult; departure tax adds another $3 or so.

You may get your tickets up to 28 days in advance, which is nice, so you won't have too much pressure on you once you get to the Shun Tak Centre; this building is a tad confusing and may be all you can handle. TICKETMATE outlets offer tickets; your hotel concierge can get them for you as well.

Now then, this is as good a time as any for a few warnings. Of all the times I have gone to Macau, the crossing has been glorious—the sun sparkles like diamonds across the South China Sea, the hills of China are delicious—the crossing has been a sea breeze. But once, just once, things were less than smooth.

Despite the fact that I checked the weather with the hotel desk, I did not read the *South China Morning Post* before departure. Had I done so, I would have noticed the word "monsoon" and the words "Number 8" along with some swirly circles drawn between China and Hong Kong. You don't have to have a degree in meteorology to know that you do not want to be on the seas during a monsoon, even if the skies are blue and the land is dry. Conditions in the sea between Hong Kong and Macau can be quite different from what's happening at landfall.

I won't bore you with the unpleasant details, but I will tell you that Ian Cook was afraid. And I was frightened by the fact that he was more afraid than I of the whitecaps, the waves engulfing the jetfoil or the fact that everyone around me was puking on my silk dress. The luggage was flying, water was sloshing into the sides of the boat and Ian's eyes were real big. "Hundreds Lost at Sea," he whispered as I reached for my barf bag.

Yes, it was bad luck. We had engine trouble; the jetfoils stopped running after ours left, due to rough seas. It rarely happens and we came out of it shaken, but just fine. But there are a few things to learn:

- Be a sport; pay for a first-class ticket. Our economy seats had us crammed in with hundreds of others, so when the rocking and rolling started, they were thrown on top of us in all their humanity. We also had the waves crashing around us. First-class is elevated; the waves would have never been seen or felt. It's more spacious. We might have turned around and flagged a helicopter to get to Macau if we were on first-class passage. We would have thought of EuroDisney and laughed. A first-class seat usually costs $3 more than an economy seat. You're worth it.

- Read the newspaper before you leave for the ferry terminal. Words such as "monsoon" and "typhoon" should set off warning bells in your brain. What's the dif? A monsoon is wind; a typhoon is rain.

- Don't think that the "authorities" are a better judge of the situation than you are. They will eventually stop running boats if things get out of hand, but if you want to be captain of your own fate, you'll get information before you leave town. The radio runs weather reports constantly. Or talk to your concierge. Remember the weather report for Hong Kong is meaningless; you want the report for the South China Sea and the pathway to Macau. It also helps to know precisely where Macau is in relationship to Hong Kong and the China coast, so you can read a map and follow the weather patterns yourself. Guangdong is the name of the coastal province of China next to Macau—if winds are blowing from Guangdong toward Hong Kong and you are riding right smack into them, well, you get my drift.

While you can come and go from Kowloon via China Hong Kong City (and I have done this very conveniently), there are departures every fifteen minutes from Shun Tak Centre in Western, and you have more choices of types of craft at Shun Tak.

Departing Shun Tak is confusing; pay attention when you line up to get your ticket. This is the second time I've mentioned this, so you can tell I think it's more than a bit confusing. Note that it can be outright difficult if you try to change tickets. We missed our return catamaran and had to buy new tickets on the jetfoil—no refunds, no exchanges, no credits.

The price of your ticket includes exit taxes for both Hong Kong and Macau. You will have to fill in immigration papers on both sides of Hong Kong and yes indeedy, you need that passport. Allow twenty minutes for the paperwork on the Hong Kong side; it's quicker leaving Macau, but you must still exit the country and go through security.

Once you have your tickets, you report to the departure area (after clearing immigration, of course). There you'll see people milling around and standing in line and you won't know what to do. Get in the line, dummy, you need a seat. Then you can mill around. There are kiosks selling food, drinks, magazines, etc.

If you arrive early—as you may well do because you are so nervous about everything that has to get done—you may board an earlier boat. No matter what your ticket says, as long as they have seats, you can get on.

Once you are on the jetfoil, you'll note they serve tea and soft drinks; they have gambling games and you can buy duty-free cigarettes. (Sorry, no perfumes.) The trip is an hour and is quite delightful, especially from the upper deck, first-class section where you can look out on the world and dream of China. Believe me, I'm the one who rides second-class in trains all over Europe and who doesn't believe in first-class, except on airplanes and the jetfoil. Don't go economy!

Oh yes, about the airport. Watch this space. Yes, a Boeing 747-400 will be able to land here, no problem. Of course, if you're coming from Hong Kong, you won't be in a 747-400. The idea is that you come directly to Macau as your principal destination and use it for day trips or overnights to Hong Kong, and then go into mainland China from Macau. You are equidistant to Canton (Guangzhou) in both Hong Kong and Macau, but you get the idea.

Arriving Macau via Ferry

You'll walk along a little gangway, enter a building, follow a walkway and go through security. You are now in Portuguese Macau. I spoke Portuguese to our taxi driver, who thought I was nuts. Better luck to you and yours.

Once you are outside the terminal, you'll note that there are bus stops and a hut for waiting for taxis. It's a little confusing, partly because so much construction is going on, and if you are used to the way it used to be, well, you'll find that everything is different.

Luggage

We were originally planning to spend the night at the Bela Vista and had overnight tote bags with us, plus camera equipment. We were rather weighted down (we always are), but were at least able to walk and carry our own luggage. Good thing. On our voyage from hell the stowed luggage was flying all over the place. There is no luggage service per se; don't bring what you can't carry. Thankfully Macau is a casual kind of place; if you lose your shirt at the gaming tables, it will be one less thing to schlep back to Hong Kong with you.

If you are staying at the Mandarin Oriental in Hong Kong and go on to stay at the Mandarin Oriental in Macau, you may arrange to have your luggage sent ahead. This is a brilliant notion.

Getting Around Macau

There are a million taxi drivers at the ferry pier who want to be your driver-*cum*-guide for a day and who will make a deal with you. It's harder to find a taxi to just take you someplace. The Mandarin Oriental is essentially across the street—it's a busy street and not easy to cross, but you can walk there if you don't have too much stuff with you. This is only one of many reasons to book the Mandarin Oriental for your stay. They will also send a car for you, if you arrange it, or send a car to take you to the Bela Vista.

When we finally did get a taxi, I told the driver exactly where to go. In Portuguese. *No fala.* This driver acted as if he didn't speak any language we spoke—and between us we do know a few—and then handed me a map of Macau so I could point to our destination. Now let me tell you something, if I did not know where we were going, its location on the map and the correct route, I would have had a nervous breakdown right then and there. Do study your *mapa turistico* while you're sitting on the jetfoil.

If this is a day trip, you want to go to see *Igresia São Paolo*. I'll guide you beyond that in a few minutes (see page 302). If you are staying awhile, you obviously want to go to your hotel. Make sure you know where it is on a map. Just in case.

If you are staying a few days, you might want to rent a mini-moke, a jeep-like affair. We had ours booked through the hotel, but gave it up when we didn't get to stay over. Prices are about $35 per day from Avis; many hotels offer a moke option as part of a package deal.

Money

Macau has its own unit of currency, called a *pataca*. It is traded on parity with the Hong Kong dollar, which is also accepted interchangeably, although change may be given in local coins.

If you have an ETC card from the Hongkong and Shanghai Bank, you can use the cash machine at the bank—you will get Macau cash. You cannot get money if you just have a passbook; you must have the ETC card.

Sleeping Macau

MANDARIN ORIENTAL MACAU

If you want to be part of it all, the Mandarin Oriental is the logical choice, if not the romantic one. This high-rise poured-concrete hotel sits right at the harbor, a sneeze from the ferry terminal. It's got about 400 rooms, including several Mandarin suites; most rooms have views of the South China Sea. It's the only large five-star property in the heart of things and it's where you want to be, if you need big and fancy.

Along with the usual Mandarin luxuries, the hotel has several famous restaurants, a beauty shop, business services, swimming pool, health club and spa and all the features you come to expect from a Mandarin property. It is the best in town in terms of luxury, location and complete facilities.

You can also get a promotional deal that will knock your socks off. Various weekday packages include Midweek Interlude and Macau Affair packages. (You know what I told you about Macau.) Packages include double accommodation, welcome fruit basket, jetfoil transfers, discounts on moke rental or tours and either a dining credit or perhaps a meal on the property, depending on which promotion you luck into. Weekday promotional rates can be as low as $115!

Call 800-526-6566 for reservations in the U.S., or Leading Hotels of the World, 800-223-6800.

MANDARIN ORIENTAL MACAU, Avenida da Amizade, Macau

HOTEL BELA VISTA

If I sound lukewarm about the Mandarin Oriental, it's only because I am wild about the Bela Vista. Book your room now, read the rest of this book later.

Once the grande dame hotel of Macau, the Bela Vista basically fell apart and became a dump. It was closed for two years' worth of renovations; it is now owned by the government and run by Mandarin. It is to die for.

Here's the problem: The hotel has only four rooms and four suites! Each is different, each is decorated to the gills with tiles and colonial furniture and touches of grandeur. Second problem: no pool or spa or health club.

If you are in Macau for a day trip, you won't mind the lack of rooms since you'll just be coming here to sniff the air and have lunch, which is not very expensive, by the way.

The hotel is drop-dead-chic gorgeous; it has colonial proportions and makes a statement of refined elegance and old money. The rooms are not cheap. In fact, you might need to sit down. The top suite in the house goes for about $500 a night. And that's U.S. dollars. It also happens to be worth it. The Macau Suite, with fireplace, is about $300 a night—and a bargain.

You can get all the charm and none of the expense by coming for lunch or tea (see page 299). The hotel is not far from downtown, although to get there your taxi may need to circle a part of the island because of one-way streets. This hotel is not really within walking distance to much of anything. Who wants to go much of anywhere once you're here?

For reservations in the U.S., call 800-526-6566. If you are booking for a holiday period, book as far ahead as possible. They may be sold out for New Year's Eve 1999.

HOTEL BELA VISTA, Rua do Comendador Kou Ho Neng 8, Macau

WESTIN RESORT MACAU

Way out on Coloane, this hotel is a destination unto itself and is marketed as such. There's plenty of places to eat; there are numerous recreational activities (including golf). There's a complimentary shuttle to and from the ferry pier, some twenty minutes away.

For reservations in the U.S., call 800-228-3000.

WESTIN RESORT MACAU, Hac Sa Beach, Coloane, Macau

Snack and Shop

It is not easy to bump into a cute place to eat lunch in Macau, so plan your day accordingly. If you come on a day trip, I can't imagine doing anything other than eating at the BELA VISTA. But there are other choices. There is also a gourmet grocery store on the main drag, and you can picnic. There may be tons of American fast-food joints like in Hong Kong, but I've never found them in my traditional shopping path. (There's a MCDONALD'S on the main drag near the Senate Square.)

Also note that eating is one of the adventures that Macau is famous for. People in Hong Kong all have their favorite places, which they may not even tell you about for fear you will ruin them; they don't want tourists crowding in.

Decide on your lunch venue before you leave for Macau, especially if you are visiting on a day trip; then plan your schedule accordingly. You will more than likely have to taxi to lunch, so budget time and funds. If you are staying for a while, these choices also serve dinner. Do note that several hotels (MANDARIN ORIENTAL, HYATT REGENCY, WESTIN, POUSADA DE SÃO TIAGO) are known for their dinner service as well.

Please note that the only one of these listed

restaurants I have been to is the Bela Vista; the others are culled from the Macau Tourist Information Bureau, friends in Hong Kong, Mary Bakht at the HKTA in New York, *Gourmet Magazine* and several guidebooks, which all agree with the others. Here goes:

HOTEL BELA VISTA

If you aren't sick of my ranting and raving about the Bela Vista, you'll simply trust me and book ahead. Weather permitting, you want to sit outside on the terrace.

The shocking thing about lunch at the BV (as some call it) is that it is very fancy without high prices. The most expensive entree on the luncheon menu is $10! The menu is huge, it's written in English and Portuguese and contains many local specialties as well as more exotic choices. The appetizers are huge; Ian's pasta could have fed two. He barely had room for his grouper and shrimp in banana leaf. The homemade cinnamon ice cream was the perfect finishing touch to a glorious day. There's a good wine list.

I am pushing BV so strongly because I firmly believe that my newfound fondness for Macau is rooted in the beauty, romance, good eats and local charm of this single hotel. The combination of Macau's funky streets, markets, antiques shops and then this gorgeous colonial restoration offers exactly what I want out of China—the best of both worlds.

By the way, if you taxi here from St. Paul's or the main area, your taxi will circle around the waterfront drive on a one-way course. Don't be alarmed.

For reservations, direct dial from Hong Kong (or call from the U.S.) 011-853-965-333, or fax 011-853-965-5888.

HOTEL BELA VISTA, Rua do Comendador Kou Ho Neng 8, Macau

HENRI'S GALLEY

You pronounce this "Henry" in the American fashion, not "On-rhee" like the French. You can also get yourself into gourmand controversy when you discuss this restaurant with foodies from Hong Kong. Glenn Vessa, who knows everything (but won't tell unless you ask), says that Henri's is very overrated and is worth skipping. I've never been. Food writers from around the world have been basking in the glory of Henri's for years. So if you are in town for a few days, you'll just have to try for yourself. (If you're here for only one lunch, you know I want you to go to the Bela Vista.)

Known for chicken, prawns, spicy dishes and a choice of Chinese food, Henri's is on the waterfront, not far from the Hotel Bela Vista, in fact. It is not walking distance from town. For reservations, call 556-251.

HENRI'S GALLEY, 4 Avenida da Republica, Macau

A LORCHA

Glenn gives thumbs-up to this choice for Portuguese cooking; it's near the A-Man Temple on the southwestern part of the main peninsula. Known for their combination of Portuguese, Chinese, Indian and African dishes. Reasonable prices. Lunch is served from 1 P.M.–3 P.M.; Dinner from 7 P.M.–midnight. Call 313-193.

A LORCHA, 289 Rua do Almirante Sergio, Macau

PINOCCHIO'S

On Taipa Island, and a good excuse to cross the bridge and see a little more of Macau than you planned on, Pinocchio's is huge, famous and the kind of landmark place where "everyone" goes. . . at least once. Fred Ferretti gives it a rave, in person and in *Gourmet Magazine*. They open at noon. You can dine alfresco. Call 27128.

PINOCCHIO'S, 4 Rua do Sol, Taipa

Shopping Macau

The main reason people come to Macau to shop is simple: The prices are lower than in Hong Kong and the specialty is antiques and "antiques." It is possible to see antiques being made in front of your very eyes. These copies are so good that you will never buy another antique again, for fear that it just came out of the back room of a shop in Macau.

Just about everything is less expensive in Macau, from hotel rooms to goods in the market to souvenirs to antiques. Every big spender from Hong Kong has his or her own private sources in Macau. Indeed, Macau is the kind of place where you need an inside track. There's no doubt that the really good stuff is hidden. And may be illegal.

The Best of Macau

Since addresses are hard to find in Macau and many places don't even have their names clearly marked, the best way for me to show you the best of central Macau's shopping area is to take you on my walking tour.

If you are visiting Macau on a day trip, take an early jetfoil from Hong Kong so that you hit St. Paul's by 10 A.M. You can wander happily for a few hours and then taxi to the Bela Vista for a 1 P.M. lunch. Book the 4 P.M. jetfoil back to Hong Kong.

1) Tell your taxi *Igresia São Paulo* (St. Paul's Church), or be able to point to it on a map. A Macau *Mapa Turistico* is handed out free in Shun Tak Centre. This particular map has a picture of the church, but no number or letter beside it, so it may take you some time to study the map and learn the basics of the town. If you have other tourist materials with a picture of the facade of the church, you may show that to your driver as well.

This church was built in the early 1600s; it burned to the ground in 1835, leaving only the facade, which is in more or less perfect condition. (It was recently restored.) Not only is this quite a sight to see, but it's the leading tourist haunt in town and signals the beginning of the shopping district. Exit the taxi at the church.

2) The church is up a small hill, with two levels of stairs leading to a small square. If you go down both levels of the stairs, you will be at the major Tourist Trap (TT) area and flea market heaven where dealers sell mostly new antiques...although you always hear stories of so-and-so, who just bought a valuable teapot at one of these stalls.

3) Before you go lickety-split down all the stairs to the stalls, note that if you go down only one staircase, there is a small alley to the side of the stairs—an alley which runs alongside the church. It's only a block long and ends just past the rear of the church, where you will find a tiny shrine.

Not that it's well-marked, but the name of this alley is Rua da Ressurreciao. It is lined with TTs, porcelain shops, antiques stores and even a ginseng parlor. You've got KENG NGAI ANTIQUANO (No. 5) and TUNG NGAI ANTIQUARIOS E ARTISANATO (No. 3), etc. Don't expect any bargains in these shops and by all means know your stuff, but begin your shopping spree here. I must say that most of these stores are rather fetching: plates in the windows, red lanterns flapping in the breeze, maybe even a few carved dragons over the doorway. They all take credit cards, and you may have a ball here. I'm suspicious of any place that's too clean and too close to a major tourist haunt such as the church, but you could spend half a day happily enjoying these stores.

4) After you've done this alley, work your way around the vendors at the main "square" in front of the church steps. Film, soft drinks and souvenirs are sold here; there are no particular bargains. I once bought a very good Chairman Mao button here (ceramic), which has become valuable in the intervening years, but nothing much here is particularly inexpensive. Be prepared to bargain; be prepared to walk...and possibly return later.

5) Now then, normal people head into town by walking down the hill to the market and shopping as they go. The way to do this is to head down the Rua de São Paulo to the Rua da Palha, passing shops as you go. This walkway leads directly to the marketplace and the Senate Square, which is the heart of downtown. There are a few cute shops this way, and I have even bought from some of them. BUT, I am sending you down the hill the sneaky, non-touristy way.

If you have the time, you may want to go down my way and then walk back up the main way, so you can see the whole hill (and shop it, of course). Also note that if you are with people and decide to split up, you can always meet back at the church stairway flea market area at an appointed time; this is a good place to get a taxi later on.

The big red stall is not a loo, it's a postal box. You can mail postcards here.

If you do head down Rua de São Paulo, be sure to look in at CHEONG WENG TRADING CO. (No. 26A), which sells handcrafted wooden items—toys for kids, nutcrackers, picture frames and non-touristy items. Next door (No. 28) is CHAN POU MANIEK HONG, where you can buy newly-made porcelains for tourists. I bought a tea mug (with lid) for $10 H.K. I bought the exact same mug in a street market in Hong Kong for a lot more, so you can see where Macau got its reputation for lower prices.

6) If you are standing with the church to your back, a major TT called NAM KWONG ARTS & CRAFTS should be to your right, with the red postal box in front of it. Shop this TT if you are so inclined, then make a hard right (under the laundry from the balcony above) onto a small unmarked street. (There are other branches of Nam Kwong in town). Once you have turned right, look to the left for an alley called Calcada do Amparo. Enter here and begin to walk downhill.

It's not going to be charming for a block or so, and you will wonder where the hell you are and why all the tourists went the other direction. Trust me, you are headed into the back alleys of the furniture and antiques area, which you will soon discover. You are wearing good walking shoes, I hope. This is called the Tercena neighborhood, by the way.

7) The reason I haven't given you shop names and addresses should be now abundantly clear—there's no way of really even knowing where you are when you walk down this hill. In about two blocks your alley will dead-end into a small street call Rua Nossa Senhora do Amparo, which may or may not be marked. These little alleys are called walkways or *travessas* and may have names (look for Travessa do Fagao).

In terms of getting your bearings, you are now halfway to the main downtown square of Macau and on a small street that branches off from Rua do Mercadores, the main shopping small street that connects the main big shopping street to the area above at the top of the hill.

This will make sense when you are standing there in the street or if you look at a map. But don't do a map too carefully, because part of the fun of the whole experience is wandering around here, getting lost and found, and feeling like what you have discovered is yours alone.

When you are back on the Rua Nossa Senhora do Amparo, you'll find a ton of little dusty antiques shops (they start opening around 11 A.M.; don't come too early)—some have names and some don't. As a starting-off point, I send you to CHEONG KEI CURIOS SHOP (No. 10)—it's written FERROS VEL-HOS CHEONG KEI in black letters over the door on a big sign—this is the musty dusty antiques shop of your dreams, and is in the core of what I call Antiques Heaven. Segue onto Rua das Estalagens, which has more antiques shops as well as some fabric shops and jobbers.

I would not begin to vouch for the integrity of any of these shops here. I can only assure you that you'll have the time of your life.

8) When you have finished shopping the antiques trade, work your way laterally across Rua das Estalagens to Rua do Mercadores. If you turn right you will connect in two short blocks to Avenida de Almeida Ribeiro, the main drag. I suggest instead that you keep moving laterally, so that you run smack into the market.

The market is called MERCADO DE SÃO DOMINGOS; it has an outdoor fruit and veggie portion tucked into various alleys, an indoor livestock portion and a dry goods portion. Wander through as much as you can take, and find yourself at the main fountain and a square (Senate Square), which instinct will tell you is the main square.

If instinct isn't enough, look for the restored colonial buildings, the tourist office, a large neon sign featuring a picture of a cow (I call this the Ma-Cow sign; Ian does not think this is funny), the main big post office, the deliciously dilapidated Apollo Theatre and the Leal Senado, which is the Senate building. You have arrived in the heart of town. After you've spotted the spotted cow (I love that cow, sorry), you'll note that there are several pedicabs —rickshaws drawn by bicycle—clustered here, you may book a ride. Or take a snapshot. It costs about $5 to get a ride to the waterfront.

There are a few shops clustered here; some are liquor stores, which specialize in old ports from Portugal, etc. After you poke around here and drop into the excellent tourist office (for postcards, no stamps), cross the street and head into the white stucco Leal Senado building just to stare—it is beautifully restored with tons of old Portuguese blue and white tiles; a garden, a library and some magnificent colonial touches.

The address of the tourist office, in case you need help, a place to meet up with the people you came with or someone who speaks English and can teach you how to use the phone or write something for you in Chinese, is 9 Largo do Senado.

The huge Post Office across the square is where you buy stamps, but beware, there can be long lines.

9) Once finished at the Leal Senado, walk to the right—this is toward the water if the Senate building is to your back. You are now on Avenida de Almeida Ribeiro, the main drag. Here you can stare at the contrasts in architecture and note the old and the new, the shabby and the luxe. The stores here include the gourmet market I was telling you about, a

branch of the local Chinese arts and crafts store NAM KWONG (No. 1) and an antiques shop or two.

I fell in love with Chinese mirror boxes while at HONEYCHURCH, on Hollywood Road in Hong Kong. I found an excellent example for 25% less than the Hong Kong price at WING TAI CURIOS CENTRE on Avenida de Almeida Ribeiro—I cannot tell you if it was genuine, or made yesterday; I can only tell you it was nice and less money than in Hong Kong. I can also tell you that schlepping a mirror box all the way home is my idea of hell. And I'm the one who judges the success of a trip by the size of the item I carried on the plane.

You can walk just about to the waterfront here, certainly to the HOTEL LISBOA, where you may want to gamble at the Atlantic City-looking casino or look at the new Bank of China across the street.

10) Get a taxi at the Lisboa; head for lunch at the BELA VISTA. Congratulations, you've seen what I consider to be the best parts of Macau. Well, the best shopping parts, anyway. Do note that if you aren't going in for the fancy lunch break, you can grab a taxi instead for the Kun Iam temple; there's more TTs and antiques shops there.

most obvious landmark—3-D popping effect —is the I.M. Pei-designed Bank of China.

2) When you get off at the ferry terminal, note that there's plenty of action going on right here—there's a vendor who sells various teas from a huge brass samovar, an excellent bookstore and a handful of rickshaw drivers who will ask if you want a ride. There's also a few street vendors selling anything from fresh flowers to film to old coins and more, depending on the night action.

3) After you browse here, note there's a pedestrian walkway tunnel which will bring you up between Statue Square and the Mandarin Oriental Hotel. If you don't use this walkway, you'll have a terrible time getting across traffic and metal bars on the curbs.

4) The MANDARIN ORIENTAL HOTEL is home to two of the most popular tailor shops in town. It's also a good place to begin your tour of hotel lobbies, which is another national pastime in Hong Kong. On the mezzanine level you will find DAVID'S (custom shirts) and A-MAN (suits). Also on the mezzanine don't miss the jewelry shop, GEMS-LAND. In fact, there's an entire mall of big-name shops right here. There's also a tiny but excellent book-postcard kiosk in the hotel. Bathrooms are on the mezzanine level, on the opposite side from the shops; you will have to tip the attendant.

5) If you're really into the whole Hong Kong scene, you might want to begin the day with a power breakfast in the MANDARIN GRILL. Leave the hotel via the pedestrian bridge that connects the Mandarin Oriental to the PRINCE'S BUILDING across the street. Explore many levels of designer shops.

6) After leaving the Prince's Building, cross the street and walk to SWIRE HOUSE (in the middle of the block and before you get to

Pedder Street). Swire House is a perfect example of an office building/shopping center. Within the Swire House arcade, you will find even more designer boutiques.

7) Leave Swire House via the Chater Road exit, take a right, and then an immediate left onto Des Voeux Road Central, where you will be in front of the LANDMARK, the most famous American-style upscale mall in town. One entrance into the building is between Gucci and the Peninsula Chocolate shop. Walk past Gucci, down a somewhat claustrophobic hallway, toward the throngs of people and center atrium. Once in the atrium, spend some time gawking like the rest of the tourists. The biggest names in design are here. If you are looking for discount shopping only, don't waste your time....Move on, or grab a bite to eat at the FOUNTAINSIDE CAFE.

The Landmark could be an all-day adventure in itself, but I'd just as soon you spent twenty minutes here to get the idea, and then beat it to the street. We're going to some outlets now!

8) Exit the Landmark via the Pedder Street door, cross at the corner of Queen's Road Central, turn right down Pedder Street, and look for the PEDDER BUILDING (No. 12: a small entryway right next to the China Building). If you get to the Mandarin House, you have gone too far. The building is a dump. The spaces now occupied by designer boutiques were once, not so long ago, workrooms. The boutiques are nice, but the hallways are not. Not every store here is an outlet and some of the outlets are not cheap. But this is as good a place as any to get a feel for Hong Kong's outlet scene and to know you've at least bettered the prices in the Landmark.

I want everyone who visits Central to spend at least a half hour in the Pedder Building, where I know you'll wake up to the shopping realities of Hong Kong. The Landmark is not the real world.

9) If you still have the energy at this point to go on, exit the Pedder Building, take a right, and then another right onto Queen's Road Central. Walk toward the HongKong and Shanghai Bank, another architectural landmark. In a block you'll hit THE GALLERIA AT 9 QUEEN'S, a small mall devoted to many tony names who have defected from the Landmark and a number of Joyce's boutiques.

10) Exit Galleria and walk underneath the HongKong and Shanghai Bank, where you'll see the Beam-Me-Up-Scotty escalators that actually lead to the bank lobby. Explore the bank if you are interested in architecture, or use this breezeway to cut through to the HILTON HOTEL. After checking out this lobby, head for SKETTI'S and a pizza lunch. Make sure lunch is well-digested if you are planning on a trip up the Peak. The Peak Tram is right outside the back end of the Hilton, but the ride down is very steep and you want to make sure lunch has already gone to your toes.

11) Finished at the Peak, you can walk to the Star Ferry and bail out now. But really, you can't be tired yet. There's lots more to see and do and now that you've gotten acclimated, you're ready to move into less Western parts of Central.

12) Walk along Queen's Road in the westerly direction, stop for a spree in the LANES, which are located before Pottinger Street. You'll pass DRAGON SEED (No. 39), a Chinese department store that will intrigue bargain and junk shoppers, and soon get to the

Lanes, with Li Yuen Street East coming before Li Yuen West (unless you are very lost). Walk to your right, going down Li Yuen Street East and shopping your heart out until you get to Des Voeux Road, then walk the few yards it takes to get to Li Yuen West on Des Voeux, turn to your left into the lane and walk back to Queen's Road along a shopping lane similar to the one you were just on. While you may not need a brassiere, do note that souvenir T-shirts cost only a little more than $1 and Hermès-style Kelley handbags cost less than $50.

13) Your last stop (well, one of your last official stops, anyway) should be the LANE CRAW-FORD department store, across the street from Mandarin Optical and farther toward Pottinger Street. This is the fanciest British-style department store in town. Prices are the highest in town also, but you can find a sampling of anything you want, from truly fine art to portrait photography, from china and crystal to Mikimoto pearls. It's a great place to work on pricing the things you plan to buy later in the trip. Figure that whatever it costs at Lane Crawford is the most the market will bear. Lane Crawford also offers top-of-the-line quality, so you'll be able to get an idea of how price and value coordinate.

14) If you aren't exhausted, while you're at Lane Crawford you are also next door to the local chemist chain WATSON'S, which sells a little of everything, including makeup, toys, perfumes, pantyhose, film, etc. There's also a branch of CHINA PRODUCTS STORE around the corner. Now you are surely exhausted and are ready to collapse for tea. On your way back to the Star Ferry, you're only a block from the Mandarin Oriental, where high tea is almost a meal unto itself.

15) Use this break to get off your feet and rest up because after dinner, you're going to the TEMPLE STREET MARKET around 8 or 9 P.M. This is a very hot night market in Kowloon, where Chinese opera is performed in the streets and all sorts of silly items—from copy watches to vibrating pillows—are sold at bargain-basement prices.

TOUR 2: ANTIQUES, TEMPLES AND MORE

Now that you've gotten used to Hong Kong, you're ready to see (and buy) a little bit more. Step this way. In your good walking shoes, please. This can be done as a half-day tour after working Central.

1) Begin your day in Central (via MTR or Star Ferry) at the foot of Pottinger Street, next to the CHINA PRODUCTS STORE on Queen's Road. Pottinger is a very steep street with scads of stalls and an equal number of steps. The stalls have very diverse merchandise, including handbags, clothing and food.

2) When you make it to the top of Pottinger Street you will be at the crossroads of Chinese antiques and curios heaven, better known as Hollywood Road. Hollywood Road became popular for antiques in the early 1950s, after the Revolution in China. At that time many Chinese had fled the People's Republic with possessions in hand. In order to raise cash, they pawned them on Hollywood Road. The tradition remained, and Hollywood Road is still the center of merchandise coming out of China. Most of what you see in the shops today is not antique, but antique repro. The true finds are in the back rooms and are saved for dealers. However, if you are an antiques collector, let the shop owner know immediately. Often it is better to have an introduction to a dealer in

town who can shop and negotiate with you.

For the majority of shoppers who want a curio to take home, rummaging through dusty shelves for the "perfect" piece is a lot of fun! Just remember that there are no Ming vases on the shelves. Ask lots of questions, and bargain. Make sure you get a receipt stating the age of your purchase. If you are buying a true antique, you are entitled to a certificate of authenticity. Customs will want to see these papers. In the more established shops, shipping is no problem and the goods arrive safely. If you are planning to buy in quantity for any reason, ask for the dealer price. Bring along your business card and negotiate on a quantity basis. Many of the shops are used to dealing with interior designers who buy for their clients.

Hollywood Road is actually an extension of Wyndham Street, with stores running for several blocks, right to the block after the Man Mo Temple. The closer you get to Ladder Street and the Man Mo Temple, the tackier the shops become, although the immediate block after the temple offers fancy dealers and TTs that pride themselves on being part of the action. Hmmmmm.

After the temple the shops become a mix of Chinese herbalists, furniture makers and curio stores. Be sure to go into a Chinese medicine shop and look at all the wonderful, exotic substances in glass jars. The wizened old men concocting remedies for any ailment you might have probably are the only true antiques left on Hollywood Road.

3) When you get to Man Mo Temple take time out from shopping for culture, religion or appreciation. You can buy any of the necessary prayer supplies right there in the foyer after you enter (we always go in the door to the farthest right if you are facing the tem-

ple). There's candles, papers for burning, joss sticks, etc. You may also say a prayer and bang the drum slowly.

4) Exit the temple and go to the corner of Hollywood Road and Ladder Street. You'll note that there is a street directional sign that says "Flea Market." Ladder Street is another of those wonderful stepped streets that looks like it has been there for centuries. Most of the street actually runs uphill, but you will be thrilled to know that you will be going downhill.

Step down just one level and you are at Cat Street, the heart of the flea market. Turn left onto Cat Street and begin to browse the stalls and blankets and huts. The shopping opportunities stretch for almost three blocks; some alleys also have vendors; there are also real, bona fide antiques shops behind some of the street dealers.

Farther along the street you will see workshops making furniture and forging metals. Dealers who sell mostly to the design trade have their showrooms in the Cat Street Galleries, which is in the middle of the block, in the Casey Building on the harbor side of the street. The actual address for the gallery is on the next street down the hill, so if you miss the building on Cat Street, walk to the end of Cat Street, turn right, duck under the hanging laundry and turn right again on Lok Ku Road.

5) If you have the energy to walk, go down the steps of Ladder Street to Man Wa Lane, taking Hillier Street. If you can't walk, you can almost roll. Man Wa Lane is confusing to shop (unless you read Chinese), but offers a wonderful photo opportunity and a unique shopping look-see. Here the chop dealers have their stalls.

6) If you have strength for one more adventure, walk the few extra blocks to Des Voeux and hang a left; you are now headed for the Western Market, which has been rehabbed and looks suspiciously like an American mall or part of Faneuil Hall. Note that there are several card and stationery dealers on the street level, which have merchandise you don't find everywhere else; there are fabric dealers on the mezzanine. There's clean bathrooms and even a good restaurant, if you need to eat. If you want a more adventurous eating experience, you are only a block from YAT CHAU (262 Des Voeux Road), where you will be examined by a Chinese doctor and told what to eat in order to be cured. Refreshed, and possibly cured, pop into the Sheung Wan MTR station and head home.

TOUR 3: HALF-DAY BARGAIN TRIPS (INCLUDES STAN-LEY MARKET)

These two tours are at opposite ends of the Hong Kong world, so divide them in half by lunch, or separate them into two different days, if you have time. We suggest lunch in or near your hotel, because you'll want to make a pit stop to drop off your packages.

1) More Outlets: Take a taxi to Hung Hom; ask for Kaiser Estates Phase I. Explore the many factory outlets in the area (see page 124), then call for a cab if you don't see one on the streets.

2) Stanley Market: Take the bus or a taxi to Stanley Market in the afternoon. Look out the windows to get a bird's-eye view of the real Hong Kong. See page 159 for directions to and suggestions for Stanley Market. Despite the fact that this market may offer no steals, we still believe in it and urge you to go.

TOUR 4: KOWLOON IN A DAY

Kowloon has many different shopping areas, each of which should be a day's adventure. In our one-day tour we will cover only our favorites; there are many more in our listings. And you will have no trouble finding adventures of your own, no matter where you wander. Begin your day early so that you arrive at the first stop (Jade Market) at 10 A.M., when it opens.

1) Begin the day with breakfast in the coffee shop at the REGENT, so you get a good view of the harbor, of Central and of Kowloon's glory. Then head for the Tsim Sha Tsui MTR station on Nathan Road.

2) Your stop is Jordan Road for the JADE MARKET, which opens at 10 A.M. If you choose to take a taxi, ask the driver for the corner of Reclamation and Kansu streets at the overfly. If taking the MTR, exit at the Nathan and Jordan roads terminal, walk past the Yue Hwa department store, past the Wing On Bank and department store, past the Hotel Fortuna, and take a left on Kansu Street. You will then see ahead of you blocks of stalls with umbrellas. These are produce vendors. The Jade Market is an enclosed area just after you pass Shanghai Street. Note that there are two tent-like buildings that make up this market. There are almost 500 dealers in total.

3) Figure an hour or two for the market—after that you'll be cross eyed or have a different notion of who the green-eyed monster is. And you may be getting hungry. Walk back to the MTR and head back toward Kowloon and the Tsim Sha Tsui station; exit at Haiphong Road, because now you're going to Granville Road, the bargain-bin capital of the world. And yes, there's a MCDONALD'S on Granville Road, so you can eat lunch. You can also eat in any of the real people places that line the

street. Ian found one he loves, but I refused to write down the name of it because it was not in English.

4) Don't eat too much lunch, because you don't want to gain weight—bargains can't be tried on in the stores in Granville Road, and they won't be bargains if they don't fit.

Granville Road is the street on your right-hand side, if the harbor is to your back and you have just passed the entrance to the Burlington Arcade. If you are having a fitting at W.W. CHAN, now is a good time to pop in. Otherwise, it's Granville Road. The first block is mostly boring; there's that McDonald's. This is also where you'll find the Taurus Building (No. 21), home to an upstairs outlet called GAT which sells mostly the Kenar label of moderately-priced American sportswear.

In the next block, you'll find shop after shop of bargain basements with bins, racks and an amazing selection of labels for less. It can be feast or famine. Dive in.

5) When you get to the end of Granville Road, turn around and walk back to Nathan Road. Cross to the mosque side of Nathan Road; note that there's an AMERICAN EXPRESS bank in the Park Lane Shopper's Boulevard, in case you now need more money. You are now headed toward the harbor, the Regent and the Pen. At the end of the mosque block, turn right on Haiphong Road. Walk over to Lock Road and turn left until you get to PAN AM PEARLS (No. 9), which is upstairs and where you'll find some of the best fake pearls in town.

6) Take Lock Road toward the Peninsula, but hang a right on Peking Road and walk one block to the corner of Peking Road and Han-kow Road to get to the SANDS BUILDING,

(17 Hankow Road). There are several outlets here. My faves include DORFIT and ORIENTAL PACIFIC. Both carry private-label knit goods (from cottons to cashmeres) at incredible prices.

7) When you're finished in the Sands Building, note there is a great Chinese department store, CHUNG KIU, also in the Sands Building, on the street level. Go up the escalators; this store is filled with junk and great souvenirs.

8) Now that you've had enough tacky cheap stuff, walk over to Canton Road (one block) and enter OCEAN TERMINAL through the OMNI THE HONG KONG HOTEL. You'll see signs for The Silk Road, which is a gallery of antiques dealers, some real, some fake. You can do this if you have the courage. Me? I'm just sending you to FOOK MING TONG, which is awfully touristy and upscale, but I feel like you deserve it after seeing some of the less tony parts of Kowloon. This tea shop has expensive but fun tea-souvenirs with wonderful packaging and beautiful shopping bags. Whether you do the Silk Road shops or not, be sure to poke in at CHARLOTTE HORSTMANN, one of Hong Kong's best-known antiques dealers. You don't have to buy anything, just touch it all.

9) If you're a glutton for punishment, you'll roam around Ocean Terminal and the miles of designer boutiques. I say, high-tail it out of there while you still have the strength.

10) Head for the PEN, their basement filled with fancy stores and a strong cup of *cha* in the lobby where the *tai-tais* gather. Gather your strength as well.

11) Fortified with tea at the Pen, you're ready for a final Kowloon-style down-and-dirty adventure: the LADIES' MARKET, which begins setting up around 4 P.M. You can take the MTR

to Mong Kok and exit the subway on Argyle. Mong Kok is the stop after Yau Ma Tei. The market is mostly on Argyle. At the market you can find Fila shirts, Japanese toys, underwear, watches, electronic goods and knits. Just about everything manufactured can be found in some vendor's pushcart. And hopefully there's even a vibrating pillow for your back, which you will need after a day like this one.

TOUR 5: E.T. PHONE N.T.

I do this via taxi and train; you may want to hire a car and driver and modify the trip accordingly. This is a Friday tour, in order to get the Sek Kong market; it works other days of the week—just skip Sek Kong.

1) Hop the taxi in front of your Kowloon hotel or from the Kowloon side of the Star Ferry; give the driver the words for the Sek Kong market written in Chinese. We're off for the New Territories. Since this is an outdoor market, let's look outside and make sure it's not raining. Since this is a Friday market, let's look at the watch and make sure it's Friday.

2) Ask the driver to wait for you while you shop this market. Allow at least an hour.

3) Back in your trusty taxi, head for the Sha Tin NEW TOWN PLAZA mall. If you have bought a lot, you could be in trouble and may have to double back to your Kowloon hotel, drop off your packages and then head for the KCR station in Hung Hom for Sha Tin. Either way, you're gonna lose the cab at Sha Tin, where you'll see the mall, eat lunch and tour YAO-HAN, a Japanese department store with a food department that is not to be believed.

4) Back on the KCR (you *can* carry all your stuff, can't you?) you are now off at Fanling, where

you'll get a taxi to the Luen Wo Market—this
is a fruit and veggie market, which is very real
and almost the edible counterpart to Sek
Kong. Be sure you are here before 3 P.M.
Photo opportunies galore.

5) Take the train back to Kowloon and collapse.
If you've done this with a car and driver, you
can reverse the order and go to Luen Wo
before Sha Tin. After you're done at the mall
in Sha Tin, refresh your soul with a trip to the
Ten Thousand Buddha monastery (if you can
stand the thought of walking up a few hills).

6) End the shopping day in the bathtub or over
drinks in a very luxurious place, perhaps the
lobby of the Regent. You need the luxury so
that you are able to contemplate the contrasts that are Hong Kong: street markets
and five-star hotels. Where in the world is
Carmen San Diego?

SIZE CONVERSION CHART

Women's Dresses, Coats and Skirts

American	3	5	7	9	11	12	13	14	15	16	18
Continental	36	38	38	40	40	42	42	44	44	46	48
British	8	10	11	12	13	14	15	16	17	18	20

Women's Blouses and Sweaters

American	10	12	14	16	18	20
Continental	38	40	42	44	46	48
British	32	34	36	38	40	42

Women's Shoes

American	5	6	7	8	9	10
Continental	36	37	38	39	40	41
British	$3^1/_2$	$4^1/_2$	$5^1/_2$	$6^1/_2$	$7^1/_2$	$8^1/_2$

Children's Clothing

American	3	4	5	6	6X
Continental	98	104	110	116	122
British	18	20	22	24	26

Children's Shoes

American	8	9	10	11	12	13	1	2	3
Continental	24	25	27	28	29	30	32	33	34
British	7	8	9	10	11	12	13	1	2

Men's Suits

American	34	36	38	40	42	44	46	48
Continental	44	46	48	50	52	54	56	58
British	34	36	38	40	42	44	46	48

Men's Shirts

American	$14^1/_2$	15	$15^1/_2$	16	$16^1/_2$	17	$17^1/_2$	18
Continental	37	38	39	41	42	43	44	45
British	$14^1/_2$	15	$15^1/_2$	16	$16^1/_2$	17	$17^1/_2$	18

Men's Shoes

American	7	8	9	10	11	12	13
Continental	$39^1/_2$	41	42	43	$44^1/_2$	46	47
British	6	7	8	9	10	11	12

INDEX

ABOUT THE AUTHOR

SUZY GERSHMAN is an author and journalist who has worked in the fiber and fashion industry since 1969 in both New York and Los Angeles, and has held editorial positions at *California Apparel News*, *Mademoiselle*, *Gentleman's Quarterly* and *People* magazine, where she was West Coast Style editor. She writes regularly for *Travel and Leisure*; her essays on retailing are text at the Harvard Business School. Mrs. Gershman lives in Connecticut with her husband, author Michael Gershman, and their son. Michael Gershman also contributes to the *Born to Shop* pages.

ABOUT THE PHOTOGRAPHER

IAN COOK is a British photographer based in London. A contributing photographer for *People* magazine, he has also worked as a reporter for British newspapers and periodicals and written numerous shopping and consumer information stories before joining the *Born to Shop* team.